The FIRST DETECTIVE

The FIRST DETECTIVE

The Life and Revolutionary Times of

VIDOCQ

Criminal, Spy, and Private Eye

James Morton

THE OVERLOOK PRESS
NEW YORK, NY

This edition first published in paperback in the United States in 2012 by
The Overlook Press, Peter Mayer Publishers, Inc.
141 Wooster Street
New York, NY 10012
www.overlookpress.com

For bulk and special sales, please contact sales@overlookny.com

First published in Great Britain in 2004 by Ebury Press
Copyright © 2004 James Morton

Cataloging-in-Publication Data is available from the Library of Congress

Manufactured in the United States of America
2 4 6 8 10 9 7 5 3 1
ISBN 978-1-4683-0057-4

CONTENTS

INTRODUCTION

It is sometimes said that, in a competition for mendacity, Baron Munchausen could lie for Germany, Frederick Rolfe, Baron Corvo, for England, Frank Harris for Ireland, Axel Munthe – the author of *The Story of San Michele* – for Sweden, Grey Owl (born Archibald Belaney and really from Hastings) for Canada, Aimée Semple McPherson for America and Casanova for Italy. To that select list could be added, if only a trifle unfairly, Vidocq for France.

The former convict and police chief Eugène-François Vidocq, and his literary ghost, finished his memoirs in January 1828 when he was, as it were, between jobs. He had been sacked, or had resigned, as the Chief of Detectives in the Sûreté and was already actively lobbying for his return to power. He was also in the process of establishing a paper mill at Saint-Mandé near the Bois de Vincennes where he proposed to employ former convict labor. However, he broke his arm in five places in a fall the following month; it was feared that he would lose the arm but in time the fractures healed. Vidocq then rather let things slip as far as his memoirs were concerned and it was not until after he had been to Dijon to obtain a copy of a pardon granted him back in 1818 absolving him of a crime committed during the French Revolution, that he looked up the printer to see the page proofs. He was not pleased with what he found, complaining that the Prefect of Police, Guy Delavau, and his henchman Franchet, had taken advantage of his absence to change the text for the worse.

So far as Vidocq – who describes himself as a sort of Faublas, the hero of one of the many semi-pornographic novels of the period[1] – was concerned, the text had been completely altered and instead of:

---

[1] The eponymous hero of *Les Amours du Chevalier de Faublas*, by Louvet de Couvray, loves three women in particular. These are reduced first by a jealous husband and then the suicide of the second. He had hoped to settle down with the third but is driven mad by his memories of the others. Jean-Baptiste Louvet de Couvray was a revolutionary and a member of the Convention nationale. He died in 1797 at the age of thirty-seven.

. . . the sallies, vivacity and energy of my character, another had been foisted in, totally deprived of all life, colouring or promptitude. With a few alternatives the facts were really the same; but all that was casual, involuntary and spontaneous in a turbulent career, was given as the long premeditation of evil intent.

The necessity that impelled me was altogether passed over; I was made the scoundrel of the age or rather a Compère Mathieu, without one redeeming point of sensitivity, conscience, remorse or repentance.[2]

Vidocq may have been a great police officer, a talented swordsman, a prodigious womanizer, and a fine raconteur, but, certainly at that stage in his career – if ever – he was not a writer. He had set down his memoirs but, in an era when length was, if not all, then a great part of it, he had come up far too short. It put one in mind of Evelyn Waugh's *Decline and Fall*, in which Paul Pennyfeather gives an award to a boy for writing the longest essay, regardless of its merit. The publisher wanted four volumes to make it worth his while. The trouble was that the public were champing at the bit and there was no way, even had he the ability, that Vidocq could bring himself to rewrite the first volume. He did, however, correct the second one and, so he said, from the point at which he joined the Corsairs at Boulogne the story was all his own. Vidocq's first ghostwriter was Emile Morice whom he sacked but, as so often happens, it was a case of out of the frying pan and into the fire. Louis-François L'Héritier de l'Ain, who was then employed, produced a further three volumes, padding things out with a version of his own, already published, novel. It is on those memoirs that Vidocq was judged for over a century. He was not helped in the least by L'Héritier's vitriolic supplement to the final volume. Nevertheless the *Mémoires* were an immediate success and were constantly reprinted.

One way of looking at Vidocq is to follow the approach to Casanova's memoirs – to take them as invention unless and until it can be proved otherwise. Over the years, however, researchers into the life of the Venetian rake, notably J. Rives-Childs, have found that much of what he wrote was accurate. He had, it was true, muddled dates, and sometimes places and names had been changed or misremembered, but essentially large chunks could be proved.

The same is true with Vidocq, particularly in the tales of his early years. It was all a large romance written to sell copies to a gullible public. Again,

---

[2] E-F. Vidocq, *Vidocq*, Vidocq to the reader. Unless otherwise stated, all subsequent quotes by Vidocq are from the English edition of 1828.

this is a trifle unfair. Not all the hyperbole was Vidocq's. For example, in the English translation of 1828–9 an appendix had Vidocq imprisoned for debt as a result of his gambling and a fictitious son, Julius, who, after being in the galleys, was now employed in Vidocq's Saint-Mandé paper mill; both stories simply added to spice up the text and neither of them true.

For years no attempt was made to separate the Vidocq of fact from the Vidocq of fiction – the hero of the novel by Dick Donovan; of the play, *VIDOCQ! The French Police Spy,* staged in London in 1829, or the 1860 version of Vidocq's life at the Brittania Theatre, or the one which played in Paris in the early 1900s. Things changed in the 1950s with the work of the historian Jean Savant who produced an annotated edition of Vidocq's life and whose research was able to confirm Vidocq's own account of many of the events in his life, particularly the later ones. Savant's incalculably valuable work does, however, come down very heavily in favor of Vidocq at almost every conceivable opportunity. A rather more inquiring note was struck by both Eric Perrin in his 1995 biography and Bruno Roy-Henry in his 2001 book. No one writing about Vidocq could be other than indebted to them and their researches. They have shown that much of what he and his ghosts wrote can now be proved to be correct.

Vidocq has been less fortunate with his English biographers, one of whom devotes only the final two pages of his book to the last thirty years of his life and manages, as has been pointed out, to make two glaring mistakes in those few hundred words.[3] Philip Stead's 1953 *Vidocq: Picaroon of Crime* is a book very much of its time when biographies included made-up conversations and contained neither annotations nor footnotes. It remains, nevertheless, a very readable account. In his 1977 account, *The Vidocq Dossier* (also unannotated), Samuel Edwards frankly admits that many of the books borrow from each other. I hope I have been able to add something to – as well as borrowing from – all these accounts and to place Vidocq more in the context of his times.

Throughout his life Vidocq changed political direction, favoring whoever was in power at the time. He was a good man to have on your side but the worry was that he might just as easily turn up in the colors of the opposition. For those not familiar with the machinations of the French throne and Empires this is a good moment to summarize events.

At the time of Vidocq's birth in 1775 Louis XVI was on the throne, to which he had succeeded in 1754. He was executed in 1793 in the

---

[3] E. A. Brayley Hodgetts, *Vidocq: A Master of Crime.*

Terror which followed the beginning of the Revolution, by which time the Convention nationale was the ruling body. This was followed by the Directory, two chambers sharing legislative power, which existed from October 27, 1795, to November 9, 1799, when it was abolished by Napoleon who established the Consulate after his coup d'état of the same date. The Consulate was a triumvirate headed by Bonaparte who, on August 4, 1802, was made Consul for life with the power to nominate his successor. On May 18, 1804, he upgraded himself to Emperor. This lasted until his abdication on April 11, 1814, when the monarchy, in the form of Louis XVIII, was restored. On Napoleon's escape from Elba and return to France – the Hundred Days – Louis XVIII fled Paris for Ghent, where he remained until the Emperor's defeat at Waterloo on June 15, 1815, and his second abdication that July. For a brief period the Emperor's son, Napoleon II, was recognized but he never reigned and died in exile. Louis XVIII died childless in 1824 and his brother Charles X succeeded to the throne. He was overthrown in the July Revolution of 1830 in favor of the duc d'Orléans, Louis-Philippe, who was placed on the throne by a combination of liberals and Republicans. His was an uneasy crown and he abdicated in 1848. In June and again in September that year Charles-Louis-Napoleon, the third son of Louis Napoleon, a younger brother of the Emperor, was elected to the Assemblée constituante. In December he was elected Prince-President of the Republic and, following a coup d'état on December 2, 1851, his powers were increased exponentially. On December 2, 1852, as Napoleon III, he was proclaimed Emperor. He was taken prisoner during the Franco-Prussian war of 1870 and died in exile at Chislehurst, in Kent, in 1873.

Although I have generally avoided its use, the Revolutionary calendar also needs some explanation. It was divided into Vendémiaire, Brumaire, Frimaire, Nivôse, Pluviôse, Ventôse, Germinal, Floréal, Prairial, Messidor, Thermidor and Fructidor, names coined by Fabre d'Eglantine, a distinguished poet of the time. It commenced in November 1793 but was backdated to September 22, 1792, the day after the abolition of royalty and the date that the Convention seized power from the Legislative Assembly, as well as being the autumn equinox. Each month contained three weeks of ten days of which the last was a day of rest. The last five days of each year were holidays as was an extra day in each Françiade, or four years, which were public holidays. The Revolutionary calendar was abandoned in Nivôse 1805, or Year XIV, a year and a half after France ceased to be either a Republic or a Consulate. I hope that readers will accept that my translations from the French are free ones.

It is sometimes suggested that the way of calculating the value of money in a currency should be made against the then living conditions. So for example in France when Vidocq was a young man a measure of flour in 1790 was 2 francs, and in 1795 in the immediate post-Revolution period the price had risen to 225 francs. Similarly the price of a hat that had cost 14 francs grew to 500 francs. Conversely 10,000 francs borrowed in 1790 could in 1796 be repaid for 35 francs.[4]

However as a very rough guide, to convert the franc in Vidocq's time to today's dollar it can be multiplied by 4.6. (The franc increased in value by a multiple of 23 between Vidocq's day and modern times. In 2002 the French Franc was converted into the Euro, and in 2009 there would have been the equivalent of five francs to the US dollar.) One hundred francs in Vidocq's time would be the equivalent of $460. A 14 franc hat would cost roughly $64 today.

During his time with the Sûréte, Vidocq served under a striking number of Préfets de Police:

Dubois, comte Louis, March 1800–October 1810
Pasquier, baron Etienne-Denis, October 1810–May 1814
Beugnot, comte Jacques, May 1814–December 1814
André, baron d'Antoine, December 1814–March 1815
Bourienne, de, Louis, March 1815
Réal, comte Pierre, March 1815–July 1815
Decazes, de, duc Elie, July 1815–September 1815
Anglès, comte Julien, September 1815–December 1821
Delavau, Guy, December 1821–January 1828
Gisquet, Henri, October 1831–September 1836

My thanks are due to Jeremy Beadle, Paul Brown, David Fingleton, Hannah Macdonald, Moya O'Sullivan, Chris Pratt of the Magic Circle, Annabel Thomas, Richard Whittington-Egan, Rosine Gandon of the Saint-Mandé Service des Archives, the staff of the British Library and the British Newspaper Library at Colindale, the Archives Nationales, the Bibliothèque Nationale, the Bibliothèque Historique de la Ville de Paris, the Musée de la Préfecture de Police de Paris and the University of Indiana at Bloomington. Any errors are mine alone.

In particular this book could not have been completed without the patient help in research and its writing of Dock Bateson.

---

[4] Michael J. Kosares, "Black Swans, Yellow Gold," www. gold-observer.com

Part One
Poacher

Chapter 1

VIDOCQ
AGAINST HIS PARENTS

*In which our hero is born and worries the midwife – steals from his
parents – runs away – thinks of a naval career but instead joins a circus
and then the army – deserts – fights at the Battle of Jemmapes – returns
home – and witnesses an execution*

IN JANUARY 1809 Sir John Moore was killed at Corunna in the
Peninsular War to liberate Spain from the French, who had occupied
the country in 1808. Later in the year, William Pitt's elder brother failed
to capture Antwerp and Lord Castlereagh and the Foreign Secretary,
George Canning, fought a duel over the fiasco. Thomas Paine, author
of *Rights of Man,* died in poverty in New York; Spenser Percival, the
only British Prime Minister to be assassinated, took office when the
Duke of Portland resigned through ill health. Gladstone, Darwin and
Tennyson were born. At the end of July, Sir Arthur Wellesley won the
Battle of Talavera and so brought an end to the Peninsular War.

In Paris during the summer of that year Eugène-François Vidocq,
future presidential candidate, already a thief, forger, suspected murderer, swordsman, womanizer and escaped convict – not necessarily
in that order – found himself caught between a rock and a hard
place. At the time living in the stews of the Marais, the slum district
a hundred meters from the right bank of the Seine, he had been on
the run from the convict ship at Brest for nearly four years and now
he was being threatened and blackmailed not only by his former
colleagues, on whose friends he had informed, but by his in-laws.
A return to the *bagne* was perhaps the least dangerous option. He
was likely to be drawn again into serious crime, possibly murder or
to be killed himself. All that seemed to be left to him was to try to do

a deal with the police. Accordingly, he went unannounced to the rue de Jérusalem, a small road on the lle de la Cité, to see Jean Henry, the head of the criminal department (known to the Paris criminals of the time as the Bad Angel), to put a proposition to him. Almost twenty years later some of what Vidocq told Henry formed the early part of his *Mémoires*.

Vidocq's birth was not quite in the same class as that of Rabelais' Gargantua, a giant who emerges from the womb calling for bread and wine, but his memoirs begin with a good bit of hearsay when he says he was born during a night-time thunderstorm on July 23, 1775, at the family home, 222 rue du Mirroir-de-Venise in Arras.[1] It was near the birthplace of the town's perhaps more famous son, Maximilien-Marie-Isidore Robespierre, born sixteen years earlier. On September 2, 1765, his father, Nicholas-François-Joseph Vidocq, who owned a bakery and shop, had married Henriette-Françoise-Josèphe Dion, who was then twenty-one. Vidocq's mother's midwife, a Mlle Lenoramand, predicted the child would have a stormy career. Never one to hide his light under a bushel he claimed that from the moment of his birth he looked like a two-year-old.

Vidocq was one-year-old when the American War of Independence began in 1776 and with it France saw a chance to get its own back on its long-standing enemy, England. However, that same year there were grain riots in northern France and when, two years later, the French entered the war, the country went into economic recession. England was duly defeated by the Americans but remained relatively undamaged, while there were disastrous financial consequences for France. So Vidocq's early life took place against a background of increasing unrest in the country.

M. Vidocq's bakery was in the place d'Armes, then one of the less salubrious spots in Arras, and Vidocq maintained it was there that he learned to fight. His victims or their parents would complain to Vidocq's but, he implies, his own admired his black eyes and torn ears. What the tormented cats and dogs of the neighborhood had to say goes unrecorded, however, for Vidocq claims he terrorized them as well as the children. At thirteen he was more than useful with a foil and by now he was spending far too much time with the soldiers from the local garrison.[2] As a way of diverting him, his father had him prepared

---

[1] In 1856 the name was changed to rue des Trois Visages. It is near the town hall.
[2] One unsubstantiated story is that at the age of fourteen he killed a soldier in a duel.

to receive his first communion, but religious instruction was a failure. It was then time to teach him the bakery trade, the hope being that, even though Vidocq had an elder brother, François-Ghislain-Joseph,[3] the young Eugène-François would take over his father's business. Apprenticeship consisted of delivering the bread and, given that the army was one of the bakery's best customers, Vidocq spent his time in the fencing rooms. When his father complained, his son was defended by the cooks who spoke of his politeness and punctuality. What his parents did not yet know about was his second career – stealing from the till along with his elder brother. It was, however, the brother who was caught in flagrante and packed off to a baker's in Lille.

For Vidocq there was a double downside to this. First, his father now wanted more speed on the round and he expected his son to be home on time. Second, the drawer which he and his brother had been plundering was suddenly locked, money being posted through a small hole in the counter instead. Vidocq explained this to his friend, a youth named Poyant, who taught him how to use glue on a feather. Vidocq was disappointed with the result; he could only pick up a few light-weight coins using this method, so it was off to another friend whose father was a blacksmith. A key was made and the money taken was spent in a bar with the local roustabouts.

It did not require his father to be brain of Arras to work out where the takings were going and Vidocq, duly caught with his key in the lock, was soundly thrashed. Accepting there was no more money forthcoming, he started taking the bread itself. Now he realized the first rule of theft – that the receiver will only pay a fraction of the full price – and to keep himself in the style to which he was rapidly becoming accustomed Vidocq started to help himself to his mother's provisions. This came to an end when, instead of wringing the necks of two chickens he had stolen, he put them in his trouser pockets concealed by his apron. Unfortunately they gave him away when they began to cackle. For this he received a cuffing from his mother, who sent him to bed supperless.

---

[3] François-Ghislain-Joseph Vidocq was born on November 29, 1772. There are only two references to him in the memoirs. He had died by August 25, 1800, when, on the death of Vidocq's father, the inheritance passed to Eugène-François and his sister, Henriette-Augustine-Josephe, known as Augustine, born on January 5, 1782. As was common in France at the time there was a high infant-mortality rate in the family. Other siblings, some of whom did not survive infancy, included Nicholas, b. November 19, 1767, d. December 28, 1767; Ghislain-Joseph, b. June 1, 1781, d. June 3, 1781; Anne-Fidèle-Josèphe, b. September 1, 1777, d. April 3, 1782; Henriette-Victoire-Josèphe, b. November 26, 1779, and François-Joseph-Constant, b. January 10, 1783.

Moving on to the bigger things, in return he decided he would steal the family plate, the one drawback being that it was all engraved with the family name. But that did not stop him, or Poyant, who took him to a pawnbroker, and Vidocq netted 150 francs, which he spent within twenty-four hours. He stayed away from home for three days before he was arrested and taken to the Baudets,[4] the local remand, short-stay prison and asylum in rue Briquet-Taillander between rue Emile-Legreue and rue Gambetta. He stayed there ten days before he was informed that he had been imprisoned at the instigation of his father, from which he correctly deduced that he would be out soon and his mother would come to see him the following day. Four days later he was released more or less on a promise of good conduct.

His parents seem to have tried their best with him. If father left the shop counter, mother would take over but Vidocq was chafing at the bit and it was Poyant who suggested the way out. Why not do things properly and burgle his parents? After all, they had to be worth a thousand crowns or more. So, one evening when Vidocq's mother was known to be on her own, Poyant went round to see her with the bad news that her son was in full debauch with a group of girls. He was fighting anyone who remonstrated with him and likely to break up the tavern which, inconveniently, was the other side of Arras. The poor woman dropped her knitting immediately and went off to find her errant lamb. Vidocq had already stolen a key, which got them into the house, but they found the till locked. A crowbar was used to jemmy the drawer and around 2,000 francs were taken and split between the pair. Vidocq, on the road to Lille within half an hour, tired at Lens and picked up a carriage to Dunkirk which – like W. C. Fields on a visit to Philadelphia – he found closed. It was on to Calais. The ultimate destination seems to have been America but the ships' captains in Calais wanted too much for his passage and so it was back along the coast to Ostend where he met his first master.

It is difficult to understand Vidocq's behavior at this point in his life. He appears to have acted without any regard for his parents or their feelings. His life seems to have been happy enough: his father does not appear to have been unduly harsh and his mother clearly doted on him. Perhaps the best that can be said of Vidocq is that he was simply displaying the rebellious nature of a young man of his age and that he was easily influenced by his slightly older contemporaries. That said,

---

[4] The Baudets was demolished in 1944.

so far as his circumstances permitted, throughout his life he would continue to do exactly as he wanted. When it comes to it he was something of a sociopath.

In Ostend, a stranger, who told him he was a ship broker, suggested they could dine together in Blakemberg and possibly with female company. Vidocq is more reticent than Casanova about the details of his early, or indeed later, loves:

> . . . some very agreeable ladies welcomed us with all that ancient hospitality which did not confine itself only to feasting. At midnight, probably – I say probably, for we took no account of hours – my head became heavy, and my legs would no longer support me; there was around me a complete chaos and things whirled in such a manner, that without perceiving that they had undressed me, I thought I was stripped to my shirt in the same bed as one of the Blakembergian nymphs; it might be true, but all I know that is, that I soon fell soundly asleep.[5]

He woke up half-naked on the docks, penniless except for a few coins which he used to settle the bill at the inn. He had returned to collect his clothes, and for his money he also received a short homily about how lucky he had been not to be stripped of everything.

For a few hours he thought that perhaps a life at sea was indeed for him; until, that is, he heard the sound of a trumpet and saw a *paillasse*, or clown, announcing a show. In a flash all thoughts of naval honors were gone. He would ask for a job in the circus.

It is not entirely clear whose travelling show Vidocq joined. He gives the name of the owner as the magician Comus who was, he says, at the time travelling with the naturalist Garnier. Unfortunately, since there were two Comuses touring as magicians more or less at the same time, it is difficult to tell which one Vidocq attached himself to.

The first, and better known, was Nicolas-Philippe Ledru, known as Cotte-Comus, born in 1731 which, assuming Vidocq to be fourteen, would put the magician in his late fifties. He had travelled to England in the spring of 1765 when he played for several weeks at a room in Panton Street in the West End, earning a reputed £5,000. He had originally only intended to stay for a fortnight. He returned to England for further seasons in 1766 – when the star of his show was the 'Learned Mermaid, the Siren of Paris' – and 1770, and also

---

[5] E-F. Vidocq, *Memoirs of Vidocq*, Chapter I.

travelled extensively throughout Europe, acquiring a huge reputation and appearing before the Emperor Franz Joseph in 1779. One of his tricks was an artificial hand which wrote the thoughts of the spectators; another was the Magic Well. Apart from running a magic act he devised a new system for nautical maps and 'an application of electricity for therapeutic purposes for illness of the nervous system' or, simply translated, epilepsy. Louis XV, who appointed him his physician, gave him the title Professeur de Physique des Enfants de France. Later he opened his own theatre in the boulevard du Temple in Paris. He was imprisoned during the Terror but survived the guillotine. He died in 1807 a wealthy man, leaving his fortune to his only daughter. It is most unlikely that, at this stage of his career, Ledru was touring with a sideshow in northern France when Vidocq claims to have met Comus.

The second Comus, who is much the more likely of the pair with whom Vidocq joined up, began travelling in the 1790s. He also went to England, probably to avoid the Terror, and after a provincial tour played in a room at 28 Haymarket for two years. After the Revolution he returned to France and in November 1805 could be found setting up his tent at the allée de Tournay, Bordeaux, where one of the advertised acts was the shooting by a member of the company at Mme Comus, who would deflect the bullet with a foil, a trick of Comus' devising. Another of his more interesting tricks was the transfer of a guinea piece from 'the hands of a Lady to the innermost of seven sealed envelopes, enclosed in seven locked iron caskets'. In the latter part of his career he was challenged by a younger magician calling himself Conus and, worsted in the competition, retired and died in obscurity and poverty in 1830.[6]

Vidocq claims that, on meeting him, he bought the clown a half-pint of gin with his last shilling to get an introduction to the menagerie owner whom he thought might give him work. Asked by Comus what he could do, he replied nothing, at which he was told that, since he had a neat appearance, he would be trained. He would be offered a two-year contract and for the first six months would receive board and lodging and clothing; after that, if he was doing well, he would get

---

[6] In his annotation of *Les Vrais Mémoires de Vidocq*, Jean Savant identifies Ledru as Comus while Eric Perrin believes he is mistaken and that Ledru had stopped travelling by the time Vidocq claims to have met him. Comus was generally a popular name for magicians. Yet another Comus, this time Ernest, appeared with Alexander Herrman in London in 1870. I am very grateful to Christopher Pratt of the Magic Circle for the help he has given me in trying to sort out the confusing identities of the Comus/Conus magicians.

one-sixteenth of the profits and the following year he would – if he was bright – get a share in the company with the others.

Vidocq was never going to last out his apprenticeship. He disliked sharing the straw mattress with the clown and, while it was one thing to clean the wooden furniture and the lamps, it was quite another to clean out the menagerie. He seems to have been particularly nervous of the monkeys who, he believed, were simply waiting for the opportunity to attack him. On his first day ten o'clock came and went with no sign of breakfast. When it arrived, it was a piece of hard brown bread which, since he could not break it with his teeth, he threw to the animals. He was due to light the lamps in the evening and when he did not do this correctly he received a beating; the same happened on the second and subsequent days. After a month he was hungry, the monkeys had torn his clothes and he was entertaining home thoughts from the countryside.

However, he must have been displaying some application because Comus put him in the charge of the acrobat Balmate with instructions to turn him into a vaulter. He seems to have made some progress and learned some of the more simple jumps, but when he tried the chair leap and the grand fling he broke his nose. He complained to Comus who, after listening to him in silence, gave him a sound thrashing. It was back to looking after the lamps and monkeys.

He was next handed over to Garnier, the naturalist, who, along with Comus, thrashed him regularly. Vidocq was to be turned into what, in later fairground parlance, would be called a geek. Given a club and dressed in a tiger skin, he was to be a cannibal from the South Seas who ate live chickens. When Vidocq refused, Garnier gave him a clip around the ear and when he retaliated the rest of the company joined in to give the newcomer a thorough beating.

Shortly afterwards he was offered a position by a puppeteer who ran a Punch and Judy show under the title Théâtre des Variétés Amusantes. He, or more likely his wife, had taken pity on him. The man was an ugly thirty-five-year-old, and Eliza, his wife, a mere sixteen:

> one of those smart brunettes with long eyelashes whose hearts are of most inflammable material, which deserve a better destiny than to light a fire of straw.

Vidocq would come in useful. All three worked in the booth with Vidocq handing the puppets to Eliza and her husband and after the show he would collect the puppets while Eliza took round the hat before the audience pushed off without paying. At the end of three days she claimed she was in love with Vidocq.

One evening, with the performance in full flow, the puppeteer called for the removal of the Sergeant of the Watch whom Punch had finished beating. Unfortunately his wife and Vidocq were locked in an embrace and she did not hear. A fight broke out between them and the booth was overturned.[7]

Vidocq may not, as he said, have been as badly made as he was clothed but clothes made the man and as he felt there was no hope of finding respectability, he decided to take the road home to Arras. He met a peddler who was going to Lille to sell powders, and elixirs, and to cut corns and pull teeth. He was, he said, called Father Godard and was getting old: if Vidocq would carry his pack, he could join him.

Vidocq seems to have had little luck with animals in general, because when they arrived at a village inn whose other guests included assorted peddlers, tinkers and quacks, he was asked if he was Godard's mountebank, or Merry Andrew, and after being given a plate of stew was sent to spend the night in the company of a camel, two muzzled bears and a crowd of "learned dogs."

Resuming their journey, they reached Lille at lunchtime on market day and set up in the square. The idea was that Vidocq should then parade Father Godard's wares, but with a full stomach, Vidocq rebelled. It was all very well sharing his quarters with a camel and carrying the pack but he wasn't going to expose himself to ridicule so near home. So he decamped.

Fortunately for Vidocq his father was out when, ever the prodigal, he returned to the bakery where his mother, poor duped woman, fed and reclothed him. There was still the problem of Vidocq père and, sending her son out of the way for the occasion, she engaged a priest to intercede. He turned the trick, the fatted calf was metaphorically killed and Vidocq jumped for joy when he learned of his reinstatement. It was accompanied by a sermon on the lines of the Prodigal Son but Vidocq maintained he never remembered a word of it.

His adventures had gained him something of a reputation with the local women, including two milliners in their shop on the rue des

---

[7] Apparently the puppeteer, whom Vidocq never named, later became the director of a provincial theatre, a post he held for some years.

Trois Visages and a married actress then appearing in the town. Soon the actress demanded exclusivity and, disguised as a girl, Vidocq turned up regularly at her house. Then, according to Vidocq, he went on tour with the actress, her husband and a pretty maid who passed Vidocq off as her sister. For once Vidocq does not seem to have taken advantage of his *patronne*. He was only dismissed when the money ran out and then it was back home again to Arras where he told his father he wanted to join the army. He was, after all, an expert swordsman.

On March 10, 1791, Vidocq appeared in the uniform of the Bourbon infantry regiment and shortly after, when some soldiers took exception to his behavior, he sent two of them to hospital. He soon joined them in the infirmary when he found one of their colleagues even more adroit than he with the foil. He was given the name Reckless and, apparently the butt of the regiment's collective wit, fought a series of fifteen duels over the next six months, killing two men. That not withstanding, he seems to have enjoyed himself. His father, no doubt pleased he had settled down, gave him an allowance, his mother kept him supplied with the niceties of life and he could be found protecting local shopkeepers and particularly their daughters. He ran up credit but was rarely in trouble with the officers.

In fact he served only a fortnight's imprisonment under one of the bastions. One of his cellmates was a soldier in his regiment who had confessed to a series of robberies, an act which could see him dismissed from the regiment and would also bring dishonor to his family. He wavered between escape and suicide with Vidocq counselling the former, with the latter a last resort. With the help of one of Vidocq's visitors two of the bars to the prison were cut through and the man was taken to the ramparts from which he refused to jump. Vidocq told him to "jump or hang" and when the man suggested he might return to his cell and take his punishment after all, Vidocq and his friend threw him over.

The story has a moral. It seems that although the soldier was lame for the rest of his life, he escaped and lived the life of an honest man. As for Vidocq, when he returned to his straw he "tasted the repose which the consciousness of a good deed always brings."

The trouble with being a soldier is that sometimes you have to fight. The next step for Vidocq was indeed war which had been declared on Austria on April 20. He was at the rout of Marquain after which General Dillon was killed at Lille on April 28, 1792.[8] The regiment was then ordered to attack the Austrian camp at Maulde and then at de la Lune against the army under the command of Kellerman, and Vidocq fought at the Battle of Valmy against the Prussians on 20 September that year. The next day the Republic was declared.

War is rarely glorious for the troops on the ground. Christopher Hibbert describes the French army of 1792:

> . . . with a strength of less than 140,000 [it] was in no state to fight the combined forces of those enemies. Over 3,000 officers had left their regiments since a new oath of loyalty omitting the King's name had been required of them after the flight of the royal family to Varennes [on June 13, 1791]. Many of those who remained exercised little authority over their men. Mutinies were common, equipment defective, ammunition in short supply. The troops and insubordinate volunteers marched towards the enemy in their wooden sabots and blue jackets without enthusiasm or confidence, and were soon retreating in confusion, throwing away their arms, and crying out, "We are betrayed! *Sauve qui peut!*"[9]

It is hardly surprising that, for much of the time, Vidocq came and went more or less as he pleased. For the present, however, he was transferred and promoted corporal of the grenadiers on November 1, taking the opportunity when celebrating to quarrel with the sergeant major of his previous regiment. Vidocq wanted a duel and pressed strongly for it. The man refused to fight on the grounds that Vidocq was of an inferior rank and so both Vidocq and his second were arrested. Two days later, on being told they would be court-martialled, they decided to desert. Enlisting, deserting and re-enlisting in another regiment or even on the other side, often for a bounty, was a common practice in continental armies of the eighteenth and nineteenth centuries. (Given that soldiers of the period were often mercenaries, there was a continual switching of sides and paymasters. The novelist William Makepeace Thackeray could well have been thinking of Vidocq when he wrote *The Memoirs of Barry Lyndon Esq.* in which the eponymous soldier-hero changes side

---

[8] Theobald Dillon (Chevalier de), born in Dublin in 1745, distinguished himself and was decorated in the American War of Independence in 1785. After the disastrous rout at Baisieux, when he tried to rally his troops he was stabbed, along with his aide-de-camp Dupont, and his body thrown on a bonfire. His wife, who had given birth the previous day, managed to escape with the child.

[9] Christopher Hibbert, *The French Revolution*, p. 145.

with near-impunity.)[10] And so, with his second wearing a waistcoat rather than full uniform and looking like a soldier undergoing punishment, and Vidocq dressed in a cap and carrying a musket, knapsack and with a packet inscribed "To the Citizen commandant of the quarters at Vitry-le-Français," they made it to that town, which was flyposted with placards urging the citizenry to join up and defend France. They bought clothes from a Jewish dealer and as civilians enlisted in the 11th chasseurs and were sent to Philippeville.

At Chalons they met up with a soldier from the Beaujolais region who had somehow acquired a portfolio of assignats, the currency in use during the Revolution.[11] He did not understand their significance but was willing to split them. Vidocq, never one to turn down a profit or fail to benefit from a fool, left him with the majority of the comparatively worthless papers, retaining the valuable ones for himself.

The two men lived well enough on the proceeds and, reaching Philippeville, still had money left over. There they were taught riding and were assigned to a squadron before being sent to join the army in time for the Battle of Jemmapes, which took place on November 6, 1792.

Vidocq's version of affairs is a heroic one. Learning that he had been identified as a deserter, with all that it entailed, he headed for the Austrian lines and was enlisted in the cuirassiers of Kinski. He was, he claimed, desperate to avoid fighting the French and so, feigning illness, stayed behind at the garrison of Louvain. There he gave fencing lessons and, doing his part for France, disabled a number of German soldiers. Unfortunately he did too convincing a job on a brigadier who, unsportingly, had him given twenty lashes with the cat. When Vidocq declined to give further lessons he was ordered to be flogged again.

Learning next that a lieutenant was going to join the army under General Schroeder, he asked to accompany him as his servant. He promptly left the officer in the lurch at Quesnoy and went to Landrecies, where he passed for a Belgian deserter from the

---

[10] During the American Civil War it was common practice for soldiers to enlist for a bounty and promptly desert, only to re-enlist under another name in a different regiment. It was a dangerous game, for if a re-enlist was discovered he might well be dispatched immediately to the front. Sometimes, however, bounties were paid simply on the basis that the recipient would not fight.

[11] First issued in 1789, assignats were a form of paper money based on the value of confiscated Church and Crown lands. They fell steadily in value and in the autumn of 1796 they were one-thirteenth of their original value. By the end of their career they had fallen to an ignominious one-seventieth of their original value.

Austrian army. He then joined the army of the Sambre-et-Meuse and ended up back at Rocroi with the 11th chasseurs where he was once more reinstated with the help of his old captain.

As with many who elaborate their memoirs, such embellishments are very often the most vague in detail. In Vidocq's case, despite all the duelling and excitement running to pages and pages of derring-do, among the most fictious and contradictory parts of his autobiography are those in which he describes his army service.

The reason, so says Vidocq's biographer Eric Perrin – and it is difficult to disagree with him – has nothing to do with his previous fictitious desertion but rather that Vidocq had backed the wrong horse and so had to invent. After Jemmapes, General Dumouriez had made a fine speech to his men but had, on the whole, failed to convince many that the path to success was to defect to the Austrian camp. His intention was to march on Paris, release the Queen and place the Dauphin on the throne.[12] Vidocq was one of the few who listened to the siren trumpet and Valance, duc de Chartres, the future Louis-Philippe I, was unsurprisingly another. On April 5, 1793, an amnesty allowed Vidocq and the others to rejoin their regiments.[13]

Throughout the parts of his memoirs dealing with his life in the army, Vidocq and his ghostwriters railed against fortune which had, they claimed, denied him his rightful place in the history of the Napoleonic wars, which would have allowed him to take his place in the pantheon of heroes. Later he modestly accepted some of the blame for this omission:

---

[12] Two of the more interesting members of the Dumouriez camp were the Fernig sisters: Félicité, born in 1776, and and her sister Théophile, three years later, daughters of a non-commissioned officer. According to Lamartine, "Their faces veiled with gunpowder, their lips blackened by the cartridges which they had torn with their teeth made these two heroines of liberty unrecognisable even to their own father." When Dumouriez fell into disfavor they left the country and did not return to France unitll 1802. Théophile became a poet and musician and died unmarried at the age of thirty-nine. Félicité married an army officer. Their brother, Louis Joseph César, comte de Fernig, became a general, dying in August in 1847, and one of their younger sisters married General Guillemniot. For a partial account of their careers, see Lamartine, *Histoire des Girondins*, t. 11, pp. 187–90.

[13] Dumouriez had an interesting if erratic career. He was born in Cambrai in 1739 and followed his father, a *commissaire des guerres,* to Hanover. By then he had been made an officer and was injured at Clostercamp in 1759. By the time of his discharge from the army in 1762 he had been wounded twenty-two times. He was then given a diplomatic mission by Choiseul to the Court of Madrid and subsequent missions to Corsica, Poland and Sweden followed. Arrested on the orders of the duke of Aiguillon, he was sent to the Bastille for six months. Even after the Restoration he remained in disgrace and never returned to France, dying at Turville Park, Buckinghamshire, in 1823.

If instead of foolishly throwing myself like a horse galloping into an abyss I had taken the place for which I was destined by intelligence and energy given me by heaven, I would have reached to heights of Kléber, Murat and the others. Heart and head I equalled them and I ought to have been like them. Theatre (posterity) failed me.[14]

However, according to the memoirs – for there had been no sex for some pages – now restored to the bosoms of his forgiving and understanding companions Vidocq, aged seventeen, became involved with Manon, a woman twice his age and the housekeeper of a gentleman. She gave him a watch and some jewelry and he never thought to speculate, let alone ask, how she could possibly have come into possession of them honestly. Manon was accused of robbery and:

> . . . confessed the fact, but at the same time, to assure herself that after her sentence I should not pass into another's arms, she pointed me out as her accomplice, and even asserted that I had proposed the theft to her. It had the appearance of probability and I was consequently implicated.

Not surprisingly, some may think; but he was in luck. After being kept on remand at Stenay letters written by Manon turned up which exonerated him and, "pure as the driven snow," it was back to the army, to the rejoicing of his captain and the contempt of his colleagues. He fought six duels in as many days and, wounded in the last, went to hospital where he remained for a month. The good captain then gave him six weeks' leave and it was home to Arras.

There, to his astonishment, he found his father had been appointed to supervise the distribution of bread in the time of its scarcity. He was under the protection of Citizen Souhan, commandant of the 2nd battalion of Corrèze. Vidocq declined to help and rejoined his regiment at Givet at the end of his leave. It was there that he was wounded in the leg. He returned to the hospital again and then had a spell at the depot where he joined the Germanic legion as a quartermaster before going off on the road to Flanders. His wound opened afresh and he was again given leave. In 1793 he returned to Arras.

Things had changed in his absence. It was now the height of the Terror, that period of executions that took place from the beginning

---

14 Charles Ledru, *La Vie, la mort et les derniers moments du Vidocq après sa confession à l'heure suprême*, pp. 13–14.

of September 1793 to the end of July the next year. Put simplistically the reasons for the Terror were twofold. The first was to purge France of the enemies of the Revolution, the second to protect the country from foreign invasion while eliminating those who might support such a course. By 1794 the fortunes of the French army were on the upturn and, in theory, there was less need for the Terror. In July the army won a significiant battle at Fleurus. *Les bons temps* were beginning to *roules*. Nevertheless, Robespierre continued with the executions, believing Rousseau's maxim that all men are born good a heart but are corrupted by society.

For once in the early part of his memoirs Vidocq meets and treats with a recognizable historical character. His first sight in the fishmarket was the guillotine operating under the aegis of a fromer priest, Citizen Lebon, whose wife had been a nun at the abbey of Vivier.

The guillotine, perfected in time for the French Revolution, was highly thought of in France. There had been a German version in the thirteenth century and in Britain both Halifax and Edinburgh had "maidens," the latter being reserved for erring gentry. The Edinburgh version had been introduced by the Earl of Morton who himself fell foul of it. The use of the dropping blade had fallen out of favour in the seventeenth century and it was Joseph-Ignace Guillotin, a professor of anatomy in the medical faculty in Paris, who reintroduced it. Earlier research had been carried out by Antoine Louis while a harpsicord maker, Tobias Schmidt, set up the first models. For a short period the guillotine was known as a Louison or Louisette. It was the public executioner Charles-Henri Sanson who pointed out two defects in the proposed device. The first was that the blade had to be of high quality and this would be expensive; secondly, there had to be what he called a communion of spirits between the executioner and his victim. It would only fall into place, so to speak, if everyone knew, and could be relied on to play, his or her part. No trouble with the nobility but what about the ordinary man or woman in the street? Would they display the necessary stoicism?[15]

The guillotine was first used, with great success, at the place de Grève on April 25, 1792, for the execution of the burglar-cum-highwayman Nicolas-Jacques Pelletier, convicted of attacking and beating to death with a cudgel a man in the rue Bourbon-Vilette and stealing a wallet containing 800 livres in assignats.

---

[15] "*Rapport de Charles-Henri Sanson au ministre de la justice sur le mode de décapitation,*" quoted by Jules Taschereau in *Revue retrospective*, Paris, 1835.

There had been some worry that the presence of a crowd might cause trouble. The Sorbonne had been closed on April 5, followed the next day by a measure abolishing religious congregations. However, it passed off well enough but people were not altogether happy. It was all over too soon and there were complaints that there was not enough pageantry attached to the spectacle. Some sang a doggerel, "Give me back my wooden gibbet; give me back my forks." Local residents also complained that, at midnight after the execution, dogs were still lapping up the blood.[16] However, one Paris newspaper commented that the device "in no way stained any man's hand with the murder of his kind and the speed with which it struck is more in accordance with the spirit of the law, which may often be severe but which should never be cruel."[17] The first political victim of the guillotine came on August 21 that year.

Born in 1765, Ghislain-François Lebon (or LeBon) had been an Oratarian schoolteacher before he accepted the Constitution and became the curé of a village near Arras. In turn he became a *prête jure*, the mayor of Arras, a deputy to the Convention and a victim of the guillotine. His rise was rapid and, after marrying, he became the mayor of Arras in 1792. He entered the Convention following the *journées* of May 31 and June 2, 1793.[18] From March 1794 he became a senior and violent member representing Arras and Cambrai.

Lebon is described as the *représentant en mission*. He was then aged twenty-nine. He travelled with his judges and the guillotine, leaving a trail of blood in his wake "in a kind of fever," said his secretary. He would return home and amuse his wife with imitations of the death throes of the victims. He attended as many executions as he could, hectored spectators and victims and ordered the bands to play the "*Ça ira.*" He would also invite the executioner to dinner.[19]

How had Lebon, a priest, come to marry a nun? It was the later spymaster Joseph Fouché, the son of a sailor and himself a former priest, who had set himself the task of destroying and reforming the clergy which he saw as capable of leading resistance to the Revolution.

---

[16] G. Lenotre, *La Guillotine et les executeurs des arrêts criminels pendant la révolution*, pp. 230–1.

[17] See Rayner Heppenstall, *French Crime in the Romantic Age*.

[18] The *journées* marked he insurrection in the Convention nationale and the overthrow of the Girondins.

[19] See Christopher Hibbert, *The French Revolution,* p. 228. Lebon was denounced for his misdeeds after Thermidor and was guillotined on October 16, 1795, in Amiens. On the credit side, he saved Cambrai from invasion but, a disciple of Robespierre, he crushed an uprising in the north with extreme cruelty. With Robespierre's death Lebon lost what protection he had and he followed him to the scaffold.

Fouché was particularly hard on celibacy, believing that not only did it set the clergy apart but it also made no contribution to the need for future generations of soldiers. On October 10, 1793, he declared that there should be no religion other than universal morality. All creeds were free and equal but they could no longer be practiced in public. Clerics who refused to marry were ordered to adopt or support the elderly or orphaned children.

A month before Vidocq's arrival in Arras, one of the guillotine's victims had been a M. de Vieux-Pont. His crime had been that he owned a parrot which had been taught to say the fatal words "*Vive le Roï.*" The parrot had been spared after Mme Lebon, the former nun – and who better – undertook to convert it. This time the victim was a M. de Mongon, the old commandant of the citadel, executed as an aristocrat. It is one of the few descriptive passages in the memoirs:

> An old man whom they had just tied to the fatal plank was the victim; suddenly I heard the sound of trumpets. On a high place which overlooked the orchestra was seated a man still young, clad in a Carmagnole of black and blue stripes. This person, whose appearance announced monastic rather than military habits, was leaning carelessly on a cavalry sabre, the large hilt of which represented the Cap of Liberty; a row of pistols ornamented his girdle, and his hat, turned up in the Spanish fashion, was surmounted by a large tri-coloured cockade. I recognised Joseph Lebon. At this moment his mean countenance was animated by a horrid smile; he paused from beating time with his left foot; the trumpets stopped; he made a signal and the old man was placed under the blade. A sort of clerk, half drunk, then appeared at the side of the 'avenger of the people' and read with a hoarse voice a bulletin of the army of the Rhine and Moselle. At each paragraph the orchestra sounded a chord; and when the reading was concluded, the head of the wretched old man was stricken off amidst shouts of 'Vive la République' repeated by the satellites of the ferocious Lebon.

Vidocq wrote of his surprise that in the midst of such scenes his taste for pleasure and amusement was not lost. Perhaps it was simply a question of gathering rosebuds. The women were just as accessible and he first dallied with Constance Latulipe, the only daughter of a corporal in the citadel, before moving on to the four daughters of a lawyer in the rue des Capucines.

If only he had confined himself to that. Instead, he met a woman who lived in the rue de la Justice who was already involved with a musician of the regiment. Now Vidocq's troubles, brought about mostly by his own misconduct, really began.

Chapter 2

VIDOCQ
AGAINST HIS WIFE
IN PARTICULAR

In which our hero goes to prison – avoids the guillotine –
marries – is duped – and finds a strange man in
his wife's rooms

A S MANY SERIAL CUCKOLDERS have found to their chagrin, from time to time the horns are on the other head. Vidocq became one of their number at an early stage of his career. Just as the midde-aged Casanova was thoroughly duped and metaphorically debagged by Marie Charpillon in London so was the nineteen-year-old Vidocq by Marie-Anne-Louise Chevalier in Arras. Casanova never really recovered from the experience. Vidocq certainly did.[1] Although he was known as the Casanova of Arras, Vidocq operated on an entirely different level from the celebrated Venetian. From an early age Casanova was mixing in society; he may have been a seigneur of fortune but Vidocq's companions were very much soldiers of fortune and at a rougher end of the scale.

Instead of staying faithful to the daughters of the lawyer, Vidocq started to court a young woman from the rue de la Justice who was, at the very least, already walking out, and probably a good deal more, with a musician from his regiment. Ever the hothead, Vidocq accused the man of boasting about his conquests and a quarrel ensued.

---

[1] Marie Charpillon led the great Casanova a merry dance during his time in London. The affair ending with an appearance by him in front of the blind Sir John Fielding, who had succeeded his brother, the novelist Henry, as chief magistrate at Bow Street. Casanova was required to find sureties for his good behavior. Charpillon later became the mistress of John Wilkes, the social reformer, and disappeared from view in 1777 at the age of thirty-one. Casanova died on June 4, 1793, at Dux at the age of seventy-three. There is a full account of their stormy relationship in his *Histoire de ma vie*.

Vidocq insulted him grossly, "inflicting on him the most degrading humiliation," he puts it happily, and a rendezvous was fixed for the following morning. Vidocq was punctual but so was a troop of gendarmes and police officers who disarmed him and took him to the Baudets. The day was January 9, 1794.

The jailer, Beaupré, dressed in a red cap and with two large black dogs always at his heel, kept strict order, and was wont to plunge his arms into the soup pot to search for keys and files. He also had an unhappy knack of saying to anyone who offended him or complained, "You are very difficult to please for the time you have left to live. How do you know that it will not be your turn tomorrow? Oh, and by the way what is your name?" Beaupré was on close terms with Lebon who visited the prison every evening and it turned out, more often than not, that the jailer's predictions were accurate.

Vidocq was in prison for sixteen days before Lebon came to see him. On this occasion Lebon seems to have dealt with him amicably enough. "Ah! Ah! It is you, François? What, you are an aristocrat – you speak ill of the *sans-culottes* – you regret your old Bourbon regiment, take care for I can send you to be cooked."

Lebon arranged for Vidocq's mother to see him and he learned that the musician had denounced him to Chevalier, a Jacobin. Once again it was Vidocq's mother who saved him. She visited Chevalier's sister and in turn representations were made. Vidocq was free after taking a series of oaths of fidelity and denunciation. "What sacrifices will not a man make to procure his freedom?" It was a theme to which he would return over the next decades.

For now, it was back to his depot and it was from there that he sallied forth to pay his thanks to Chevalier and his large, dark-eyed sister, Marie, a woman five days older than himself:

> I was polite; she construed literally some compliments which I paid her, and from the first interview she so greatly misinterpreted my sentiments as to cast her regards on me.

There was even some talk of marriage but Vidocq's parents thought he was too young and so he returned to his regiment and to soldiering, under the command of General Vandamme.

It was the usual Vidocq story of adventures with women, learning that a good-looking man – and who might that be? – may be given change from a barmaid to whom cash has not been paid. He seems to have been with his division for about three months before it was ordered forward to Stinward. The Austrians had signalled that they were marching on Poperingue and at first Vidocq's division defended and then fell back towards Stinward. He was wounded in a hand-to-hand sabre duel with an Austrian Hussar and two months later was sent to rejoin the battalion at Hazebrouek.

When it came to it Vidocq said little about the Revolution in his memoirs but here was an exception. He saw, for the first time, the Revolutionary army, men with pikes and red caps and a transportable guillotine which it was claimed secured the fidelity of the fourteen armies they had on foot. The local peasantry was terrified but Vidocq, warrior that he was, quarrelled and fought with one of the sansculottes who dared to upbraid him about his gold epaulettes. The regulation was that only worsted epaulettes should be worn. Fortunately for him he was sent to Cassel and told to join the 28th battalion of volunteers. The intention was now to drive the Austrians out of Valenciennes and Condé.

Vidocq and his colleagues were quartered at Fresnes and in the farm where he was billeted he met Delphine, the "remarkably handsome" eighteen-year-old daughter of a river pilot staying in the house. Earlier the Austrians had made off with the man's supply of grain and his boat. On a reconnaissance Vidocq had seen they were still unloading it and he proposed a raiding party. It was only a partial success. On the negative side, two of Vidocq's companions were killed; he had two fingers broken and the pilot was captured and given a good beating. On the positive side, the pilot's wife recovered a bag of money hidden in the grain and before setting off to Ghent to look for her husband, now a prisoner of war, she handed over a portion to Delphine.

Vidocq and Delphine now returned to Lille for convalescence, rest and recreation, where it appears such a good time was had that marriage was discussed. At this stage in his life Vidocq seems to have been uxorious because the question of a union with La Chevalier had already been mooted as well.

This time, however, the pilot's wife had apparently found her husband in Ghent and they signalled their consent. Vidocq was to set out for Arras to obtain the license and the consent of his own parents. He had, however, forgotten his hospital ticket, which he would be required to present to the authorities, and went back to the hotel to collect it.

It was around six in the morning when he arrived and there was no answer to his knock on Delphine's room. He knocked again and she opened the door rubbing her eyes. His suspicions were aroused and he suggested, to test her, that she should go with him to Arras. She agreed but continued looking in the direction of a cupboard. When, after a short struggle, the door was opened there, under a pile of dirty linen, was the doctor who had been treating him for his broken fingers.

Here we have Vidocq, the abuser of women. He justified not beating her on the grounds that she was not his wife and also, more pragmatically, that he was in a foreign town and something approaching a deserter in wartime. However, out of the window went her clothes and suffi- cient money to get her to Ghent. The remainder of the money Vidocq kept on the spurious grounds that he had captained the "splendid expedition" which had led to its liberation from the Austrians.

He decided to stay in Lille, had an affair with another woman and was found abroad dressed as a woman. (Not, perhaps, as strange as it sounds; Vidocq was happy to appear in travesty, throughout his life, sometimes to avoid recognition or arrest, sometimes as a joke. There might even be a suggestion that he was something of a cross-dresser.) He was taken to the police where he decided to remain silent to protect both the woman and himself, now that he was a fully fledged deserter. Like so many others, Vidocq was never happy in confinement and a few hours was all that was needed to soften him up so that he had soon told all to a senior police officer. After that, it was boys together. The commandant general of the division heard the no doubt embellished story which made him "laugh to excess." Vidocq was released and told to rejoin the 28th at Brabant.

Just as prison was no home for Vidocq neither was the army. He set off instead for Arras to see if he could get Chevalier to persuade Lebon – now a leading follower of Robespierre and at the height of his power if not his popularity – that there could be an extended leave. There could, and it was back to Marie to say thank-you in what a few decades earlier Casanova would have called proof positive of his affections. "The habit of seeing her daily familiarised me with her ugliness."

So it came about that at 6:30 on the evening of August 8, 1794, Vidocq married nineteen-year-old Marie-Anne-Louise Chevalier, the daughter of Bonaventure Chevalier and Marie-Françoise Lacour. She may only have been five days older than he but, despite his adventures, she was rather more experienced in the ways of the world. It was not a marriage about which he was enthusiastic and it resulted solely from the fact that he could not keep his breeches buttoned.

In the words of the old music hall joke, she was neither pretty nor ugly. She was, according to Vidocq, pretty ugly but, as Georg Christoph Lichtenberg (philosopher and aphorist) remarked, "What they call 'heart' is located far lower than the waistcoat button." She maintained she was pregnant. "Familiarity blinded me to her ugliness," Vidocq repeated, but "things proceeded to a point when I was not astonished to hear she was enceinte."

In fact she was not, but that did not help our hero. He had been given the option by Lebon of marriage or the guillotine and "of the two evils I chose the lesser." During their relatively brief marriage they lived at 73 rue du Saumon, near Vidocq's parents.

Neither seems to have behaved well towards the other. Soon Vidocq was meeting up with his friends in a tavern, or cabaret, called *La Bouteille Noire* and it was not long before he had run through Marie's dowry and she, high-metalled racer that she was, had replaced him with a more mature forty-eight-year-old soldier.

Now Vidocq returned to his regiment but, sent back to Arras on something of a confidential mission, he found all was not well at home:

I arrived at 11 p.m. I went to my wife's home and called out – no reply. I heard a sabre fall on the floor and put my ear to the door. I heard the window open and someone jumped into the street. Down the staircase I ran and I detained a man dressed only in a vest. I gave him a *rendezvous* for the next day.

Chapter 3

VIDOCQ
AGAINST WOMEN IN
GENERAL

In which our hero finds himself in prison again – finds another
mistress – takes up gambling and becomes a thieves' ponce or protector –
and helps to separate a Baroness from her fortune

T HE SOLDIER IN QUESTION WAS Pierre-Laurent Vallain,
the adjutant of the 17th on leave.[1] In France, divorce was now
an option. The Legislative Assembly of 1792 had passed a law which
made divorce available for almost any reason and so inexpensive that
it was within reach of all except the most indigent. This freewheeling
law was, however, changed in 1803 by the more restrictive Napoleonic
legislation, which in turn was repealed in 1816. From then until 1884
there was no divorce in France when the Nanquet law essentially
re-enacted the 1803 legislation. During the Revolution it was said that
"unfettered by law, divorce became rampant and society was plunged
into an orgy of sexual chaos."[2]

The option was one which appealed to Vidocq; it did not, however,
appeal to the authorities. For Vidocq, there was also the question of
honor slighted. The day after finding the half-dressed adjutant major, a
scene witnessed by neighbors, he went to Vallain to demand satisfaction
and was promptly arrested.

The honor of the chaste Marie had to be protected and Lebon, who
initially believed not only was the fault Vidocq's but that he was also a

---

[1] Vallain was then aged forty-three. Born on November 18, 1751, he served with the chasseurs
from 1792 to April 3, 1796. He retired two years later.
[2] Max Rheinstein, *Marriage, Statutory Divorce and the Law*. In Paris from 1792 to 1803 in a
population of 555,000 there were 51,827 marriages and 12,431 divorces. See also Roderick
Phillips, *Family Breakdown in Late Eighteenth-Century France 1792–1803*, p. 1.

deserter, on hearing the evidence, instead made him promise to leave the city. At the time Vidocq may not have been clever with women but he was intelligent enough to see how the political wind could change and that Marie might even welcome a guillotined husband. He delivered the message from his original assignment and fled back to Tournai in search, so he said, of his own adjutant general who had gone first to Brussels and then to Liège before going on to Paris to appear at the bar of the Convention.

As for Vidocq's wife, Vallain did not last and she later formed another relationship, this time with a lawyer. Charles-Joseph Leduc succeeded Vidocq and Vallain in the matrimonial bed of Marie. She had a son by him, Emile-Adolphe, whose birth was registered on January 8, 1799. She claimed that Vidocq was the father but this was impossible since at the time of conception he was in the *bagne* at Brest. "One knows the impossibility of communication in these places," Vidocq remarked years later to his friend, the lawyer Charles Ledru.[3]

Having fled to Tournai in 1794, Vidocq set out by coach to join his superior officer in Brussels and found that he was travelling in what might reasonably be called queer company. His companions, now wearing the uniforms of officers of various rank and regiments, were none other than the men whom he had met in the Lille taverns. They too seem to have been surprised that he was now a mere soldier and he explained that the reconstitution of the battalion had deprived him of his rank. The half colonel among them who paid for everything assured him of his protection.

By the time Vidocq reached Brussels the adjutant general had already gone so he returned to Liège. There, when Vidocq learned the officer had gone to Paris, he simply waited for him, believing it would only be a fortnight before he returned. A fortnight became six weeks and Vidocq's money, or, strictly speaking, that of the pilot's wife, went with the days. He returned to Brussels where he cast about for ways of earning:

> I must confess that I had begun not to be over scrupulous in my choice of these means; my education had not made me a very precise man in such matters, and the injurious society of a garrison, which I had been used to from my childhood, had corrupted a naturally honourable mind.

---

[3] Charles Ledru, *La Vie, la mort et les derniers moments du Vidocq après sa confession à l'heure suprême*. Since the mother had not divorced Vidocq, the boy took his name under the then civil law. It was a question of like father like notional son because Emile-Adolphe Vidocq received six years with hard labor in 1820 for theft, desertion and conspiracy. Marie-Anne-Louise Chevalier later married François Pernot and died on July 27, 1855.

Not a thought, then, about the theft of a neighbor's fowls, the persistent looting of the bakery and shop, the sale of the family silver, nor even, if he was having trouble remembering so far back, his financial treatment of Delphine.

The type of woman with whom Vidocq kept company in this period of his life did not generally have a settled time. In *The French and Their Revolution*, Richard Cobb describes them as being *en marge*, and it is easy to see what he means when he writes:

> Girls continued to be kicked in the stomach, beaten, whipped, tarred, and feathered, dragged by the hair across the room, made love to on the tables of wine-shops, on the ramparts or in rural ditches, their clothes torn, their skirts pulled up, even in the middle of a Paris street, as joyfully and with about as much impunity as under the old regime.
>
> For the country girl up to Paris, nothing would have changed; *la Paysanne Pervertie* of 1775 would remain *la Paysanne Pervertie* of 1794, though her chances eventually of being abducted by a Duke would have been considerably diminished and the range of promotion open to her greatly narrowed.[4]

There is no reason to suppose things were any better in small towns. Did Delphine really think that Vidocq was genuine in his protestations of matrimony? It is hardly surprising that she should have preferred to carry a doctor on the side as some sort of insurance when he cantered off into the distance.

Women, even if ultimately unfaithful to our hero, were never hard to come by and he stayed with Emily, the one-time mistress of General Van der Nott who, abandoned by her lover, was slipping a little in society. Days were passed in the Café Turc or the Café de la Monnaie watching the cardsharps pluck the pigeons. In conversation with a young man the rules of life were explained to him. The sharps came daily, the pigeons only once. Vidocq began to study how it was done and, he claimed, was often tempted to tell the pigeons how their feathers were being removed; "[it] proved that there was still something good in me." He was, on this occasion at least, able to resist the temptation. And it was just as well for him that he did.

Soon he was approached and given ten louis by one of the thieves. He had been noticed and, with the sharps fearful that he might in

---

[4] Richard Gobb, *The French and Their Revolution*, pp. 361–2; see also Archives Nationales, BB 18 744.

fact warn a pigeon and aware that he was big and strong enough not to be intimidated, Vidocq was now put on the payroll. If you accept his version of events, quite by accident Vidocq had become a thieves' ponce. His protestations that this was robbery by another name were met with the response that the merchant who, in the counting room of a morning, would not dream of cheating a person of an hour's interest, would be happy to rob him at the gaming table in the evening. "How could I answer such unanswerable arguments? I had nothing to reply but to keep the money, which I did."

Everything was really going rather well. Vidocq's mother, good woman, had come across with another 100 crowns and this enabled him both to live things up and also to repay the devoted Emily a little. Then came another set back: Vidocq was arrested at the Théâtre du Parc and asked to produce his papers.[5] He said he had none and was taken to the Madelonettes, a local prison. There he gave his name as Rousseau, and his birthplace as Lille. He claimed he was in Brussels for pleasure and had not thought to acquire any papers. The best he could do for himself, however, was to ask to be taken under escort back to Lille. For a small bribe it was agreed Emily could go with him. What he certainly did not want was ultimately to reach Lille where he would surely be recognized as a deserter.

At every stop it was Vidocq – in reality his mother – who paid for the wine and food, convincing his escorts by his generosity and relaxed manner that he was no risk. Back at Tournai he paid for a good supper and with the guards sleeping on the table, he and Emily formed a rope of sheets and, escaping via a second floor window, slipped off to the suburbs of Lille. There he donned the uniform of a chasseur, put a black patch over one eye and the pair set off for Ghent.

Now, according to Vidocq, a really rather touching moment occurred: the errant Emily was reunited with her father. An emotional farewell followed with Vidocq promising to return as soon as he had dealt with some matters in Brussels, and soon it was back to business there poncing off the café cardsharps. It took him three weeks and fifteen louis to obtain the necessary forged papers to show he was indeed the Rousseau he had claimed to be and eventually these arrived delivered by the once respectable Belgian army officer, Captain Albert Labbe, now a member of the celebrated robbers

---

[5] In *Le Vrai Vidocq* Jean Savant says the arrest was over a brawl.

the *Chauffeurs*, a man whom Vidocq would meet again some years later.[6]

How was it that Vidocq and these others seemed to exist outside the Revolution and the terror it brought with it? The answer is that probably for the majority it was quite possible to lead a life largely unaffected by it. This, however, was not so much a rejection of it as by it. "It had nothing to offer the vast body of the poor or vagrants, beggars, the rich, the old."[7]

In the Café Turc he once again met the renegade officers with whom he had travelled to Brussels the first time. He told them of his adventures and was awarded an immediate sub-lieutenancy in their 6th chasseurs. So now Vidocq joined the *armée roulante*, what was effectively a two-thousand-strong bunch of guerrillas plundering the countryside. Promotion and transfers were rapid and informal and Vidocq became a captain of the Hussars and ended back in Brussels billeted with a middle-aged baroness who insisted he dine with her and other guests.[8]

Vidocq explains his entry into society, saying that while he would never have passed in Paris, a little gaucherie did not matter in Brussels. Ultimately, however, he was obliged to introduce his leader, Auffray the soi-disant brigadier general, to the baroness at a supper party. Again it was the more mature man who was seemingly preferred but when the next day Vidocq went to complain he was told that the tête-à-tête night before had been about him.

Auffray had devised a scheme so that Vidocq could marry the baroness who had an annual income of 100,000 florins. He had already spun the poor woman a story that Vidocq was himself of noble birth who had fled to Hamburg with his parents. It was only a version of the old Spanish prisoner swindle. His father had an arrest warrant out against him. Vidocq had returned to France to retrieve his fortune hidden under the floorboards at the beginning of the Revolution, when he was denounced by a man he thought was a true friend. Vidocq had narrowly escaped the guillotine, and as an old friend of the family, Auffray, had procured him a commission under a false name. At the end of the pantomine he would reveal himself as count B. The problem of Vidocq's existing marriage was easily solved. Marie had married Vidocq, not count B and so that did not matter at all. The new

---

[6] Arch. Nat. F[7]16 468.
[7] R. Cobb, *Reactions to the French Revolution*, p. 30.
[8] Bruno Roy-Henry suggests that this may be the baroness d'Ixelles.

count's lack of education and sometimes rough manner were explained by the political events which had ruined his childhood. The only thing Auffray asked was a pension of 1,000 crowns payable in advance and a premium of 30,000 francs for having ennobled the baker's boy from Arras.

Vidocq went back to the baroness and played along. Money was immediately put at his disposal; she would also send some to his impoverished parents. Auffray told Vidocq that, as far as the swindle was concerned, he was the parents and would arrange this. All was going well once more until the authorities, alarmed by the growing strength of the *armée roulante*, clamped down and Auffray fled to Niort where he was arrested. Vidocq was now developing an unhappy touch of the seconds – bigamy, now swindling this poor woman – and for once his conscience was mildly pricked. He went to the baroness and, if he did not explain all, he indicated that it was not what it seemed. She left immediately but only after instructing her butler to hand Vidocq a casket containing 15,000 gold louis.

Easy come, easy go. After a short visit to Amsterdam he made for Paris, arriving at the beginning of March. This was a very different Paris from the one that had witnessed the Terror two years earlier:

> As before the revolution, the streets are full of fine carriages drawn by the well-groomed horses resplendent in new harness; and on the cushioned seats are charming women in costly silks and muslins – dresses so scanty that some of the wearers seem almost as naked as Greek goddesses. Gilded youths ride in the Bois, wearing yellow, brown or scarlet frock-coats and tight-fitting white nakeens. In their beringed hands they carry elegant gold-knobbed riding-whips, which they are glad to use now and again to belabour the once so dreaded terrorists. The perfumers and the jewellers do a roaring trade. Five hundred, six hundred, a thousand dancing-halls and coffee-houses appear like magic. Villas are built, houses bought and sold; theatres are packed; speculation and betting are rife; gambling for high stakes goes on behind the damask curtains of the Palais Royal. Money is afoot once more, autocratic, bold, defiant.[9]

It was in Paris that, to his dismay, he found the cardsharps of the city were in a different league from those in Brussels whom he had studied so assiduously. He also had the misfortune to fall for a girl, Rosine, who separated him from almost all of the rest of the baroness's money. A

---

[9] Stefan Zweig, *Joseph Fouché*, p. 117.

milliner's bill here, some jewelry to be paid for there. In fact, she was being directed in the scam by her pimp who had retreated to Versailles from where he ran the operation until Vidocq had almost been picked clean. For our hero it was time to return to Lille, where he faced more trouble.

This time it would be with Francine Longuet with whom he took up. Vidocq seems to have chosen a series of women who were constitutionally incapable of more than a few hours' fidelity. Worse, he seems to have been unable to recognize the type with whom he set himself up. Were Vidocq's girls prostitutes in the strict sense of the word or camp followers and good-hearted tarts? Probably a mixture of both. Was Vidocq a romantic or a pimp? Certainly he would never admit to being the latter but, reading between the lines, he came close to being one.

In fact, the relationship between prostitute and pimp in Vidocq's time was very different from that of later years. According to the Paris detective Alfred Morain, the concept of the bully or pimp, as we now know him, does not seem to have existed in France until the last quarter of the nineteenth century. Before then Vidocq and the others had a much more subservient relationship with the women earning for them.[10]

---

[10] Alfred Morain, *The Underworld of Paris*, p. 39.

Chapter 4

VIDOCQ
AGAINST THE GYPSIES

*In which our hero joins up with a quack doctor – meets another
of his many nemeses – brawls and is sent to prison – and allows
himself to be used in a prison escape*

V IDOCQ WAS STILL, for the time being, going under the name
Rousseau and, given the raffish society, including officers of
the 13th chasseurs, in which he was moving no one seemed to worry
too much that in previous encounters they had known him by other
names. He was now reduced to giving fencing lessons at the local *salles
d'armes* and was not doing too well at them when, through café society,
he met a man known as Christian Rentier, "with bushy eyebrows and
sun-burned from his outdoor life." Would Vidocq like to travel with
him? Yes, but in what capacity? Vidocq saw himself as too old to be a
clown or the valet of monkeys and bears once more.

It turned out that Rentier was another itinerant doctor, this time
one who cured secret – by which he meant venereal – diseases with an
infallible recipe. A man of many talents, he also cured horses, citing as
his own testimonial that he had cured the horses of the 13th chasseurs
when their own vet had despaired of them. Vidocq arranged to meet
him at 5 a.m. the next day at the gate leading to the Paris road.

Vidocq turned up with a boy carrying his trunk only to be told there
would be no need for that because the expedition would be a short
one on foot. Boy and trunk were sent back to the inn and Vidocq and
the good doctor made for a farmhouse some five leagues away which,
said Rentier, they had to reach by midday. There the farmer produced
bags of crowns and spread them on the table. He and Rentier then
counted out 300 crowns and divided them, with Rentier taking an extra

six, three of which he gave to Vidocq as a share of the profits. When Vidocq asked what profits, he was told that if Rentier was satisfied with him, in due course all would be revealed. The game continued for four days with Vidocq receiving two or three crowns every evening, and then Rentier, whom Vidocq considered to have some ability with animals, set out his stall. Vidocq was to take a certain powder into a farm through the back gate and put it in the manager of some of the animals. He protested, saying he would not do it unless Rentier told him exactly what was going on.

Rentier was reticent. His mother had belonged to a gang of gypsies and the previous year she had been hanged at Temeswar. He had been born in a village in the Carpathian mountains. Gypsies, or more properly Romanies, spoke a language they were forbidden to teach anyone and, moreover, they were forbidden to travel alone which accounted for the fact that they moved in bands of between fifteen and twenty. The band in which Rentier moved had worked its way across France poisoning cattle and then curing the sick beasts, but now they found the peasants were at last catching on and business was taking a dive. Rentier had gone to Lille on private business and was due to meet up with the remainder of the team at the fair at Malines. Vidocq could tag along or not, as he wished. He wanted to. No more seems to have been said about doctoring the cattle.

The gypsies had not reached Malines by the time Vidocq and Rentier arrived so they headed for Brussels, where in the faubourg de Louvain at midnight they stopped before a "wretched-looking house with blackened walls and with straw bales instead of windows." The door was opened by a crone and they were let into a room where about thirty people were "smoking and drinking, mingling in licentious positions." The men all wore blue smocks and underneath sported blue waistcoats with silver buttons. A woman in a scarlet turban was performing "a wild dance with the most wanton postures."

Vidocq feared that the company might turn on him and that his poor mother in Arras, who no doubt continued to dote upon him, would never find out what had become of her little lamb, but the men welcomed them both. The women too embraced him and Vidocq was assured that they were under the protection of a duchess, or mother, of the group. Why should Rentier stay there when he had been meticulous about the cleanliness of the places they had stayed the previous three days? Apparently that was another requirement of being a Romany: if you didn't stay in a Romany house when one was available, you were considered to be a false brother. Vidocq noted that at least the straw was clean.

The next day everyone was up and about smartly; the women neatly dressed as Zealand peasants, the men in vests of the style worn by people from Poissy. Vidocq was told he was not needed, given some more money and told to go off for the day. He did not consider himself obliged to stay at the Romany house and he booked himself into an inn, and took a turn round the fair where he ran into Malgaret, an old acquaintance from the recruiting battalions. Who were these people watching Vidocq? No one that he knew. Malgaret was not deceived. The people, Vidocq's companions of the night before, were robbers no less. Malgaret would show him. Indeed Malgaret did show him and, as they watched, here was a purse taken from a farmer, there some jewels being lifted from a shop.

But who were the people apart from being robbers? Malgaret did not really know. He had done six months in the Rasphuys prison at Ghent over a game with loaded dice, and while in the prison had shared a cell with a couple of the men working the market today. They had told him the tricks of the trade. They came from Moldavia where there was no legitimate occupation for them except that of public executioner. Instead they travelled Europe mending saucepans, changing money, repairing crockery and curing cattle into whose mangers they had previously thrown emetics or other mild poison. When they changed coins they would use sleight of hand to steal and when they knew a farmer had a stash, they would, in return for a share, point out the property to burglars. All of this alarmed the upright Vidocq greatly. . .

Worse was to follow. Malgaret suddenly saw one of the men from Rasphuys approaching them. It was Rentier. Of course, Vidocq could have nothing more to do with gypsies and jailbirds and so he and Malgaret teamed up to find the latter's friends in Courtrai. They were not there and what money Vidocq had received from Rentier went on the gaming tables. For a man who had wandered the roads of northern France for some years Vidocq was remarkably naïve, or at least he portrays himself as such. Malgaret was in league with the other gamblers. Vidocq would have done better to have stayed with the gypsies. He returned to giving fencing lessons again and a benefit exhibition, which produced 100 crowns. And after that it was back to the demimonde where, at the Bal de la Montagne, he met Francine Longuet, the girl whose acquaintanceship would prove seriously discomforting to him.

Francine appears to have been just as much attached to him as Rosine, who had taken his money in Paris, frequently protesting her fidelity. "I thought myself if not the happiest of men at least the most loved," wrote Vidocq. Wrong; her claim of fidelity was not something which prevented her giving private "interviews" to a captain of engineers in an inn in the place Riourt. In came Vidocq the beater and both she and the captain received a thrashing. She fled, the captain remained and, in a most ungentlemanly and unsporting way, preferred charges.

Vidocq may have been unhappy that Francine shared her favors but he himself does not seem to have been in the slightest bit faithful. While he was in prison awaiting trial, numerous young women came and gave ready evidence of their affections. Vidocq was the type of man who could not see a petticoat without chasing it. The penitent and, according to Vidocq, jealous Francine repined.

Now she wanted to withdraw both her and the captain's complaint. The judges smelled bad fish and complicity, and in September 1795 Vidocq received three months' imprisonment. He went first to the Petit Hôtel and then he was transferred to St. Peter's Tower where he had a room known as the Bull's Eye. Francine was allowed to go with him for part of the day.

It is from this point that some of his memoris can be verified and it was now that his fortunes began the serious downward spiral which would last for a decade and a half.

Two of the other prisoners in St. Peter's Tower were ex-sergeant majors Grouard and Herbaux, the latter the son of a Lille bootmaker, who were waiting to go to the galleys. There was also a laborer, Sebastien Boitel, who had been sentenced to six years' imprisonment for stealing garden tools.[1] Boitel continually protested the harshness of his punishment and it was decided by Herbaux and Grouard that they would forge a discharge. Because of the noise in the common quarters of the prison Vidocq was approached to see if his cell could be used. He, poor man and continual dupe, thought they were merely drawing up a pardon and agreed to lend them the cell for four hours a day.

---

[1] In the more heartrending pro-Vidocq accounts of Boitel's imprisonment, bread is substituted for the tools; See Jean Savant, *La Vie aventureuse de Vidocq*, p. 27. Arch. du Nord (Lille) XIV/1 97/122 Dossier Coquelle.

It took them eight days in all and, two days after that, two of Boitel's brothers arrived and dined with him at the jailer's table, something which seems to go against the story of the impoverished man stealing to feed his large family. At the end of the meal a messenger arrived bringing the order for the laborer's release.

The next morning the local inspector of prisons appeared, saw the order, pronounced it a forgery and said that Boitel should not be released. Told he had gone the night before, the inspector had the jailer arrested. Vidocq approached Grouard and Herbaux but they assured him they were as surprised as anyone. All they had done was draw up a petition.

The day after that Vidocq was brought before a magistrate where he protested his innocence. Grouard and Herbaux were put in solitary confinement and Vidocq only then, he claimed, learned the truth from a man he describes as Boitel's bedfellow. The supposedly impoverished Boitel had offered 100 crowns for anyone who could get him out. The pair had charged 400 francs. Others in the plot included the jailer and one of Herbaux's friends, Stofflet. Herbaux had persuaded Boitel to put up the money which, he said, was to be shared with Vidocq.

Vidocq tried to persuade Boitel's bedfellow to make a declaration exculpating him but sensibly, with no wish to be regarded as a nose (or *avoir manger le morcel*), with all the risks that entailed, the man declined. Vidocq was assured he had nothing to fear and was persuaded not to tell the judge. It all sounds very flimsy indeed.

Boitel did not last long on the outside and, on his return to Lille, happily named all his co-conspirators. Again Vidocq, blindly confident that there was no case against him, failed to say anything to the judge. He alone seems to have been surprised when, at the end of his three months, he was not released but instead was arraigned as "an accomplice in the forgery of authentic and public documents." Were it not for his undoubted intelligence and ability one might be tempted to think that Vidocq was a few swallows short of a liter bottle.

Later, rather than sooner, the franc dropped and Vidocq began to realize just what trouble he might be in. He now seems to have been a remand prisoner and the presently faithful Francine Longuet was allowed into the prison to look after him when he became ill. Once he was convalescing he regarded his incarceration as insupportable and devised an escape plan. The best way out, he believed, was in the disguise of a senior prison officer, someone whom the gatekeeper – who had been in turn a *galérien*,[2] and then in the *bagne* at Brest before being sent to Lille – would not dare to challenge. The man was regarded as an asset by the authorities and was promoted to the position of gatekeeper on the basis that a former poacher must know all the tricks of escapers. Francine brought in the clothing concealed in a large muff and then it was just a question of waiting until the prison officer made a visit. One of Vidocq's friends caused a distraction by asking him to examine the food he had been given. Vidocq changed and was gone. The gatekeeper doffed his hat as he passed by. The escape had cost Vidocq 300 francs.

The problem Vidocq now faced was that of many an escaper. It was not merely getting out of the prison; that was, as he and others have repeatedly shown, relatively easy. The trick was staying outside. He went first to a friend of Francine's where she joined him. For a time he remained indoors but then he began to regard the friend's house as little different from that of prison. Off he went for a morning walk and returned without incident. He did the same the next day and had the misfortune to meet a police sergeant who had seen him in prison. It was then standard practice for police officers to tour the prisons looking the inmates over to see if they knew them. When the man asked if he had really been released, Vidocq knew the game was up. Vidocq bought himself some time by asking if, before he was returned to St. Peter's Tower, he could go and see his mistress who was in a house in rue de l'Hôpital. At first Francine could not understand why he had wasted his money in escaping only to give himself up but he then indicated that he needed warm cinders. In a deserted street on the way back to prison he threw the cinders in the man's face and was off.

Once again he seems to have behaved with no discretion at all, ducking, diving and dining all over the city. He was nearly caught in a tavern in the rue Notre Dame but, with a show of bravado worthy of the Scarlet Pimpernel or Fan-Fan La Tulipe, heavily disguised he asked one of the police if it was Vidocq he sought. Told it was, he lured the officer and his colleagues into a cupboard under the pretense of hiding them until he gave a signal and was off. Not, however, before he revealed his real identity.

He claimed he made two more escapes before he was caught and sent back to St. Peter's Tower where now there was no private room

---

[2] Galley sentences were common from 1500 onwards and there is evidence that vagrants were rounded up for this specific purpose. The galleys were abolished in 1748 and the men were put to work at the naval arsenals.

for him, instead a dungeon which he shared with another escaper, Calendrin. It was clear there would be no deceiving the gatekeeper in the same way again and this time a hole was dug in the wall. Fifteen prisoners tried to escape on the third night and the first eight got clean away. Lots were drawn for who went next and Vidocq won. He undressed to enable him to get through the hole more easily but he became stuck. The guard dragged him out and, bruised and scraped, he was sent back to the prison at the Petit Hôtel where he was fettered hand and foot, the left wrist chained to the right ankle, and vice versa, and put in a dungeon.

Ten days later, after promising not to try to escape again, he was returned to the main prison community. Previously he had led what he saw as a sheltered prison life among robbers, forgers and cardsharps but now he was in with the professionals, including another man from Arras, one Desfosseux, who had first been sent to the galleys at the age of eighteen, had escaped from the *bagnes* three times, and was due back on the next consignment. Throughout his life Vidocq was a good listener and, with an ear to escape, he talked to the man – who was convinced that the guillotine would eventually claim him – about his exploits. He also made friends with some of the captured members of the *Chauffeurs*, that disparate band of some forty or fifty robbers (Vidocq had earlier met one of their members, Albert Labbe) who were the scourge of the northern French countryside under the leadership of the notorious Salembier. Vidocq names his fellow prisoners as Chopine (the Nantzman), Louis Duhamel known as Lilleman (from Douai), Auguste Poissard (the Provençal), Caron the Younger and Caron the Hunchback, and finally the Bruxellois known as Daring.

The Bruxellois' act of bravery which had gained him his nickname was indeed fairly spectacular. Trapped in a slipknot while trying to lift the latch of a farmhouse door – his hand inside, his arm outside – unable to release himself and, fearing his colleagues might kill him in case he betrayed them, he took a dagger and cut off his hand at the wrist before escaping. He was afterwards also known as Manchot, or one-armed. As with all good stories, it was said to have happened in a dozen or more places in the north of the country but Vidocq maintained it occurred in the vicinity of Lille. Manchot was later executed.

Strictly speaking, the bands of robbers, known as the *Chauffeurs du Nord*, operated between approximately 1795 and 1803 in north, eastern and central France, carrying out their robberies at night when, their faces masked or covered in soot, they entered isolated farmhouses, garrotted their victims and burned the soles of their feet to force them to reveal where their money was hidden. Afterwards it was a case of rapine, looting and arson. Blame was generally laid at the door of the English and the Royalists who were said to have hired them. When, from time to time, some members of the bands were arrested, judges declined to convict out of fear for their personal safety.

In the prison, with many bound for the galleys, escape was again the order of the day and after eighteen prisoners had been taken before an examining magistrate and placed in an anteroom, when a gendarme put down his coat and hat Vidocq donned them, seized a fellow prisoner as if marching him to another judge, and managed to get past the corporal of the guard. Again there was the same old problem. Where to go? Vidocq's partner fled to the provinces but Vidocq went back to Francine who, it might be thought, had by now well and truly repaid her debt for getting him arrested in the first place.

It might also be thought that when Vidocq escaped all the gendarmerie had to do was to go to rue de l'Hôpital or wherever Francine was working, and arrest him. They do not appear to have done so and again it was Vidocq's inability to keep his breeches buttoned that led to his return to prison. He and Francine, who now sold her furniture to raise funds, decided to escape to Belgium but before the flight a former girlfriend, Eliza, reappeared. Supper was followed by a night with her, and Francine was fobbed off with the story that he had been chased by the police and had hidden out until the next day. A friend apprised her of the true story and Francine threatened to have Vidocq rearrested. Prison would at least put a halt to such heterosexual infidelities.

Vidocq thought that Francine might cool down but, prudently avoiding her, went to the house in which they had been living, forced a shutter and took his clothing. Five days later he went to a seamstress whom he knew and whom he thought might act as a go-between in the reconciliation. Again he misjudged things. When the woman returned there was a host of gendarmes and other police. Back to the Petit Hôtel. What the authorities wanted to know was who had been sheltering him. When he refused to tell them he was stamped with the mark of a convict and sent back to his cell in rags.

Vidocq was not convinced that Francine had actually betrayed him and he could not see the benefit to the seamstress in doing so. After twenty-four hours in solitary confinement he was brought before another examining magistrate where all was revealed. The police case was that, far from merely forcing the shutter, he had been there with Francine, there had been another quarrel and he had cut her with a knife. It was produced, the blade and haft covered in blood. A porter who had carried Vidocq's luggage had also noticed he had blood on his hands.

The next day he was confronted by Francine, who fainted, and he was then charged with her attempted murder. She had been stabbed in five places. The police thought that the only reason Vidocq had shown up at the seamstress's home was to find out if she was actually dead. Now the loyal Francine told the magistrate that she had stabbed herself in despair but, given her previous attempt to withdraw her charge in the original assault case, it was thought she was simply trying to protect Vidocq:

> At the age of twenty I was suffering under the weight of the twofold accusation of forgery and assassination, without having even dreamt of committing such crimes. I even reflected whether I would not hang myself at the bars of my cell with a straw rope.

Here again we see Vidocq the self-exculpator. This one act of folly in sleeping with another woman and another of kindness in allowing his cell to be used for the petition-cum-forgery had produced consequences far beyond any he could have expected and far beyond any punishment he could reasonably have felt justified. In the end this second charge was dismissed. Vidocq explained that he had cut himself on the window after he had broken the shutter and Francine maintained her new story. That still left the forgery, however, which was in abeyance because, while Vidocq had been having his own adventures, Grouard had also escaped.

Now he was back with temporary prisoners and when the turnkey forgot to lock the door one morning Vidocq was off and flying. Unfortunately, he was seen by the jailer who was drinking in a public house opposite. The hue and cry went up and Vidocq, temporarily safe in rue Saint-Saveur, realized he had to get out of Lille. At night the gates of the city were closed and manned by gendarmes. Vidocq went to the bastion of Notre Dame, tied a rope around a tree, threw the end over the city wall and proceeded to slide down. He went too fast, burned his hands, let go of the rope and fell some fifteen feet, spraining his ankle.

In agony he managed to persuade a carter to take him to the next village where the man and his wife put him up for the night. Vidocq explained that he had been smuggling tobacco, and once he had fallen had been abandoned by his colleagues. After a fortnight the carter, who had been told Francine was a go-between for the smugglers, took a note to her and she sent back 110 francs in gold. Vidocq left for Ostend, intending to sail for either India or America.

He was to be disappointed once again. The only captains he could find were Danish or Dutch and they refused to take anyone without papers. The small pile of money was diminishing and Vidocq (or his ghostwriter) had a bit of philosophizing to do:

> Money certainly does not produce wit, nor talents, nor understanding; but the quiet of mind which it superinduces, the equanimity which it affords, amply supply the place of these qualities.

For now, Vidocq decided to join the smugglers of whom he had heard so much; not that he wanted to, of course. Vidocq had always a healthy sense of self-preservation and he was not keen on nights on windswept rocks being shot at by customs officers. Still, needs must.

So, "with great repugnance," he went to see a man called Peters, who might be in need of additional help. He found the man in a cellar but not in any sort of good humor: no sooner had Vidocq introduced himself than Peters proceeded to give him a good beating. He had, Vidocq reasoned as he escaped, been taken for a spy. For his part, Peters had every reason to be worried about Vidocq being a spy. At this time, smuggling, a staple occupation for the poor in France, carried heavy penalities. A second conviction for smuggling on foot with no weapons carried six years in the galleys; a first conviction for smuggling in an armed band would earn nine years and a second conviction would result in life imprisonment.[3]

Vidocq now went back to the dealer who had given his name to Peters and was this time told he would need to say "Beware of the sharks," a term for customs officers. He also took the precaution of filling his pockets with stones in case he needed to defend himself. He did not need them. This time Peters welcomed him and Vidocq was put under the care of a man from Bordeaux to show him the ropes. There were some fifteen members of a motley crew – Dutch,

---

[3] See Olwyn Hutton, *The Poor of Eighteenth-Century France, 1750–1789.*

Danes, Portuguese, Swedes, two French and no English. The second night Peters came into the communal bedroom and told them that the *Squirrel* had been making signals prior to landing and they should prepare for it. More joined and two women and some countrymen brought horses. Barrels were dropped into the sea tied to a rope which was retrieved by a Newfoundland dog, and Vidocq, in one of the three teams, began hauling in the booty, while the other teams stood guard against customs officers. The *Squirrel* stayed well offshore to avoid the risk of running aground. The barrels were loaded onto the horses which were then ridden off. Then, as the third delivery was being unloaded, the customs officers arrived. Two of Peters' men were killed but the customs officers were reluctant to attack and Vidocq and the others faded away. At dawn he was back at Peters' house and stayed there for forty-eight hours with a fever brought on by the cold and fear. He told Peters the work was too hard for him and he wanted to go back to Lille. He was given 100 francs and he set off, watched by Peters' spies who made sure he went where he said he was going.

Once back in Lille, and using the name Leger, he wanted to meet Francine whom he decided to take to Holland where he hoped to set up what he called "a small establishment." Unfortunately, he was again careless and was spotted by two gendarmes out drinking. Vidocq looked shifty and they followed and arrested him. He did not have a passport and was held for the arrival of men from the Lille brigade. It was only a matter of time before a senior officer cried, "By Jove 'tis Vidocq," and once more it was back to the Petit Hôtel.

Any suggestion that an eighteenth-century French prison had any more of a reforming effect than one of today is unsustainable. Many of the men whom Vidocq had known before his last escape had been released and rearrested for new offenses. Among them was Calendrin who had lasted only two days on the outside before he was charged with a new burglary. It was escape time again.

Not, thought Vidocq, that easy a matter. The dungeon in which the cream of the prisoners were held was seven feet square with walls six feet thick, strengthened with planking and crossed and riveted with iron. The door was cased with wrought iron and the small two foot by one window had three separate iron gratings. But guards are there to be bribed and Vidocq and his cellmate, Duhamel, paid six francs to a trusty prisoner acting as turnkey who, for the money, procured two files, a ripping chisel and two screwdrivers.

Chapter 5

VIDOCQ
AGAINST THE FEETWARMERS

In which our hero escapes yet again – meets the dreaded
Chauffeurs again – takes to the sea – is sentenced and heads
for the Bicêtre

V IDOCQ NEXT SET about cutting a replica of the dungeon key from a large carrot, made a mold of bread and potatoes and, from the pewter spoons the prisoners were allowed, he finally succeeded in making a key. Then, on the day of the breakout scheduled for the evening, Vidocq learned his term in the dungeon had expired and that he could rejoin the main prison population. He was not pleased. He was, however, advised that to escape with men like Salembier and Duhamel, who had been with him in the dungeons, was simply asking for trouble. They would probably kill someone within twenty-four hours of being on the outside. The information was correct. Salembier and Duhamel escaped and joined up with a band of around fifty *Chauffeurs*, of whom twenty-eight were executed at Bruges within a month.[1]

It was Francine who again provided help for the next escape when, with Vidocq wrapped in the tricolore, he again fooled the guard, Baptiste.[2] Francine was arrested and questioned but, apart from admitting she had supplied the material for the tricolore, she claimed she knew nothing of the use to which it had been put.

---

[1] Vidocq incorporates them into his faction novel *Les Chauffeurs du Nord*.
[2] If some of Vidocq's escape stories seem too good to be true there is clearly some historical evidence to back them up. Leonard Betrand, a clothing merchant imprisoned at La Force, escaped but was rearrested, this time for passing counterfeit money. When asked how he had managed the escape he said he had found a mason's gray coat and, wearing it, went to the prison secretary claiming he could not find the person he was looking for, gave the name of a prisoner who had been released and walked out. Arch. Nat., Judgements, 5th Provisional Tribunal.

Her protestations did her no good and she received six months imprisonment. Vidocq managed to leave the city and once again joined a troupe of strolling players at Courtrai, run by the juggler and quack physician Devoye, some of whom were his former prison companions who had also escaped. The troupe then performed in Ghent and went on to Enghien for the five-day fair. After Vidocq had, he maintained, taken over the major roles, out of jealousy one of the clowns informed on him. He was never one to keep his head below the parapet.

Back in Lille he discovered that not only had Francine been sentenced but that the guard, Baptiste, was thought to have been in the plot and that he too was now in his own prison. He had been helped there by other prisoners who claimed he had taken a 100-crown bribe from Vidocq. As for our hero, now regarded as a most dangerous escaper, he was sent to the prison at Douai and was soon back in chains in the dungeon.[3] And who did he find there in the vermin-ridden straw? None other than Desfosseux, the fellow criminal from Arras, along with a young man Doyenette, sentenced to six-teen years for burglary. Vidocq had money left over from his time with the troupe and bought food and provisions. In return the others explained the next escape attempt; this time it would be via a hole in the paving stones of the dungeon. It took them fifty-five days to dig the tunnel, one man at a time taking turns. A body had been made from straw so that guards looking into the dungeon would assume everyone was in bed. Then, freedom. Unfortunately there had been a miscalculation and the tunnel ended not on a riverbank but in the river itself. The cell was flooded and the trio were obliged to call for the guards for help.

Meanwhile, Baptiste, the jailer at the Petit Hôtel, was awaiting sentence over Vidocq's escapes. It seems that convicted but unsen-tenced prisoners had a certain amount of freedom, and Baptiste, in return for promises by Vidocq to exculpate him, had brought in a knife and two large nails which Desfosseux had used to dig out what ap-peared to be cement between ceiling tiles but which was in fact pieces of whitened bread. The plan was discovered and the pair were soon back in fetters, chained together. Desfosseux, who like many prisoners kept one or more files in a container up his anus, removed the fetters and then, chained once more, performed the trick again telling the

---

[3] It is still possible from Tuesday to Thursday to visit the cells from which Vidocq made his attempts and finally escaped.

guards that he had a well-known herb which melted iron. It was something to keep the prisoners amused and the guards on edge.

In fact it was another false key which got them all out while they were seeing their counsel prior to a court appearance. All they had between them was six francs. Vidocq claims that Desfosseux was going to commit another burglary and that he did not want to be involved. It also seems that his clothing was still in a fair state of repair while the other two were in rags. He went into an inn on the pretense of buying them all food but instead ate and drank his fill then walked out of the back door.

Four days later he reached Compiègne where he sent a message to his mother asking for help. Now he was going under the name of Lannoy and he applied to join a regiment of Hussars at Louvres but was only employed to curry the horses. His freedom was short-lived: he ran into another gendarme who knew him from Douai and, despite an attempt to brazen it out, it was prison for him once more. There he learned on the grapevine that Grouard and co. had decided someone should confess to forging the Boitel pardon and – since he had not been there at the time – the decision was taken that that someone should be Vidocq. The only comfort was that Desfosseux and Doyenette were back in custody in the same prison. They had been arrested at Pont-à-Marcq. Why hadn't Vidocq returned with food for them? Unfortunately, just as he was buying the food, a gendarme had turned up and he had been obliged to flee himself. They accepted the story and, given that their trials were rapidly approaching, there were further plans for escape.

Prisoners came and went; one batch included the Duhesme brothers who were also members of the *Chauffeurs* and who had been denounced by a neighbor. One of them had a knife and he gave Vidocq a file. As a Justice of the Peace accompanied by gendarmes was beginning a strip search, Vidocq swallowed it. It seems that the authorities were still looking for the seal which had been used to stamp Boitel's pardon and it was suspected that this was what he had swallowed. He was placed in fetters, the sole occupant of a dungeon in the town hall prison, until he passed it. When, after eight days, the seal had not appeared he was due to be returned to the prison proper. Usually prisoners had to walk, but Vidocq, feigning weakness after his dungeon ordeal, was placed in a carriage and while on the road jumped out. The gendarmes, wearing jackboots and carrying sabres, were soon left far behind and this time he reached Dunkirk. Somehow he had received money sent by his mother and he made friends with a man who arranged to get him a passage on a Swedish brig.

Vidocq seemed to have had just about as much luck with seamen as he did with women. He agreed to go with his newfound friend to St-Omer to buy biscuits where he was promptly arrested. For once he blames only himself:

> . . . my turbulent character would not allow me to remain quiet in a pot-house row and I was arrested as a riotous fellow and taken to the watch-house.

Without papers he was sent back to Douai and the dungeons where he tried yet another escape with a bayonet stolen from a member of the National Guard, which he used to dig a hole in the wall. The escape route was discovered by the jailer's wife, who saw the debris from the digging when going to feed her rabbits. Now it was a stand-off in the prison cell, with Vidocq and his companions surrounded and threatening to kill the first man who entered. Meanwhile, one of them continued digging in the forlorn hope they could still break through the wall. Disgrace, dungeons, fetters and, worse, the Boitel trial, followed.

Even by Vidocq's standards he was unlucky. On 7 Nivôse, the fifth year of the French Republic (or December 27, 1796), the jury of the criminal court of the division of Cambrai returned a verdict that the allegation of forgery had been made out, that César Herbaux had committed the forgery, intentionally and with an intent of doing wrong; that Vidocq was guilty in like terms; that the others, including Boitel, were acquitted.

Each received eight years in the galleys. Anyone condemned to the punishment of irons, imprisonment in the house of correction, or to confinement had first to be placed in the town square of that place, tied to a post and set on a scaffold for six hours. If he was condemned to the rack it was only four hours and a mere two for imprisonment. Inscribed in large letters on a board above the head of the convicted man were his name, profession, residence, the reason for his sentence and the judgment passed on him. The only positive thing was that he was not branded. It was now a question of an appeal or of waiting to be sent to a *bagne*.

Vidocq maintains that this was the only real crime for which he was ever sentenced; brawls did not count. Over the years rumors abounded about Vidocq being sentenced to death for a variety of murders, that he had been the equivalent of a stagecoach robber, and that he had been sent to the galleys for life as a housebreaker and robber. When it came down to it, these rumors would stand his reputation in good stead, but for the present he was not happy:

> . . . when I assert that I should be believed for it was at last but a prison joke, which, if proved, would at present only subject the offender to a sentence of corporeal punishment. But it was not the suspected accomplice in a foolish forgery that was to be punished; it was the disorderly, rebellious, and impudent prisoner, the chief of so many plans of escape, of whom an example must be made and I was sacrificed.

Despite his annoyance Vidocq decided not to appeal against either his conviction or sentence. He explains this by saying that the prisoners were to be sent to Bicêtre and then on to the *bagne* at Brest. An appeal would keep him several more months at Douai. He was now being guarded more closely and he believed that his best chance was to escape on the way either to Bicêtre or the port.

In Vidocq's case he and his companions each had a fifteen-pound ball attached to their leg irons and the men were secured two by two with an iron wrist-cuff. On May 20, 1797, they set off for Bicêtre. Vidocq, often one to make bullets for others to fire, had persuaded fourteen companions, one of whom was Desfosseux, to join in a mass escape in the forest at Compiègne. The guards must have displayed a singular lack of curiosity and a reluctance to make an internal search for Desfosseux still had a number of files and saws about his person. Within three days the fetters had been cut and plastered over to prevent the guards seeing the marks.

As the plan unfolded, the prisoners leaped out of their carriages and tried to make for the woods but the guards prevented them. The men then tried to throw paving stones at the soldiers but with one charge it was all over. Two prisoners were killed and five others seriously wounded. The survivors, including Vidocq, soon begged for mercy. Then Hurtel, the warder-cum-officer who had ordered that the prisoners should have the iron balls attached to their leg irons, stuck a knife into one man who did not comply quickly enough with the orders to get in the carriage. There was another mini-riot, quickly suppressed by the dragoons, but afterwards Hurtel kept well in the background.[4]

The convoy made its way to Senlis where the jailer doubled as streetkeeper and the prison was left in the command of his formidable wife. When she heard them digging at the walls she threatened them with the bastinado (beating the sides of the feet with a stick) and they stopped. The day afterwards they reached Paris and then it was on to Bicêtre, the prison-cum-lunatic-asylum-cum-hospital-cum-poor-house at Sceaux some seven kilometres north-east of Paris and which housed around three thousand, including the staff and their families.[5] Vidocq and the others arrived there on May 20, 1797.

What did Vidocq look like in adult life? The register at Bicêtre recorded him as aged twenty-six, five feet six inches tall with blond hair, beard and eyebrows, a round forehead, a long aquiline nose, gray eyes, a medium-sized if askew mouth, a long and round chin, an oval face with a scar on the upper right lip and pierced ears. His life had so far anticipated that of an unsuccessful minor outlaw in post–Civil War America. There had been a number of what, in criminal circles, are called touches, but, mixing metaphors, there had also been a large number of roundabouts.

In one of the more comtemplative passages of his *Mémoires*, Vidocq wrote of Bicêtre:

> On reaching the end of the avenue which looks on the road to Fontaine-bleau, the carriages turned to the right and entered an iron gate, above which I read mechanically this inscription – *Hospice de la Vieillesse*. In the forecourt many old men were walking clothed in grey garments. They were paupers; and stared at us with that stupid curiosity which results from a monotonous and purely animal existence; for it often happens that a person admitted into a hospital, having no longer his own subsistence to provide for, renounces the exercise of his narrow facilities and ends by falling into a state of perfect idiocy.

The prison of Bicêtre was a quadrangular building which enclosed a series of other buildings and courtyards – the great court where the prisoners exercised, the kitchen court, the dogs' court, the irons court (the *cour des fers*, where prisoners' irons were fitted), the punishment court and the idiots' court, on which Vidocq had first set eyes.

---

[4] Very occasionally the convicts managed a successful escape on the way to the galleys. One instance was in November 1827 on the road to Morlaix. See Index to the *Gazette des Tribuneaux*, 1827–8.
[5] It was closed in 1836.

By the time Vidocq, Desfosseux and the others reached the inner courtyard of the prison they were surrounded by some sixty inmates. The irons they still wore were a status symbol and Desfosseux, among old friends and acquaintances, made the introductions. There still seems to have been the opportunity to buy drinks from a shop on the premises and, once his irons were off and he was clothed in a half-gray, half-black smock, Vidocq was led there. Food could also be bought and Vidocq recounts the story of a guard dog named Dragon which sat on a roof – "the most incorruptible of all the guards' – until it was fed with a leg of mutton and so missed foiling an escape. As a result he was beaten and sent back to the dogs" court where he subsequently died.

The most troublesome of the prisoners were sent to an older building with underground cellars in which Gruthus-Duchâtelet, the man who betrayed the celebrated robber Cartouche in return for a commutation of his death sentence, lived for forty-three years. Early in his sentence he had escaped from Bicêtre, but had been recaptured on June 5, 1724. He was then taken to the Bastille and later back to Bicêtre, where he remained from June 12, 1749, until his death on July 3, 1750. To see a moment's sunshine the man would feign death, something at which he was so successful that, when he did eventually pass on, Gruthus-Duchâtelet had actually been dead for two days before the guards removed his iron collar.

As an associate of the *Chauffeurs*, Vidocq had something of a reputation preceding him and he was made head of his dormitory and given a proper bed. However, not everyone was delighted with him. One convict, François Beaumont, said to be one of the most "impudent of thieves," picked a quarrel with him and, fighting him at savate – the old French-style foot boxing which Vidocq surprisingly maintained he had never seen – gave him a good beating. He was taken aside by another old hand, Jean-Baptiste Goupil, and taught the art.[6] From then on he was left alone.

The description of Beaumont as the most impudent of thieves is an accurate one. Even the police were not safe from his predations.

---

[6] The fighting style of savate was born in the cabarets and streets of the working-class suburbs of Paris but it was not until the early nineteenth century that it really came to be recognized. It was popularized by Michel Casseux, born in 1794, who opened a salon in Courtille and instructed, amongst others, the duc d'Orleans, the designer Gavarni and Lord Seymor, "Milord l'Arsouille." Casseux wrote the first treatise on the sport, *L'Art de la Savate*. Others who ran schools included Louis Lebouchier whose gymnasium on the quartier du faubourg Montmartre was frequented by Rossini and Théophile Gautier.

Later the celebrated Jean Henry, who negotiated with Vidocq, fell prey to Beaumont. The man obtained an imprint of the keys to offices in the Préfecture and, arriving in an all-black outfit of the type worn by magistrates and public officials, said he was the keeper of the Bureau Central and that he required a soldier to accompany him. He placed the soldier on guard and at his leisure helped himself to watches, jewels and diamonds. Unfortunately most of the property was found on him. After several attempts at escape he was wrapped in more and more chains and apparently died from exhaustion.[7]

As for daily life in the prison, it seems little different from that in many of those of today. In Bicêtre, designed to hold twelve hundred men, there was serious overcrowding; the guards were brutal but could be bribed with a bottle of wine or money, robbers stole from the weaker prisoners and homosexuality was rife. "Men condemned for those attempts which modesty shrinks from naming, openly practised their detestable libertinism," wrote Vidocq. Suspected informers were given bad beatings with the guards turning away indifferently. There was also another version of the Spanish prisoner swindle. Addresses of rich people living in the province from which a new prisoner came were obtained and what was called a "Letter of Jerusalem" was sent, in which, in time-honored tradition, the addressee was told he had been singled out as a man of integrity and discretion. The writer had, it seems, managed to secrete a cask of money and jewels from thieves who had attacked him on the road. Could the addressee help in return for a share of the contents? Vidocq says that, surprisingly, about one in five of such letters was answered. Some people actually came in person to Bicêtre.

The guards did not mind. If the prisoners received money that meant more for bribes, and they also looked the other way over the making of false two-sous pieces which were circulated in Paris, of making false passports and, importantly, false hair, essential in any escape attempt since the prisoners had their heads shaved. All these were concealed in metal tubes inserted in the rectum.

As for the new fish in the prison, they were stripped of their clothes and jewelry, which was sold for the general good. If they were slow in removing their earrings these were pulled out. Nor was it any use trying to sleep with your valuables under the pillow. In such a case, a weight was attached to the man's foot and, as he sat up, the goods were snatched. It was survival of the fittest.

---

[7] Arch. Nat. F7 10351.

Of course the quality of life in prison would depend on the force of personality and circumstances of the prisoner. Pierre Griffard, sentenced to a year for the theft of a handkerchief on the place de Grève, fared quite well. Imprisoned in La Force he wanted to remain there for the whole of his sentence. A shoemaker by trade, he had set up a shop and was afraid he would lose work if he was moved.

On the other hand, Antoine Chapuis, who was training for the law and who spent three weeks in the same prison, complained:

> I have been robbed of four écus, of six livres, of most of my linens – hand-kerchiefs, socks, collar, even a pair of pants. I had to pay for a bed and pay to save my life from the brigands around me.[8]

In winter those who had been stripped of their possessions could keep warm in the straw but, once on the chain to the *bagnes* with nothing but packing-cloth trousers and a smock, they often failed to survive the first night on the road.

As for Vidocq, he did not favor even one night on the road to the *bagnes*. It was a question of another escape. He and his colleagues reasoned that they could get into the asylum part of Bicêtre and so successfully did they dig that on the night of October 3, 1797, thirty-three of them reached the idiots' court. Now all they needed was a ladder. Instead, all they could find was a pole and in doing so disturbed one of Dragon's replacements. The prison inspector heard the noise and sent for guards who approached the men with fixed bayonets; it was all over in a trice and the men were returned to the dungeons. One man however, Vidocq's friend Desfosseux, was missing. He had hidden in a bath before getting into a room with one of the more insane members of the asylum. He stayed there for a day but, when he tried to leave the cell, the idiot set about him hitting and biting him. Desfosseux was for once happy to give himself up.

After eight days in the dungeon Vidocq was sent to rejoin the other prisoners who were in high spirits since they had made a haul from the Spanish prisoner letters. It was, however, only a matter of time before they were to start out on the long road to Brest. One of the prisoners who was to go with them was Pierre-Thomas Richard, who had been involved in one of France's most spectacular and much-talked-of crimes – the robbery of the Lyons Mail.

---

[8] Z 3/16 Arch. Nat. Paris Provisional Criminal Tribunals 1791–2.

Chapter 6

VIDOCQ
AND THE MEN FROM
THE LYONS MAIL

*In which we read the story of Vidocq's fellow galérien Pierre-Thomas
Richard – of a terrible murder, mistaken identities and thrilling
escapes – possible miscarriage of justice which has fascinated
writers for two centuries*

THE FRENCH POSTAL SYSTEM evolved during the reign of Louis XI. In 1464 the mounted messengers who carried his administrative orders to the provinces became a regular body working fixed routes. It was a matter of time before members of the aristocracy were given permission, for a payment, to use the messengers for their own private letters. Originally carried in saddlebags, by the eighteenth century the volume of mail had grown to the extent that the couriers used chaises or carts for the lighter goods, which now included parcels. Heavy goods went by diligence and barge. The Crown then contracted out, granting monopolies to *fermiers généraux* who paid heavily for the privilege. In turn the *fermiers* recouped and made their profit by charging the rank and file for delivery. Acceptance as a *fermier* was highly prized. A substantial deposit and sureties were required and a sale of a position produced considerably more than the salary. They also served as an informal news agency.

The *fermiers* more or less survived the fall of the ancien régime although they were now more closely administered. By 1796 they also served as an express, if uncomfortable, stagecoach. Up to three passengers could be taken and only hand luggage could be carried because speed was of the essence. Passengers paid more than the regular fee for a seat on a stagecoach and to purchase a ticket

a passenger had to present his passport and papers at the Bureau
Central des Postes. Curiously, even though valuables were carried,
there was no armed guard to prevent hold-ups.

There were staging posts, usually, but not always, inns every ten
miles and with fresh horses coaches could travel at about eight miles an
hour. Mails travelled all night so with between forty and fifty changes
the Paris–Lyons Mail would arrive in not less than a day and a half but
certainly within two days.

On May 26, 1796, the Government Mail Coach, driven by the
fifty-year-old Jean-Joseph Excoffon, left rue Martin after he had
taken dinner at the Pewter Plate inn. As is often the case in romances,
this was to be one of his last journeys because he was in the process of
selling his business. The largest consignment was of boxes of coin and
assignats worth seven million francs intended for Bonaparte's army in
Italy. His fourteen-year-old son Maurice and Citizeness Dolgoff saw
him off. There was one passenger, Pierre Laborde, a wine merchant,
whose papers suggested he came from Lyons. He had no luggage at all,
something which was not unusual, but carried a large cavalry sword.

The first stop was Villeneuve where a postboy was picked up for a
double stage. The Lyons Mail then stopped in Montgeron where four
strangers had been dining earlier in the day. Lieursant was the next
stage and after that Melun. When the Mail did not arrive there that
evening or during the night, the next morning a search was made.
Excoffon was found slashed and dead in a field. The body of the postboy, who had made a run for it in his stockinged feet, was found some
distance up the road. One hand had been cut off. A spur, presumably belonging to one of the attackers, was found nearby. Of the wine
merchant there was no sign.

The thieves had taken the horses, and that of the postillion was
found in Paris near the Minimes de la Place Royale. Then came a report that one Etienne Couriol of 200 rue du Petit Reposoir had taken
four sweating horses to a Citizen Morin at 227 rue des Fosses Germain
l'Auxerrois. They fitted the description of the horses of the strangers
seen in Montgeron and Lieursant where the wife of the landlord of
the White Horse recalled stitching the fastening of a spur for one of
the men.

A warrant was issued in Melun for the arrest of Laborde, and
Couriol was traced to the house of a receiver, Pierre-Thomas Richard.
By now Couriol and his mistress, Madeleine Breban, were long gone

and had to be retrieved, a week later, from Château Thierry, some sixty miles east-north-east of Paris. They were staying in the house of a man named Gohier, a former military contractor. In Couriol's possession was approximately one-fifth of the value of the stolen assignats. Charles Guénot from Douai, who had the misfortune to be in Gohier's house at the time, was also arrested and then released, being told to collect his papers from the Central Law Courts in Paris in a week's time. Sensibly Madeleine Breban turned State's evidence.

The *juge d'instruction* was named Daubanton and it was while he was conducting his preliminary investigation on May 11 that a curious incident took place. Two barmaids from Montgeron, Marie Grossetête and Marie-Victorine Sauton, were waiting to give their evidence when Charles Guénot came to collect his papers accompanied by Joseph Lesurques, a tall fair-haired man. The girls were convinced that this was one of the four men responsible for the robbery and Lesurques was duly arrested. Couriol was then brought up and the girls were even more convinced that he was the man who had actually paid for lunch for the four.

Lesurques' story was simple. He had done military service and had retired with the rank of sergeant. His wife had brought him a dowry and he had played it up buying and selling Church and Crown lands, producing 12,000 francs income. No effort seems to have been made to check this. Daubanton now had Richard, Couriol, Guénot, Lesurques and Richard's servant Bruer in custody. Soon after David Bernard, a Jewish livery stable keeper, joined them.

At the trial, conducted not by Daubanton but a superior judge, Citizen Judge Jérôme Gohier – described by the executioner Charles-Henri Sanson as "harsh" – Madeleine Breban tucked Couriol away neatly saying he had been absent from home on the night of the robbery. His case had been more or less hopeless anyway. That left Lesurques as a robber who, apart from having the additional problem of the spur being identified as belonging to him, was in a very different position. He called sixteen witnesses including Hilaire Ledru, a painter of some note.[1]

Unfortunately like so many in the dock, Lesurques wanted just a little too much to ensure his acquittal and called a jeweller, Legrand,

---

[1] Hilaire Ledru (1769–1840), who studied art at Douai, would later paint the well-known and touching pictures of Lesurques' farewell to his wife and family. Generally his pictures were of sentimental subjects and although for a time his work was much appreciated he fell out of fashion and died in poverty.

who had a shop in the Palais-Royal arcades. Legrand produced a sales account showing that Lesurques had spent some time with him on Floréal the 8th. Unfortunately the figure eight had been written in different ink over a nine, which had only partially been erased.

Judge Gohier was not pleased:

> So, to save a criminal, criminal forgery is to be employed! Not content with lying, Lesurques, you will try this method of leading Justice astray! We know what to think of proceedings like that and the morality of people who use them.

And if his lawyers thought they were blameless they did not escape unscathed: "Counsel for the defence, I should like to think that you, at least, are acting in good faith."

The jeweller Legrand was put in custody overnight but the next day, accepting he had made a mistake, he was discharged. It is impossible to know at this remove why the lawyers had not spotted the alteration but from that moment their client was doomed.

Judge Gohier summed up for the jury at 10 a.m. on August 6 and the jury returned their verdict that evening. Guénot and the servant, Bruer, were acquitted. Lesurques and the others were sentenced to death. Lesurques was defiant:

> Doubtless the crime of which I stand accused is horrible and deserves death, but if it is dreadful to commit murder upon a public highway, it is no less so to use the forms of law to strike an innocent man. The moment will come when my innocence is recognised, and then will my blood spurt upon the heads of the jurors who so lightly condemned me and the judge who influenced their minds.[2]

Couriol took the opportunity to accept his guilt but to say that Bernard, the stable keeper, was innocent. All he had done was to hold the horses and watch the division of spoils, while Lesurques was absolutely innocent and had taken no part in the affair at all.

The receiver Richard, Vidocq's fellow *galérien*, received twenty-four years' penal servitude and the others were to be executed in red shirts to signify their guilt. Their goods would be confiscated. Lesurques wept, his wife fainted and the reporter from *Le Messager du Soir*

---

[2] The quotations in this chapter are taken from Charles Oman's *The Lyons Mail*.

wrote that he thought the judge had been unfair and that Lesurques was innocent, so beginning a campaign on the man's behalf.

Daubanton went to watch the trial as an interested spectator and almost immediately afterwards saw Couriol, who was now prepared to tell all. It was, of course, held against him that he had not told all before but, as Rayner Heppenstall points out in his account of the trial, Couriol must have thought he had an outside chance of an acquittal.[3] To say anything would have vitiated that completely. Now he exculpated Lesurques and brought up the names of Dubosq, Vidal and Roussy, also giving their addresses. The wine merchant Laborde, who was the passenger on the stage, was really Durochat, who lived in the rue des Fontaines; Dubosq lived in the rue des Petits Champs (last house on the left), Vidal in the rue Martin and Roussy in the rue de Valois (facing the dram shop). The broken spur belonged to Dubosq. Durochat and Dubosq had been the ringleaders. Durochat had held Excoffon's arms and Dubosq had been the first to stab him.

Now Madeleine Breban added a few more details. She had in fact seen Lesurques that evening, something she had denied at the trial. They had dined at the receiver Richard's house. Lesurques and Dubosq did resemble each other being about the same height and weight. Dubosq did wear a blond wig, however.

Without damning himself completely this had really been the first opportunity for Couriol to speak, not that the Court of Appeal saw it that way:

> Since he [Lesurques] is rich it would not be difficult for him, after conviction, to procure any number of witnesses. We cannot understand why this innocent citizen did not with the powerful and sublime accents of truth, demand from Couriol in open court the declaration now so tardily made.

The Minister of Justice thought it would be inhuman to "allow men's torment to be prolonged when they are destined to inevitable death, and any deferment is a prolongation."

Lesurques left seven louis with the jailer to give to the jeweller, Citizen Legrand, adding the rather curious comment, "who helped a bit to get me assassinated, but whom I forgive with a good heart." He was allowed to wear a white shirt, protesting his innocence, when he was executed on October 29 on the place de Grève, following David

---

[3] Rayner Heppenstall, *French Crime in the Romantic Age*.

Bernard who had to be carried to the scaffold and held upright when he was strapped to the bascule and tipped, and then Couriol.

Before his death Lesurques handed Charles-Henri Sanson a letter to be given to the press:

> Citizen Dubosq – I do not even know you and I am going to suffer the death which was reserved for you. Be satisfied with the sacrifice of my life. Should you ever be brought to account, remember my three children and their mother, who are disgraced for ever, and do not prolong their agony. Confess that you are the man.

Sanson was asked to send it to all the papers and this he did.

Was Lesurques innocent? Daubanton, who then began to sacrifice his judicial career, certainly thought so. His property, which was confiscated, was certainly a good reason for a verdict of guilty and many have been convicted on no more satisfactory evidence. On the other hand, for a man of property Lesurques was keeping what might in those days be called queer company, dining with a known receiver. The possibility is that he was what is known as the putter-up, or financier, something Couriol might not have known. Lesurques, more than others, would have been in a position to have a man inside the post office. It can be argued that if he was involved he would not even have gone to the Law Courts, but, since he was genuinely not actually on the robbery, there would be no reason for him to think he might be identified.

The first of those named by Couriol to be caught was Durochat, who, curiously, had no previous convictions. He was arrested in the spring of 1797. He had, he said, only joined the conspiracy on the understanding that there would be no bloodshed. Daubanton travelled with him from Melun to Paris, taking a meal with him alone. The story goes that the magistrate picked up a knife to slice off the top of an egg and Durochat asked if he were not afraid of him since it was his knife.[4] It was then that Durochat confirmed the name of Pierre Vidal. Durochat was executed in the great square of Versailles on August 10, 1797.

Before his death Durochat, whose real name was probably Joseph Verot, talked. He had been in prison in Lyons where he had picked up with a man, Pierre Pialin, or Pialat, who went by the names of Vidal and Lafleur, and was also known as *le gros Lyonnais*. Durochat confirmed

---

[4] Vidocq has the same story in different circumstances in his memoirs.

that there was a man inside the post office. He had already put up the Brest Mail as a potential target but it had been abandoned because of the rebellious Chouans operating in the area.[5] It had been Roussy who had done the stabbing of Excoffon. He also took the opportunity to implicate his old friend Vidal who had been arrested on an unrelated theft.

As for Vidal, he had refused to answer questions. There was the evidence of Couriol and Durochat against him but they had both been guillotined. At one time he had kept a wine shop in Lyons and had been given twenty years at Grenoble for highway robbery with violence but he had escaped after a year. There was some evidence that he had been in Paris shortly before the attack on the mail coach and he had left Paris almost immediately afterwards saying he had to go back to Lyons to see his dying (if non-existent) father. As for the informers, he did not know Couriol, nor did he know Durochat and he certainly did not know the still-wanted Dubosq. The waitress Marie Grossetête identified him but then she had already identified Guénot and that was certainly wrong.

As was standard practice, all the prisoners at Versailles were allowed to mix and, if they could, to pay for the meals served by Citizeness Humblot, the chief warder's wife. Provided they did not complain about her cooking they were more or less guaranteed privileged treatment. Vidal spent around 200 louis d'or on cuisine, which amounted to around £200. Much of the money was provided through his lawyer Lebon.

On February 27, when the Humblots went to Pontoise to see friends, Vidal and Jean-Guillaume Dubosq, who, under an assumed name, was in prison on other charges unconnected with the Mail, escaped, freed the latter's plain but devoted mistress Claudine Barrière, also in prison for theft, and, since there was no one guarding the corridors, were off. Dubosq fell as he climbed out of the prison and broke a leg. He was found by the night patrol; Barrière went back to her cell and Vidal was clear.

Vidal lasted only a few months on the outside. All but the smartest escaped criminals tend to gravitate back to their own environment where presumably, and for the most part incorrectly, they think they will be safe and this is just what Vidal did. On June 6, 1797, he was found back in Lyons at the home of a professional thief, Châtre.

---

[5] *La Chouannerie*, the Royalist insurrection in Brittany and the Vendée during the Revolution, derives its name from the Breton dialect for owl. It is said to have applied to the hooting signals given by its members during the night. *Les Chouans* (1829) was Balzac's first successful novel. For an account of the war in the Vendée, see Henry Jephson, *The Real French Revolution*.

He had no papers, said he was a trooper from the 10th Hussars and when this did not wash accepted he was Pierre Pialin who had escaped from Grenoble. Unfortunately for him Pialin was a name connected with the Lyons Mail and it was back to Versailles where, on December 3, 1797, he was executed.

No one seems to have been that bothered that Dubosq had tried to escape. Sometimes said to have been born in Basle and sometimes in Besançon, he was a brilliant organizer, a cat burglar rather than a highwayman and an escaper to rival or even surpass Vidocq. He certainly began his criminal career in Besançon where in 1785 he stole the plate chest of the archbishop.

Shortly after Dubosq's fall from the roof the prison doctor, Du Clos, reported he was out of danger, there was no question of gangrene, the bones were knitting and so Claudine was allowed to nurse him back to full health.[6] After four months, however, Dubosq was still bedridden in a cell overlooking a private garden and with a large fireplace.

He escaped on August 28 apparently still unable to put a foot to the ground. The pair had taken bricks out of the fireplace and made their escapes through a gap eighteen inches square. After the escape Dubosq, who must be one of the most entertaining criminals of this or indeed any other period, wrote a letter of thanks to the unfortunate Du Clos. To help in the search Daubanton employed a convict, Durand, who claimed to know everything about Dubosq, certainly where he was hiding. Durand, sent out guarded by three gendarmes, gave them the slip and disappeared. As for the widow Lesurques, she was living on the rent from some land which had not been confiscated on her husband's conviction, along with handouts from friends and sympathizers. It was two years and a month before, on September 4, 1800, Dubosq and Claudine Barrière were found.

On August 30, 1800, the Perfect of Police received an anonymous letter to the effect that the pair were living under the name Barrière at 11 rue Hautefeuille. When the police raided the house they found a number of disguises, a good deal of housebreaking equipment, eight forged passports, a number of blank identity card, Claudine Barrière but no Dubosq. She, ever loyal, said she had not seen him for a fortnight.

Foolishly Dubosq did not stay away from the area. He was caught the next day, albeit disguised, in the passage des Petites Ecuries at the back of rue Hautefeuille. This time he was kept in fetters until he went

---

[6] Report of Du Clos to the Municipal Council of Versailles, 26 Ventôse.

on trial on December 19, 1800. It was an occasion for *le tout Paris* who attended the four-day trial en masse, taking over the local hotels and inns to see this man. Would he provide the spectacle they hoped for? Would he, against all odds, escape again? The answers were yes and no respectively. To prevent the latter two gendarmes positioned themselves between him and Barrière.

By the time of the Dubosq trial the "Lesurques is innocent" campaign was growing. The presiding judge was Chollet, and Anthelme Brillat-Savarin, the gourmet and later noted chef, appeared for the prosecution.[7]

The evidence against Dubosq was thin. The unhappy Legrand was called to produce his papers. Legrand, exposed at the first trial as a receiver and launderer, had lost a good deal of his legitimate clientele and had spent some of the four and a half years since the Lesurques trial in asylums.

His papers, he said, had been given to Daubanton and were never found. Six officers from Bicêtre said they had never confused Dubosq and Lesurques. Nor, on the second day, did things improve for the prosecution. The barmaids said Dubosq was not one of the men at Montgeron. In all, the nine witnesses who had identified Lesurques stuck to their guns. None would admit to a mistake even when Dubosq was persuaded to put on a blond wig. Things did improve on the third day when the receiver Pierre-Thomas Richard was brought from the galleys at Rochefort, regarded as being the worst of all the *bagnes*. Just as Judge Gohier had been against Lesurques so Chollet took against Dubosq. When Richard purported to identify him and Dubosq commented, "He didn't say a word of this at his trial," Chollet intervened, "There is always a time for the truth. A pity it hasn't come to you yet."

Dubosq did not help himself, keeping up a steady stream of satirical comments, some directed at Richard whom he suggested was hoping to slip away on the way back to Rochefort. Other shafts were aimed at Couriol's mistress who had now become Madame Ferret, the wife of the executioner of Dijon.

What was also admitted in evidence against Dubosq were the depositions of Durochat and Couriol. Durochat said that Dubosq had

---

[7] Anthelme Brillat-Savarin (1755–1826) came from a family of magistrates. In 1789 he was a member of the Assemblée constituante but during the Terror he fled to America. A man of wit and culture he wrote the classic collection of *pensées*, anecdotes and aphorisms. *Physiologie de goût or Méditations sur la gastronomie transcendante*.

been so upset at the loss of the spur that he had thrown its pair down a public latrine.

The jury, sent out at 3 p.m., returned at 5:15 with what looked suspiciously like a compromise verdict. Dubosq had not been present at the robbery but he had been an aider and abetter. His mistress Barrière had received some of the stolen property. It was not a verdict which appealed to Lesurques' supporters who had hoped for nothing less than the identification of Dubosq as the man with the broken spur. Jean-Guillaume Dubosq was executed in Versailles on January 24, 1801. Claudine did her six hours in the pillory and was taken to serve her ten-year sentence at Dourdan, twenty miles south of Versailles. Richard came out of the affair best of all. In good Vidocq tradition somehow he did manage to escape on the way back to the galleys.

The last man to stand trial was Roussy, known as Luigi Bernoldi, sometimes as Ferrari and sometimes as Scotti, who had been on the Paris police files from 1790. He had been arrested five times and had a fine record. Twice he was acquitted, twice he escaped from police custody and on the fifth occasion he escaped from prison.

Shortly after the robbery of the Mail he left Paris, carried out a swindle in Lyons and went to Italy where he lived with his mistress, Sophie Godard, in Genoa. His family was not well thought of and it is likely that his father had been executed as a poisoner.

From Italy he went to Spain where he was in difficulties in Saragossa and ditched his mistress in Madrid. He then took to robbing churches of plate and was in jail in Madrid in early 1803. He had been sending some of the proceeds to Bresson, a soi-disant brother-in-law, in Marseilles.

He was extradited at the request of no less a person than Charles-Maurice Tallyrand-Périgord, Napoleon's confidential adviser. Unlike Dubosq he was identified by forty-eight witnesses. Despite this he denied knowing any of the Lyons Mail gang and tried to establish an alibi that he was in Genoa at the time of the robbery. He was executed on June 30, 1803. Before that, however, he made a statement before a priest, Grandpré, in which he wrote:

> J'ai décalere que le nome le Lesurques est innocen; mes sete décalaracion que je done a mon confessor il ne poura le décalarer à la justice que six mois après ma morte. Louis Bernoldy.

And in January 1804 it was duly released, published in the press and raising the whole controversy once again. The statement really amounted to a confession, but why not go the whole hog and name Dubosq? After all he had been dead three years. It could hardly hurt him.

Lesurques' supporters pointed to the ill-worded statement as being that much more genuine. Opponents of the miscarriage of justice theory argued that the priest, a Lesurques man, had worried this partial confession out of a now very frightened villain. Neither side could explain what was undoubtedly correct – why Bernoldi had wanted the note held back for six months.

Lesurques' son, Paul-Joseph, died in the retreat from Moscow and over the years Joseph's widow Jeanne Lesurques fought on and received partial compensation in 1821 and a further sum in 1832. The first payment was not an acceptance of innocence but rather an acknowledgement that the practice of confiscating all the family property was now unjust. She made no more appeals and died at the age of seventy-three in September 1842 without having cleared her husband's name. The cause was now taken up by her daughter who had married and become Mélanie d'Anjou. She had no success whatsoever and, when told there was no question of a personal interview with the Minister of Justice, threw herself off the Pont d'Austerlitz in 1845.

Now Mélanie's son Charles took over, beginning his efforts when he came of age in 1846. He battled stubbornly, appealing to the Minister of Justice, the Minister of War and Louis Napoleon Bonaparte, not forgetting the Empress Eugènie, petitioning, regularly but unsuccessfully, until 1854 when he retired ultimately defeated. One further curious aspect is what happened to the monies the widow had received, which amounted to around the equivalent of £20,000. Nothing remained for Mélanie's children.

Even so that was not the end. In 1868 the Court of Cassation published an *arrêt* to the effect that the convictions of Lesurques and Dubosq were not irreconcilable and around the same period the Minister of the Interior ordered that graffiti on the family tomb in Père Lachaise reading, "*A bas l'inique sentence!*," "*La plus grande de toutes des degradations de l'espèce humaine,*" and the like, were to be erased.

Was Lesurques innocent, unluckily mistaken for the master criminal Dubosq? In his analysis of the evidence Charles Oman, Professor of

Modern History at Oxford, really came down on the side of the Dubosq jury. He believed Dubosq was the putter up, the master thief, but he was not an assassin. The louche Lesurques, with his daily dealings with the fence Legrand, could well have been a highwayman, the man who lost the spur. He would not have been the first, or the last, thief who despite owning a substantial portfolio, for one reason or other – excitement, power – could not stop.[8]

The story of the Lyons Mail was turned into novels and melodramas both in French and English. They were great successes and the play by Charles Reade became a standard thriller on the Victorian stage with Sir Henry Irving and later his son in the dual role of Lesurques and Dubosq. Irving, who was invited to put the piece on at Windsor Castle for the King and Queen and Portuguese royalty, was said on one occasion to have so terrified the horses when he drove them across the boards that they reared and bucked to such an extent that in their turn they frightened the members of his gang, who fled to the wings. The piece plays havoc with the facts, culminating in a thrilling quick-change scene where Lesurques is led to his death while Dubosq hides in a gallery counting the steps Lesurques must take to the guillotine before he is safe. It seems last to have played at the then newly restored Liverpool Playhouse in the late 1960s. There was also a British film with Sir John Martin Harvey leading the cast.[9]

---

[8] This dual personality theory is not all that far-fetched. Oman cites the case of a Mr. Freeman who, in the third quarter of the eighteenth century, leased the splendid manor house of Swinbrook. Freeman installed himself with a retinue of servants and entertained lavishly, paying his bills in gold. Unfortunately his residence coincided with a series of daring robberies by a gang of four masked men who plundered mail and private coaches in Warwickshire and Worcestershire but never within striking distance of Swinbrook. All was revealed when one of the highwaymen was killed and found to be Freeman's butler.

[9] *The Times*, September 13, 1968.

Chapter 7

VIDOCQ
AGAINST THE PRISON SHIPS

In which our hero is taken to Brest – finds it not at all to his
liking – escapes – tricks a dead man's parents – disguises himself
as a nun – so disguised shares a bed with two women – and
has all manner of other adventures

FITTED WITH IRON BOLTS at the neck, bound into groups of thirty making up two or three hundred men, Vidocq and the other convicts would leave Paris for the prison ships at Toulon or Brest.[1] The chains of men left Paris on an irregular basis when the *bagnes* had vacant places and the city's prisons were becoming overcrowded. The men were placed in long carts facing outwards, thirteen a side. Pictures show them seated rather like chickens on spits but with their legs hanging over the seating. On the journey, surrounded by armed guards and creating often horror, sometimes compassion, and always curiosity, they formed a long column of flesh and iron which crossed France in a month. Their work on arrival would be to carry heavy loads, turn wheels, drive pumps or pull cables. Others would work as joiners, and some of the more trusted were used in building ships. The most dangerous remained chained to their beds or, during the day, to tables.

It was on November 20, 1797, nearly a year after his conviction, that Vidocq and the others learned that a new chain was being put

---

[1] The *bagne* at Brest was designed by the local architect Antoine Choquet de Lindu, built on the left bank of the river Penfeld from 1750 to 1751 by a convict labor force of between two and three thousand. Wake-up call was at five o'clock in the morning in summer and six in the winter. Work started between seven and eight. At night the men were chained together and to benches. The *bagne* was replaced by a moving prison in the form of the Panopticon. Prisoners, who could not see or hear each other, never left the vehicle and were allowed only to read religious texts. They sat on zinc and oak funnels which emptied onto the highway. See Michel Foucault, *Surveiller et punir*, pp. 263–4; *Gazette des Tribunaux*, June 15, 1837.

together. At 11 a.m. Viez, its captain, along with a Lieutenant Thierry, appeared and asked if there were any "return horses," or escaped galley slaves. Like schoolboys and their master the prisoners gathered round the men endeavoring to curry favor. Viez seems to have conducted the interview with a good deal of humor, chaffing Desfosseux about a lucky escape from the guillotine and telling him how much better off he would be back at the meadow than being a head shorter. Then they were sent to the *cour de fers* for a cursory medical examination before being fitted with irons. They were given back their own clothes but any hat brims and coat collars were removed to prevent an escape, or at least to ensure the wearer was noticeable. Prisoners who did not have their own clothes wore a gray and black smock and packing-cloth trousers. They could take with them a maximum of six francs. Vidocq did not think much of this last precaution. Louis could always be hidden in hollowed-out sous.

The prisoners were matched in height and then fettered and attached to a six-foot chain with a sort of iron triangle known as the cravat. This meant that the prisoners could only move as a body. Putting on the iron collars was dangerous for them. Even if they kept still their heads were grazed; if they moved or caused a nuisance, their heads were split open. Finally, heads and beards were shaved. The guards of the chain, known as Argousins, were generally from the Auvergne, and would, between trips, return to their jobs as messengers or coalmen.

At five o'clock, the fettering done for the day, it was time for singing and general horseplay in as much as the chains would allow. Vidocq and the other escapers took care to join in. Sullen, withdrawn prisoners were regarded as potential escapers. From time to time a returnee would start the prisoners' song, "La Complainte des Galériens:"

> *La chaîne*
> *C'est la grêle*
> *Mais c'est égal*
> *Ça n'fait pas d'mal*
>
> *Notr' guignon eut été pire*
> *Si comme de jolis cadets*
> *On nous eut fair raccourcir*
> *A l'abbaye d'Monte-à-regret.*

Vidocq's immediate companions included a schoolmaster convicted of rape and an ex-officer of health serving a sentence for forgery. The latter thought conditions at Brest were not too bad, certainly better than at Toulon where it took up to eight days to find all the beans in a pot of soup.

During the evening three prisoners were set upon by the others. They had been pointed out as informers by a prisoner known at Bicêtre as Mademoiselle, "one of those degraded wretches who abandon themselves in Paris to a course of the most disgusting debaucheries." The Argousins were not keen on intervening, and one prisoner, Petit Matelot, was so badly beaten that he died four days later. Vidocq claimed the credit for the survival of the others saying that one of them, Lemière, whom he had known in the *armée roulante*, had helped him with an earlier escape.

At six o'clock the next morning they set off. They were placed in the long carts and the journey began. The first stop was at St-Cyr where there was a search for concealed files and also for watch-springs which, it was said, could cut through fetters in three hours. Food was the aforementioned bean soup and bits of half-spoiled meat. The officers and senior guards ate at a separate table and, in a scene which anticipated *Oliver Twist,* when a prisoner asked for water he was told to put out his hand. When he did so he was beaten. Only the very few prisoners who had money fared better. Afterwards they slept, still chained together, in a stall on soiled straw.

The passing of the chain was something of a spectacle with, like today's Tour de France, the public turning out in force, in this instance to guess what crime which man had committed. Broadsheets were handed out recalling the crimes of those on the chain and sometimes identification through tattoos was possible.[2]

One of the cordon, usually one of the most dangerous and troublesome, was always made to walk as a loose coffle and the others were allowed on occasions to do so. As they made their way through villages women were insulted and shops subjected to what would

---

[2] It was thought some 100,000 came to watch the departure of the chain of 1836 which carried the priest-murderer Delacollonge, who had dismembered his pregnant mistress, and Lacenaire's companion François, who behaved extremely badly. Efforts had been made to disguise Delacollonge but the *Gazette des Tribunaux* helpfully described him. Nevertheless, it was François who had displayed no shame when he had been exhibited on July 18 and now "blessed" the crowd. There was considerable looting and fighting on the way between Bicêtre and Sèvres. *Gazette des Tribunaux,* July 18, 21, 22, 23, 1836; *La Phalange,* August 1, 1836. For an account of that chain, see Michel Foucault, *Discipline and Punish,* pp. 257–62. The last chain left Bicêtre for Brest on October 1836. It contained 72 convicts. The *bagnes* were abolished in 1854.

today be called streaming or wholesale robberies. The Argousins would pretend to control the prisoners but in fact they would benefit from the looted goods either by buying them cheaply or exchanging them for some extra cups of wine. Nor were they averse to stripping and robbing the convicts they thought might have money. At Rennes some of the men gang-raped a nun who had brought them tobacco and money.

They reached Pont à Lézen after twenty-four days and were immediately put in a form of quarantine to allow them time to recover from the journey and also to see if they had any contagious diseases before they were sent to the *bagne*. First, they were bathed in pairs in warm water and then supplied with two sailcloth shirts, one red shirt, two pairs of trousers, two pairs of shoes and a green leather cap. Everything was marked GAL (for *galérie*) and the cap bore a badge with the man's register number stamped on it. An iron ring was put on each man's leg but they were not coupled. Once again Vidocq's thoughts turned to escape.

Security was not tight and prisoners told Vidocq that it was not that difficult to get out of the holding room and climb the walls. To make things easier the men were fed with enormous loaves weighing eighteen pounds and he took the opportunity to hollow one out and stuff it with a shirt and trousers. For no good reason Lieutenant Thierry did not regard Vidocq, who had for the duration been on his best behavior, as a potential escaper. His generous attitude was rewarded by an attempt in which a colleague cut his irons with a carelessly abandoned chisel and Vidocq all but vaulted the prison wall. He fell heavily, limped back and, turning his charm on a female nurse in the prison infirmary, more or less escaped punishment.

Three weeks later he was transferred to a *bagne* moored in the middle of the bay at Brest which housed the more troublesome of the prisoners. There the men were kept in rooms with what he describes as twenty night camp couches for the use of six hundred men. As might be expected, newcomers were the butt of jokes and attacks by the older hands. Homosexuality was rife in the *bagnes*. Alvarez, a magistrate who made a tour of them at the beginning of the nineteenth century, found that "the most perverted, the most vile will be king." He believed that homosexual "marriages" were commonplace and estimated that three-quarters of the population of the *bagnes* practiced sodomy. Homosexual rape was prevalent, with clergy and teachers who had molested young children a principal target. By 1846 little had changed. Brest was regarded as a homosexual *soute-neurs'* paradise.[3] Vidocq tells the story of a former bishop at Antwerp who, to avoid rough treatment, used to participate in mock confessions and blessings. He was known as Monsignor and, during his sentence, became the innkeeper for the convicts at Brest.

Initially Vidocq was chained to a man whom he describes as a half-idiot, a vine-cutter from Dijon who was so broken that he answered to whistles. This did not suit his purpose. Vidocq feigned illness and the vine-cutter was soon shackled to another man. This time Vidocq was chained to a man serving eight years for stealing chickens from a church. This man advised Vidocq that if he was thinking of escaping he should do it before the guards got to know his face. He should also avert suspicion by seeming to resign himself to a long stay. This could be done by buying a small mattress, straps to support his fetters and a wine keg. Vidocq also bought a sailor's outfit which he put on under his convict's smock.

The next day he marched with his company to work on a pump. Manacles were examined and found to be intact. Behind a pile of planks his partner helped saw through the last of the fetters; then, doning a wig, Vidocq was gone again.

But, as always, the problems were not in the escape so much as in the immediate aftermath. For a start, Vidocq did not know Brest. Eventually he reached the only gate of the city which was manned by a guard, a man named Lachique. Convicts regularly tried to escape but they could be detected fairly easily because of the limp caused by wearing fetters. Vidocq was fortunate; he had not yet developed one. To help him pass the guard, who was reputed to be able to spot a convict at forty paces and more, Vidocq bought a pitcher of buttermilk. Now he sat down with Lachique and had a smoke with him before passing on his way.

He was well on his way before the sound of the cannon fired to announce the escape of a convict – and also signalled a 100-franc reward for anyone turning the man in – was heard three-quarters of an hour later. After that, the peasantry turned out armed with clubs and guns to help in the search. Someone passed close by Vidocq but he was well dressed and also apparently had a full head of hair.

---

[3] Marcel Leclère, *La Vie quotidienne dans les bagnes*, p. 196.

His adventures immediately after his escape follow the normal Vidocq pattern. He spoke with two young women who led him to an estaminet, where he recognized one of the guards. Things did not go right for him at all that day. In the bar he fell in with the local mayor and told him he wanted to get to Brest. "It's five leagues," said the mayor, who offered him a bed for the night. Or he could go back with the prison guard who would show him the way. Vidocq switched track. He had left his pocket book, passport and money in Morlaix. Very well, the guard would walk with him that way as he had to collect another prisoner. On the way Vidocq got the guard drunk and made his escape. Two days later he was stopped by gendarmes. He told them he was Auguste Duval, a deserter (whose name he had learned at Brest), and was taken by them to the naval prison at Pontainau, near Lorient.

Now Vidocq's luck changed for the better. A young sailor on an assault charge told him that if Vidocq would buy breakfast he would give him some essential information. The information was indeed valuable. Auguste Duval had been dead for two years but Vidocq looked reasonably like him and, with a tattoo of an altar on his left arm, he might be able to pass himself off when he was confronted by Duval's parents. Vidocq duly received a prison tattoo, managed the deception and was sent to the prison at Quimper where, by feigning dropsy – a trick he had learned at Bicêtre – he managed to get into the prison hospital. There he bribed an inmate to steal the habit of a nun working in the prison and he was over the wall and gone.

The nun in question was, so his memoirs say, the fifteen-stone Sister Françoise, and Jean Savant suggested that Vidocq believed that she would be charitable enough to cover up the loss of her habit.[4]

Then came a short and improbable interlude where, as the *religieux*, he shared a bed with the two daughters of a farmer who gave him food and shelter. Despite the tendency of the more attractive one to cuddle up to him, naturally he treated them as the farmer, if not the reader, would have expected. The next morning it was off to the Ile Feydeau, where he had heard of an inn used as a thieves' hideout. There he spent a few days meeting up with some others who had also escaped from Brest. They wanted him to join them in a burglary but he nobly declined and, scraping together what cash he had left, he set off for Nantes.

---

[4] Jean Savant, *La Vie aventureuse de Vidocq*, p. 48. She was probably part of the prototype for Sister Simplice in *Les Misérables*.

Once again in his memoirs Vidocq is at pains to emphasize that he was unwilling to commit crime. It is easy to see why. On his own admission, his enemies would almost certainly have tried to have him charged and returned to prison. There are many who do not regard Vidocq's crime – assuming he was guilty of the forgery – as anything more than trifling. Philip Stead, his biographer, is one of them:

> It may be said at once that the crime which had caused Vidocq to receive a prison sentence was not a grave one; many would not regard it as a crime at all, for it consisted simply of contriving an arrested person's escape.[5]

To have behaved as a common criminal even in the face of the vicissitudes he was undergoing would have ruined the image he had so carefully built. Surely, though, there was a danger that one of his former companions might come out of the woodwork to say that, far from clumping off into the dawn dressed as a shepherd, there he was unbolting the windows and helping himself to the silver plate? It should not have been a problem. These adventures had taken place thirty or more years earlier where many of his old companions would now be dead; many would have been transported or in the *bagnes* on a long-term basis. Many could not read. And if they did come forward, who would believe them? It was, however, a risk Vidocq, even to spice up his future memoirs, could not take.

---

[5] Philip Stead, *The Police of Paris*, p. 94.

Chapter 8

VIDOCQ
MEETS FRANCINE AGAIN

*In which our hero meets some old friends and becomes
involved with the dreaded Chauffeurs*

V IDOCQ WALKED FOR A day and two nights, eventually arriving
at a town which appeared to be in the midst of a battle. A number
of houses were in flames and soldiers were using chalices from the
churches to water their horses. Others were dancing with country-
women who were prostituting themselves for bread. Vidocq thought he
might have been in the wilds of America but, in fact, he was at Cholet,
in the Vendée, still something of a Royalist outpost. The soldiers were
there to prevent outbreaks by the *Chouans*.[1]

The next day was market day and, spinning a story to a cattle dealer
that he was a deserter from the 36th demi-brigade trying to get to Sceaux
to see his parents, Vidocq arranged to drive some oxen to Paris. He did
so well that he was given a bonus of 40 francs but, because he had an-
noyed the other drovers, was also challenged to a fight. With his knowledge of savate his opponent was no match for him and Vidocq garnered
further praise by going softly with him. Now decked out in new clothes
consisting of a smock, leather gaiters and a hat covered with waxed cloth,
Vidocq ventured into Paris where, on the rue Dauphine, he met Captain Villedieu of the 13th chasseurs whom he had known back in Lille.
It is surprising how often, wandering throughout France, Vidocq keeps
meeting old friends and acquaintances. In fact, at this stage his memoirs
closely resemble the form of the traditional picaresque novel.

The two men took a coach to Sceaux and dined in a private room at
the Grand Cerf where Villedieu admitted that if he did not get out of

---

[1] For an account of the war in the Vendée see Jenry Jephson, *The Real French Revolutionist*

France he was a dead man. Vidocq, acknowledged King of Escapers, must help him get clothes so they could travel to Switzerland together. In true Henry Fielding style, Villedieu now told him his story. He had, he said, met up with a jeweller, a M. Lemaire, and, better still since the husband travelled a good deal, his wife, Josephine. One day Josephine told him her husband had been found with unstamped plate and as the house was likely to be raided everything must be packed as soon as possible. The valuables went into the captain's portmanteau and were left at his lodgings. Nothing would then do for Josephine but that Villedieu should go with her to Courtrai to intercede on behalf of her husband.

Villedieu and Josephine became lovers, Lemaire was released but Villedieu had already begun pawning the valuables left with him as he ran up huge gaming losses. He confessed all and, in turn, was told Lemaire was indeed a *Chauffeur* working with the celebrated Salembier and his brothers. The jewelry had come from a country house robbery near Courtrai. Villedieu could make good the losses by going on a few raids with him.

And so Villedieu joined up with Salembier. The first raid in which he accompanied Salembier, Duhamel, Chopine and Calendrin was a successful robbery near Douai pointed out by Duhamel's mistress who had been a maid there. Others followed but the Salembiers were caught after three raids on the same night. The elder confessed and gave up some forty-three others, including Lemaire and his wife. There was a warrant out for Villedieu as a known associate. What was Vidocq going to do?

Nothing very much. He did not completely trust Villedieu and he was himself an escapee. The farmer who had been employing him to drive cattle wanted to go to Nogent-le-Rotrou and Vidocq went with him. Four days later he returned to Paris and begged time off to see Villedieu. He was too late. There in a newspaper was news of Villedieu's arrest. He had made a good stand severely wounding two police agents. He was executed two months later in Bruges, calmly watching eighteen associates guillotined before he took his turn.[2]

Vidocq took the arrest of Villedieu as an ill omen and made for his parents' home in Arras where he learned his wife was now pregnant by her lawyer friend. He took a position as sacristan with a local curé who, because of the political climate, was still obliged to say mass in private.

---

[2] Arch. Guerre, Contrôle du 13e chasseurs, du 20e d'infanterie.

Vidocq also taught schoolchildren but again his inability to keep his britches buttoned let him down. He began to give private lessons to some of the older girls and a complaint concerning impropriety was lodged. He denied it, but as he was about to give a lesson to a girl in a hayloft, he was seized by four youths who stripped him and gave him a beating before stealing his clothes.

Vidocq made for his uncle's house near Mareuil covered only with a mat he had found by a pond. Eight days later, when the wounds had healed, he set out for Arras with a view to going to Holland. On the way through Brussels he learned that the baroness d'Ixelles, who had given him money all those months earlier, had gone to London.[3] For his part he made his way to Antwerp, Breda and then to Rotterdam where he met up with a Frenchman who wined and dined and then shanghied him. Vidocq awoke on a Dutch brig-of-war. He was not pleased and was one of the ringleaders in an abruptly quelled mutiny. His defense against the subsequent charges was that, since he had not signed articles, he was entitled to escape as best he could. Later he gave the other sailors fencing lessons and stayed on the vessel for some two months until he learned that the French were looking for their countrymen on board Dutch ships. This time Vidocq was allowed to leave and joined a Dunkirk privateer, the *Barras*, on which he stayed for six months before it was laid up in Ostend. Papers, which in his case were always in short supply, had to be produced; after giving the name Auguste Duval, he again tried to escape. This time he did not even manage to clear the quay. He was caught and given a beating after a washerwoman tripped him up.

Eight days later he was marched to Lille and the Egalité, a military prison, where he was able to mix with the other prisoners who included a man he had known on the *Barras*. Invited to share dinner with the man and his wife, he reasoned that he might persuade the woman to bring him some clothes to aid escape. As with all good feuilletons, he was in for another cliff-hanging episode. The sailor's wife was none other than the Francine.

Vidocq passed her off as his sister and the journey was continued the next day. He was surprised to find that the route they were taking was to Douai instead of the more usual road to Sens. The intention was to drop off some of the more tiresome prisoners at Arras.

---

[3] She did indeed go to London where she mixed in exiled royal circles. See Bruno Roy-Henri, *Vidocq du bagne à la préfecture*, p. 338.

Francine was waiting for him at the first stop and she managed to smuggle 200 louis in gold to him. There was also a painful and touching scene in which she blamed herself for the infidelity which had led to all his troubles and, in a scene worthy of the last act of some grand opera, he forgave her. Then it was on to Douai where there was, surprise, surprise, more misfortune; the gatekeeper was Dutilleul, who possibly knew him, and there was also Hurtel, who certainly did. Both identified him but, when he claimed to be Auguste Duval, Rauson, the public prosecutor, was not sure. Vidocq's mother was wheeled in. If he is to be believed, Vidocq had a quick mind except where young women and gambling were concerned. He told the magistrate that it was wrong to give a woman false hope of seeing her son and Vidocq *mère* took her cue. Game to Vidocq. Then the authorities learned that Duval had a tattoo and Vidocq happily showed them his left arm. Set to Vidocq. Then, when he heard that he was wanted in Lorient for desertion, he decided to admit that he was Vidocq. Match to the tribunal.

It seems Vidocq thought that he might have a chance to escape but there was no opportunity on the way back to Bicêtre where, waiting for the galleys, was none other than his old friend Captain Labbe from Brussels, who had received sixteen years in the galleys for a serious housebreaking offense in Ghent.[4] It was only on promises of good behavior that Viez, about to lead another coffle, did not carry out his threat to have them both in wrist cuffs and collars. This time they were to go to Toulon.

Along with them went a man named Jossas, known in the provinces as the Marquis de Saint-Armand de Faral, and one of the most celebrated thieves in Paris of the period, generally working with false keys. One of his greatest exploits was obtaining a duplicate key to a cash box held by a cashier in Lyons. To do this he instructed a young female accomplice to collapse inside the bank, bleeding from the mouth and nostrils. As is well known, the recommended method of stopping a nosebleed is to apply a cold key between the shoulder blades where, in her case and providentially, there was a wax pad which took the impression of the key.

The son of a silk-maker at Saliès in the Haut-Garonne, in his youth Jossas had been in the service of a rich colonel from whom he learned deportment, manners and speech which allowed him to pass

---

[4] Albert Labbe, known as Captain Albert, was head of the fifth chain on the journey to Toulon. He later escaped, was recaptured and sent to a *bagne* at Antwerp, from where he escaped at the end of October 1814. See Arch. Nat F⁷10354.

in polite society. Very often he appeared as a Creole from Havana and, a handsome and ingratiating man, was able to obtain a number of dowries from the unfortunate parents of daughters whom he appeared to wish to marry.

He seems to have had some qualities. Told there was an apartment in the rue du Hazard which would provide booty he broke in, found only a pile of pawnbroker's tickets and left a note apologizing for the broken furniture and five louis for its repair.

This was to be Jossas' third visit to the *bagnes*. He escaped on February 1803 but was recaptured and died at Rochefort in 1805.[5]

The chain left Bicêtre on June 22, 1799 and at Chalons the coffle was put on a boat going down the Rhône, until they eventually reached Avignon. It took a total of thirty-seven days to reach Toulon and they arrived on August 29.

Vidocq was sent to *Le Hasard*, formerly a frigate, and along with the other escapees had three years added to his sentence. Now he was put in double chains in Room 3, a vast dormitory. He and the others were not required to work, something which would have given them the opportunity at least to reconnoitre an escape. Instead, they lay down on a bench, attacked by ticks, unable to wash, and were given a few blows every day by their Argousin jailers. They were not happy.

There were some notables among Vidocq's companions. The executioner of the *bagne* was one Vidal who had avoided the guillotine at the age of fourteen when he was sentenced as part of a gang of robbers. Instead he received a twenty-four-year sentence and during it he knifed another prisoner. The sentence was converted into one of hard labor. Then, when a convict was sentenced to death, since Toulon did not have a public executioner Vidal offered his services. He was temporarily released when the Terror provided more regular clients but after that period of bloodletting he was sent back to the *bagne* where he was chained to the bench with the galley guards, out of reach of the other convicts. He was also used to administering the bastinado.

Other inmates included the jewel thief and possible murderer Deschamps and the housebreaker Louis Mulot, son of Cornu, whose daughter Florentine had been required to carry the head of a farmer in her apron after she had shown some repugnance towards the family trade. Poor Florentine: she was later executed with her father, mother and another brother at Rouen.

---

[5] His name is sometimes given as Jaussas. Arch. Nat. F⁷ 10343.

Unsurprisingly Vidocq did not like his conditions. Here he was at the age of twenty-four – certainly by his own account – at worst a petty criminal, chained to a bench with murderers. He began to work on a guard whom he calls Father Mathieu and charmed him into letting him have tools to carve children's toys. Other prisoners joined in and for a short while there was a regular cottage industry. Unfortunately the prisoners made the toys too well and since none ever broke the local market was soon flooded. Now, on the basis that escape from a prison hospital is generally easier, Vidocq feigned pain in his legs. He made one break for it but had covered no more than thirty yards before he was hauled back.

He escaped for the last time on March 6, 1800, and again it was a woman who helped him. Earlier, he had persuaded the trusting Father Mathieu that he was in danger from his fellow prisoners and was placed among the regular convicts. Jossas alone knew of Vidocq's intentions. Now he was out of chains and with Mathieu out of sight, he removed the screw from the yoke and ran to another ship, *La Meuron*, where he was mistaken for a new crew member (he had discarded his red shirt). Vidocq was a good mimic and was soon chatting away to an Argousin in the man's own dialect. He leaped in a boat and rowed away, hoping to get out of the Italian gate at Toulon. He did not, however, have the necessary green card and was walking in the dock area when he was accosted by a prostitute, Célestine, who offered to help him.

Chapter 9

VIDOCQ
MEETS A BAD ANGEL

*In which our hero visits Lyons – begins his career as a mouchard – and
sets up home in Paris before meeting his in-laws again – and after that
he both begins to see the light and meets a Bad Angel*

A S THEY WALKED, Célestine pointed out a funeral to Vidocq,
advising him to join the procession of mourners and that way
make his escape. His adventures were, of course, not yet over and they
followed the familiar pattern. Once again he fell in with thieves, or
rather poachers, because he had joined a form of guerrilla organization
composed of men who had refused to become soldiers. Unfortunately
their leader, Roman, after starting with the best of intentions, had
turned highwayman. Vidocq now had a series of problems. First,
there was his natural reluctance to steal. Secondly, and much more
importantly, if he was captured with this band, given that he was an
escapee he would almost certainly be guillotined. His problem was
solved when he was accused of the theft of a purse belonging to one
of the troupe. When it was seen he had been branded as a *galérien*
they were all for shooting him, but he displayed his usual cunning.
He persuaded the leader to have all the men draw straws, saying that
the one with the longest would be selected by the guilty man. In the
end it was the man with the shortest straw who turned out to be the
guilty one. He clearly had bitten off a piece to ensure that his straw
was not the longest. All the others were of equal length. He had not
read Berquin from whom Vidocq borrowed the idea.[1] The man had
the purse hidden in his belt. Vidocq, however, was expelled from the

---

[1] Louis de Berquin was one of the early leaders of the Reformation in France translating the
works of Luther into French. His protection by Marguerite de Navarre, sister of François, was
not enough to save him and he was executed in 1529.

organization. They did not want a known *galérien* in their midst. He was given fifteen louis and told to go away and to keep quiet for the next twenty-five days.

And so, after all this time, Vidocq approaches what might be described as the end of Act One, Scene One of his life. Now he made his way across France, to Orange, where he fell in with some wagoners, told them he was a deserter and asked for help. He paid to be passed off as one of their sons but, by the time he reached Lyons, he had spent all his money with them.

He put up in a dormitory at a cheap inn and awoke to hear two men discussing the burglary of a jeweller. One of the men was Neveu, who had escaped from Toulon just a few days before Vidocq, along with Charles Deschamps, who had got away shortly after. Vidocq was provided with food, drink, clothes and a girl but the price was that they wanted him to join them along with the Quinet brothers, who were then wanted for the murder of Catherine Morel, the wife of a mason, and half a dozen more.[2] When he would not, they informed on him to the police and so for the first time he too became an informer.

Vidocq was arrested at Adèle Buffin's tavern in the passage Saint-Côme and put in the prison at Roanne. From there he wrote to François-Louis Dubois, Napoleon's commissary general of police in Lyons, and was taken to see him. The deal he proposed was that he would give up the Quinets in return for his own release. Dubois was by no means convinced. Very well, said Vidocq, he would escape and then give himself up as a gesture. He knocked down his guards at the street corner and returned to Dubois at the Hôtel de Ville. Dubois was impressed and Vidocq, freed, went back to his false friends. It seems they did not think he suspected them and they discussed their next project openly in front of him. This he faithfully relayed to Dubois who, in turn, passed it to Ganier, the Inspector General of Police.

Two days before the job went off Vidocq thought it prudent to be arrested again and went back into prison in Roanne in solitary confinement, being joined there the next day by Neveu and the others. When Vidocq was released into the general prison population, Neveu, who appears to have been brighter than the rest, suspected Vidocq was the informer. Vidocq brazened it out, which was just as well for him for the prisoners in general had a reputation for killing informers. Neveu later apologized for being suspicious.

---

[2] See Arch. de Lyon, I/25 Dossier Morel.

The police had information that a Parisian gang was travelling to Lyons but when the names were put to him Vidocq did not recognize any of them. He was to be released the next day and he turned his attention to Neveu, taking his chance by telling him that he had indeed informed on the gang. Neveu had already received an approach from Dubois and in turn decided to join him as informant in the hope of his own release. Vidocq arranged for Neveu to go with him and point out the Paris crew in a series of bars and halls. The pair then failed to return to prison. Neveu was arrested for another job two days later and, with him safely in custody, Vidocq denounced the Parisians who had, it seems, been planning to rob the congregation of a church after mass. In return he was given safe conduct to Paris.

Of course, Vidocq, temporary safe conduct or not, was still an escaped convict. He made his way to Arras where an aunt went to find his mother and he, in the meantime, was hidden in a small room. He still could not let well alone and three months later he was out on the town at a Shrove Tuesday ball where his partner spoke to another girl who had a grudge against Vidocq. They gossiped and the police arrived. He knocked one of them down and using an iron key as a false gun escaped from two more and was soon back in his bolt hole. He stayed there another two months before, using the name Blondel and with a pack of lace to sell, he made his way to Paris, got rid of the lace for a small profit and then returned home.

Allowing for some errors in Vidocq's timescale this must now be the summer or autumn of 1801. In December he survived an attempt to capture him by leaping into the river and hiding in a sewer, but an application to be allowed to spend the remainder of his sentence in the Arras asylum was refused. He had now transferred his hiding place to a convent but he was again getting restless and, changing clothes with an Austrian prisoner who was also being held in the locality, he moved in with a young widow dressed in his new uniform. This relationship seems to have lasted eleven months before he told her of his deceit. It does not seem to have fazed her in the slightest.

> So much are women generally smitten by anything that bears the appearance of mystery or adventure! And then, are they not always delighted with the acquaintance of a wicked fellow? Who, better than myself, can know how often they are the providence of fugitive galley-slaves and condemned prisoners?

asked Vidocq smugly.

It was another eleven months before someone betrayed him and the police were round again. Together with the widow he escaped, making for Rouen, and actually sent for his mother. For a year he was happy but then the widow seems to have behaved like so many other of his women: she tired of him and found another lover. For some time he shut his eyes and ears but reasonably he feared that she might also, in some way, betray him and off he went, passing as a travelling merchant on the long circuit of Nantes, St-Germain and Versailles. And mother came too, setting up house with him first at 14 rue de la Monnaie and then in Versailles, at 38 rue de la Pompe.

Criminals have traditionally been devoted to their mothers and vice versa. It is a poor criminal whose mother will not attend court to say that he is a good boy at home in an attempt to mitigate the sentence he is to receive. Vidocq's mother does seem to have been exceptionally tolerant of her erring lamb's bad behavior in the early part of his career. In turn, she seems to have been rewarded after the death of her husband until Vidocq established himself in the police, with a lifetime on the hoof as her son moved from one parlous situation to the next.

Denunciation did indeed follow and, despite his efforts to show he was really Blondel, it was off to the prison at St-Denis. To his dismay he found that he had been condemned to death in his absence. He and other similarly dangerous prisoners were transferred to Louvres, near Douai.

This time Vidocq had some luck, for the Procurator-General was none other than Rauson who had prosecuted him ten years earlier and sent him to the *bagne*. Now he suggested that Vidocq present a petition for the commutation of his sentence. Meanwhile, he had a surprise if not welcome visitor. Along came Mlle Chevalier to serve him with divorce papers.

Always impatient, Vidocq could not wait for the result of his petition. After five months' incarceration, he was by now allowed to dine with the concierge, Wettu, and the agent, Hurtel. Again Vidocq had money, for it was he who was paying for the wine, which he poured generously. On November 28, 1805, after another drinking bout with them, he dived through their window into the river Scarpe and swam beyond the Douai city limits. It would be the last that officialdom would hear of him for four years.

Vidocq next made his way to Paris where his mother, who had remained in Versailles, now joined him. At first he laid low, seeing only a jeweller,

Jacquelin, of whom he says ambiguously, "I was compelled to a certain extent to make my confidant, because he had known me at Rouen under the name of Blondel."

It was at Jacquelin's that he met the woman whom he declared to be the love of his life, a Madame de B whom he calls Annette, a very different person from Francine Delphine, Emily and the others. She appears to have been the deserted wife of a merchant who left France for Holland when his business failed:

> I liked her wit, understanding, kindly feeling and ventured to tell her so; she saw soon, and without much trouble my assiduity and regard; and we found that we could not exist without each other.

With Annette in tow, Vidocq resumed the life of a travelling sales-man, and had a narrow shave at Melun when a commissary of police threatened to examine his papers. He returned to Paris just in time to hear of the execution of two men at the place de Grève, sentenced to death for the robbery/murder of a woman in place Dauphine. They had apparently gained entry by telling her they had news of her son. Vidocq fancied he knew one of the men and indeed he did. One was Armand Saint-Leger, an old slave and former *galérien*, and the other Herbaux, who had begun Vidocq's serious troubles with the forgery of Boitel's release. He went straight away to the prison to see if this was the Herbaux he had once known and indeed it was. In a highly dramatic moment their eyes met and then Herbaux went on his way to the guillotine. While at Bicêtre Herbaux had, it seems, expressed his regret at what had happened to Vidocq. The encounter with Herbaux was something of a revelation on the road to Damascus for Vidocq.

> I sought to lay down an impassable line of demarcation between the past and the present; for I saw but too plainly that the future was dependent on the past; and I was all the more wretched, as a police, who have not always due powers of discernment, would not permit me to forget myself.

And so, armed with Jacquelin's passport which he had borrowed, and schooled by Annette in the details of her family, he set off for Lower Burgundy where he travelled for a year more or less untroubled. It was at Auxerre that he met an old associate from Bicêtre named Paquay and again was obliged to make his excuses and leave when it became clear that Paquay wanted a helping hand in some robberies.

He agreed to meet him when the river boat sailed for Soigny and took the opportunity of sending a denunciatory letter to the lieutenant of the gendarmerie. Not without some self-recriminations:

> How pitiable is the condition of a fugitive galley-slave who, if he would not be denounced or implicated in some evil deed, must be himself the denouncer!

Accordingly the letter told the police that one of the authors of the robbery at the coach house in Auxerre was sailing and the police would do well to put some men on board – until eventually superseded by the railways, the *coches d'eau* were a principal form of transport in the latter half of the eighteenth and first half of the nineteenth centuries. Paquay was arrested and in turn denounced Vidocq. Then it was back to Paris where the police had already raided his warehouse, which meant that he could no longer pass as Jacquelin. Now he purchased a tailoring business in the cour St-Martin. Another eight months went by in domestic bliss with Annette and his mother but, inevitably, he was recognized once again, this time by two men who had also escaped from the *bagne* at Brest. One of them, Blondy, had also helped him escape at Pont-à-Lézen, the other was a man called Deluc. They were on their way, they said, to Chalons-sur-Marne but, as would any good blackmailers, promised to see Vidocq again. Worse was to come. In the rue de Petit-Carreau he met his former wife, looking considerably down at heel. On to the payroll she also went.

As if things could not get any worse, they did. One morning Vidocq was told to go to 23 rue de l'Echequier and, to his horror, found there not only the former Mme Vidocq and her nieces but also his bête noire, her father, who had just served six months for stealing plate. When he returned home he found Annette and his mother in tears. Blondy and Deluc had returned and now they wanted Vidocq to point out some houses they could burgle. The following night they were back again with plate and gold watches. Vidocq must buy it off them. He did.

Then came another request. Could they and a third man, St-Germain, borrow Vidocq's wicker cart and go to Senlis? Certainly. A few days later St-Germain was back. The other two had been caught. As for the wicker cart, it was covered in blood which he told Vidocq had been from the body of a wagoner they had murdered. Vidocq took his cart to Bercy and burned it.

Now, if he wanted to retain any stability in his life, he really had only one option open to him: he had to try and strike a bargain with the police. But what had he to offer and what sort of bargain might they just possibly entertain? Nothing very much, was the answer. The officer he wanted to see was the snuff-taking Jean Henry, who had been appointed by Louis-Nicolas Dubois,[3] and was head of the second division, essentially in charge of serious crime and security. His bureau was in the rue Sainte-Anne near the quai des Orfèvres. One line of his work was the recapture of escaped convicts and the surveillance of released criminals. Regarded as a valuable and very clever officer, a man devoted to his work and with little social life, he was known to his colleagues in the style of the time as Father Henry and to the criminals as the Bad Angel. He joined the police in 1784 and remained with them until the 1820s, gaining his reputation during the Revolution when, working with limited resources, he led the Bureau Centrale de Sûreté.[4]

Vidocq was shown in to see him and put such cards as he held, if not his name, on the table. If the police would leave him alone, he would put a string of names to the authorities. Henry was not impressed. First, Vidocq must come up with the names and he would evaluate them. If the information was accurate and useful then things could be taken a stage further. Vidocq wanted more; once he started informing he was a dead man. Henry would not budge, however, and the disappointed Vidocq returned home.

Another of Vidocq's biographers, Henry Jagot, has described Henry as a psychologist, a man who looked for secrets, comparing, studying, building cases; free-spirited but with an eye to detail at the same time and one whose theories were generally correct.[5] It really is a measure of Henry's discernment and style that he did not have Vidocq arrested on the spot but preferred to play a waiting game. On the plus side would have been the immediate recapture of an escapee. He must have thought, however, that, to mix metaphors, the game was worth the candle and there was the possibility of what Chesterton later called a twitch upon the thread. He could also have had Vidocq followed but he knew that here was a man who had survived a long time on

[3] Louis-Nicolas Dubois (1758–1847) is sometimes confused with François-Louis Dubois (1758–1828), who gave Vidocq safe conduct from Lyons after he had informed on the Parisian gang who had come to the city. The confusion appears to stem from an article by G. Montorgueil in *L'Eclair* in 1910.

[4] Pierre-François Réal, *Indiscretions*, t. 1, p. 252.

[5] Henry Jagot, *Vidocq*.

the outside and could easily lose a tail in the stews of the Marais, with its narrow streets and courtyards, let alone those around the Canal St-Martin. If they were to do business, there would have to be an element of trust and if Vidocq even saw the police on his tracks Henry would also have forfeited any possible trust the meeting might have engendered.

For a time it seemed as though things had worked out well with Vidocq. Two months went by and, when there was no word from St-Germain, Vidocq started to believe that he also might have been caught. Then, at dawn on May 3, 1809, Vidocq was awakened by a series of knocks on his warehouse door. He climbed out of the window and into the next-door apartment of a brass-worker, Fosse, where he hid behind a curtain. The gendarmes failed to find him but the Fosse family did. They were curiously incurious about the whole thing and arranged for a pie with a message to be sent to Annette.

In turn Vidocq went to Chevalier, repossessed a suit of clothes he had bought for him and took him to pawn some of the man's silverware for 100 francs. Vidocq must have expected that once out of his sight, Chevalier would denounce him and he was right. Annette had already been arrested by the time the pie was intercepted and she spent twenty-five days in solitary confinement under threat of being taken to St-Lazare, the prison for prostitutes and adulterous women.

Meanwhile, Vidocq lodged at the house of a currier, Bouhin, who promised to get him a passport. If nothing else, Vidocq does seem to have been able to inspire confidence in others because Bouhin told him he was a coiner as well as a currier and made some five-franc pieces while he watched. Now another of the panic attacks, to which Vidocq seems prone, set in. If he was found in Bouhin's home with the coins, who was going to believe that he was not involved? The place de Grève loomed large particularly as Bouhin was the long-term associate of a Dr. Terrier, whom Vidocq saw as a gallows' bird if ever there was one. When Vidocq offered the advice that theirs was a dangerous business, the good doctor was scornful, saying he had been in the business for years, adding ominously that Vidocq should mind his own affairs. Now, with Annette due for release in a week's time, he decided to wait before leaving Paris. That was on the Tuesday. Three days later, at 3 a.m., he heard a knock on the door, went to the staircase and climbed on to the roof where he hid behind the chimneys. This time he was easily found. He was arrested on July 1 and was taken to Henry, who, on July 20, ordered him to be sent to Bicêtre to await the next galley chain.

Chapter 10

VIDOCQ
AS SUPERGRASS

*In which our hero returns to prison – we learn of some informers and
their motives – he treats with Henry – and at great personal risk proves
his worth to the authorities*

B ACK IN PRISON AGAIN, Vidocq was fêted by the other inmates.
Here was a repeated, inventive and courageous escapist and the
convicts fawned on him, seeking his advice and opinion and asking
him to settle their disputes.

As for his long-term future, he really now had no other option but
to work for Henry on the policeman's terms. He would become an
early example of a supergrass. The decision made by the supergrass,
as opposed to the common or garden informer, to assist the police has
almost invariably been taken at a moment when his professional life,
for one reason or another – very often because he has been arrested
and finds that death, transportation or more recently a long term of
imprisonment are looming large – has become impossible to sustain.
It also happens when he finds that his life on the outside is similarly
threatened by his employers or former friends. What he must do is cut
himself as good a deal as is possible.

Possibly the first of the British supergrasses was a professional
housebreaker, John Smith. On December 5, 1705, one hundred and
four years before Vidocq struck his own deal, Smith appeared at the
Old Bailey on four indictments including the theft of 50 pairs of men's
shoes, 900 yards of cloth, 400 lb. of Chinese silk and 128 pairs of gloves.
Ironically, in the case of the shoes an accomplice gave evidence against
him to the effect that they had been stealing as a team for some six
years. There was accomplice evidence in the second case (the cloth)
which was dismissed and he was acquitted over the matter of the silk.

There was nothing much he could do about the matter of the shoes; he was caught in the shop with the goods packed up neatly awaiting disposal. Since, at the time, conviction for theft where the value of the goods was more than five shillings carried the death penalty, he was sentenced to be hanged.[1]

Smith appeared at Tyburn on December 12, having travelled west from Newgate prison, a journey which coined the expression "to go West" well before either Mae West or the American journalist and politician Horace Greely put their names to a version of the phrase. There he was hanged, or rather half-hanged because, while he had been swinging on the gibbet for between seven and fifteen minutes, his reprieve was announced. He was cut down and resuscitated.[2]

A reprieve, then, was not necessarily a complete escape for a prisoner. It was more in the way of a stay of execution. Many would be subsequently pardoned and a good few not. Smith was fortunate; and it may be that fortune favors those who help themselves because on February 20 he received an unconditional pardon. By March 3 he had informed on 350 pickpockets and housebreakers who had joined the army to avoid detection.[3]

In the first quarter of the eighteenth century England had a thief-taker, much of whose career closely resembled that of Vidocq who could almost, according to his enemies, have used him as a blueprint. He was the celebrated criminal-cum-policeman Jonathan Wild, who lived a double life with conspicuous success. Wild, who carried a silver-mounted staff as an emblem of his self-styled rank, was a broker for stolen goods and an informer. Provided no questions were asked and there were adequate rewards the goods were returned to the warehouses from which he had often arranged

---

[1] The practice was for a merciful jury to return a verdict that the prisoner had stolen goods to the value of 4/11d and so avert the death penalty. Even if they did not do so there were still a number of ways in which the prisoner could escape the gallows. There was the Oath of Clergy under which, if verses of the Bible could be read (or memorized), the prisoner went free. There was also branding which, as the years went by, was often carried out with a cold iron. Smith had, however, run out of these options.

[2] Failed executions were not all that uncommon. In November 1740 the seventeen-year-old William Duell had hung for half an hour before he was cut down from Tyburn and resuscitated. He was later transported. In 1782 John Hayes was revived after his hanging and was later given a passage to America paid for by a surgeon from Gough Square, London. Douglas Hay et al., *Albion's Fatal Tree*, p. 104.

[3] From 1706 onwards Smith appeared on an infrequent basis in the London courts until, in 1720, he was sentenced to transportation. At the age of sixty-six he had been found trying to break into a warehouse. There is a full account of his activities in James Bland, *Crime Strange But True*, pp. 183 *et seq.*

their theft. Indeed he seems to have provided a role model for some policemen to the present day.[4]

Wild's career was an interesting one. Born in Wolverhampton in 1683 he was apprenticed to a buckle-maker. He married and left his wife. In 1708 he was imprisoned for debt and was discharged four years later when he set up house in Drury Lane in London with his mistress Mary Milliner, a prostitute whom he had met in prison. Initially he was what was called a twang, the pickpocket who would take the wallets of Milliner's clients – in those days intercourse with prostitutes was almost invariably undertaken vertically. He began his criminal apprenticeship proper with a Charles Hitchin, a City Marshal, who taught him the trade of receiver which Wild was to perfect.

From then on he set up a loose association of thieves, pickpockets and highwaymen. He was described in the Newgate Calendar as the Prince of Robbers. He also set himself up as a thief-taker and opened an office near the Old Bailey where he acted as agent between thief and victim, often later arresting the former. If anyone threatened to expose him he brought a capital case against the man, fabricating a felony charge. At the time no convicted felon could give evidence against anyone else. It is difficult, at this distance, to understand why anyone at all went near him but for twelve years he was able to maintain a successful double life. By 1718 he had already designated himself as "Thief Catcher General of Great Britain and Ireland" and had issued himself with his silver staff.

It was not as if the authorities were unaware of the dangers of the receiver-cum-thief-taker. In 1691 anti-pawnshop legislation had driven the receiver underground and in 1718 Hitchin, now suffering from the predations of his protégé, had published a pamphlet, A True Discovery of the Conduct of Receivers and Thief Takers, In and about the City of London, denouncing Wild. A bill – later known as the Jonathan Wild Act – was passed making it a felony to receive rewards under the pretense of retrieving stolen goods. In the debate over the bill, Wild was denounced again but, for the moment, he was adroit enough to circumvent trouble.

In 1723 Wild was still sufficiently confident of his invulnerability to make a petition to the Lord Mayor and Aldermen for the Freedom

---

[4] For a full account of Wild's life, see The Thief Takers by Patrick Pringle. The character MacHeath in John Gay's The Beggar's Opera was based on Wild.

of the City of London "in return for his services to justice." He had, he said, sent sixty men to the gallows. By now he had a branch office in the care of a manager, had become a successful slum land-lord and owned a country house tended by a butler and a footman. A hundred years later Vidocq had achieved something of the same position.

Wild's end came when he was indicted under his own Act, so to speak, for receiving ten guineas as a reward for helping a Mrs. Steham to recover stolen lace, the theft of which he had arranged. Convicted, he was hanged on May 24, 1725, despite another petition to the Lord Mayor of London. He tried to commit suicide, taking an overdose of laudanum the night before his execution and, still drowsy, was pelted by the mob on the way to Tyburn.

However, not everyone was pleased with the death of this celebrated informer:

> It is remarkable that since the Dissolution of Jonathan Wild, not one Felon has been convicted capitally, which by some is attributed to a Reform amongst the Rogues and by others to the Want of a proper Person to detect them.[5]

It was very much the same sort of comment made after Vidocq's retirement.

Horace Bleakley is, however, a champion of Wild:

> Nature intended Jonathan Wild for a sleuth, and had he been born two centuries later it is probable that he would have won a responsible posi-tion at Scotland Yard. For ten years at least, from 1715 until he died, he was by far the most efficient thief-taker in England. Fear was unknown to him. He was as tenacious as a bull-dog. Whenever he had resolved to clasp hands on a mill-ken or a bridle-cull – as burglar and highwayman were termed in his jargon – he ran his quarry to earth at whatever hazard. Scores of times this intrepid man arrested some armed desperado single-handed or rounded up a dangerous gang with a couple of his henchmen.[6]

And much the same could be said of Vidocq, although when it came to it he was rather more astute in his dealings. It is easy to see how in England he became known as the French Jonathan Wild.

---

[5] *Daily Journal*, July 5, 1735.
[6] Horace Bleakley, *The Hangmen of England*, p. 47.

Generally the supergrass, which is what Vidocq was aiming to become, has to have both reasons and self-justification to enable him to live with his conscience. The principal reason is to obtain some form of benefit, usually in the form of a reduced sentence. Sometimes it is actually revenge for a slight, real or imaginary; for some it is money; often it is a combination of these and other reasons. But coupled with them there is always an excuse; some have found religion; others are tired of the wickedness which surrounds them; some seek to repair the damage they have done in the past.

Of one twentieth-century criminal the detective Jack Slipper wrote:

I was less impressed, though, by the reasons O'Mahoney gave me for wanting to become a supergrass. He told me he was sick of crime and wanted to make a complete break from it. If he grassed on everyone, he said, no one would ever invite him onto another team, and that way he wouldn't be tempted back into the criminal world. But supergrasses need excuses – excuses they can make to themselves – more than they need reasons.[7]

One hundred and sixty years earlier Vidocq set himself up to clear his conscience and cut himself out of the coffle at the same time. He was, he wrote, disgusted by his fellow prisoners:

. . . the more I read of the souls of malefactors, the more they laid themselves open to me, the more I pitied society for having nourished in its bosom such offspring . . . Decided at any event to take part against them for the interest of honest men, I wrote to M. Henry to offer my services afresh, without any other condition than that of not being taken back to the bagne, resigning myself to finish the duration of my sentence in any prison that might be selected.

The truth was, of course, very different. Vidocq was now experiencing any number of serious difficulties. He might, for the time, be lorded at Bicêtre, but sooner or later he was going to encounter the men on whom he had informed at Lyons, or Paquay from Auxerre, or Blondy or Deluc or St-Germain or any of a dozen others of their friends. His life expectancy was plummeting. He could no longer run, nor could he hide. He wanted out.

In the late summer of 1809 he asked to see Henry again, promising the real names of convicts in the prison. But now, with the

[7] Jack Slipper, *Slipper of the Yard*, p. 114.

police officer holding all the cards, things did not work out quite as Vidocq had hoped. In desperation, he did supply some of the information Henry wanted, passing over the names of escapees who were in custody under false identities. He was also able to provide some testimonials to the effect that he had tried to earn his living honestly. He was transferred to La Force in the Marais and, to explain his non-appearance on the chain, it was put about that he was under a capital charge.[8] The deal was simple. For the moment, provided he came up with sufficient and accurate information he would not be returned to a *bagne*. If he failed, he could expect to join the next coffle.

An alternate and more romantic, if inherently improbable, version of events is that he assisted in the recovery of emeralds stolen from the Empress Josephine. In return Vidocq was summoned before the Emperor who ordered he be given a suitable post in compensation. There is no doubt the jewels were stolen and recovered but there is no record of Vidocq's assistance in the matter. As part of his reward it is most unlikely he would have wanted to go back to La Force with all the dangers that entailed.[9]

Vidocq now submitted a petition asking not to be sent to the galleys but before Henry could make any long-term arrangement, there was the problem of the constant rumor that Vidocq had been a *Chauffeur*.[10] One thing over which the authorities used to baulk – although in the face of expediency their attitude had softened considerably over the years – was that they were generally not prepared to accept a murderer as a supergrass. In 1810 the Prefect Dubois confirmed to the Minister of Police, Joseph Fouché, that there was "no indication that he was the head of a band of warmers and garrotters not even that he was just a warmer or garrotter."[11]

---

[8] La Force prison stood between rue Pavée and rue de Roi-de-Sicile near what is now the rue de Rivoli and the St-Paul metro station. Built in 1265 by Charles, King of Naples and Sicily, it had been known as l'Hôtel de Sicile. Later it became the home of the La Force family and on the advice of Jacques Necker, the Swiss-born banker and adviser to Louis XVI, it became a prison and, like others of the time, it was divided into a series of courts separately housing debtors, children, people who had not paid to have their children fed, women, beggars and criminals proper, whose worst examples lived in what was known as *la fosse aux lions*. During the Revolution it housed a number of political prisoners and in August 1792 was the scene of the massacre and mutilation of one hundred of its inhabitants including Marie-Thérèse-Louise de Savoie-Carigan, the widow of the debauched and guillotined Prince de Lamballe and now the confidante of Marie-Antoinette who was also imprisoned there. La Force was pulled down in 1845.

[9] See Samuel Edwards, *The Vidocq Dossier*, pp. 33–4.

[10] Arch. Nat. BB 21 166. February 27, 1810.

[11] Arch. Nat. BB 21 166. Letter, March 16, 1810.

Now the way was clear for Vidocq to begin his steady supply of information. At the same time he continued to be the fountain of advice and assistance to the inmates as well as running his kangaroo court. One of Vidocq's early triumphs was his peaching on a man named France, otherwise called Tourmel, one of a gang of *galériens* on the run who were committing a series of robberies in Paris. He had hidden two notes of 1,000 francs each at the time of his arrest and he gave them to Vidocq to act as his banker. There had been a robbery at an umbrella shop in the passage Feydeau and France had maintained he was of no fixed address. The police, on the other hand, were convinced that he had one and, moreover, that there would be a good deal of stolen property there if they could find it. It was up to Vidocq to wheedle it out of the man. He soon learned that he had been living in the flat of a known fence, Josephine Bertrand, at the corner of rue Montmartin and rue Notre Dames des Victoires near what is now the Bourse and by no means the gentrified area it is today. Vidocq's difficulty was not in passing the information on to the police – that was done through the faithful Annette – but to deflect attention from himself as the informant. He is not forthcoming about how he managed it, merely saying:

> I, however, succeeded; and so little did he suspect that I had abused his confidence, that he told me all his troubles.

The police seem to have behaved with some dexterity in protecting their man. An agent gained the confidence of one of the other lodgers who said that no one had seen any movement in the flat for about three weeks. The worrying word "disappearance" was bruited and the commissary thought it necessary to intervene. The door was broken down in the presence of witnesses and there was the stolen property as well as housebreaking tools. But what had happened to the woman Josephine Bertrand, said to live in the flat? She was never found but another girl, Lambert, known to be France's mistress, was arrested in the rue Montmartre. France was taken for the "on-the-spot" identification beloved by the French police. He claimed the neighbors were mistaken but he was found guilty and received a fairly modest eight years in the galleys.

However, not everything went according to plan. Now attention was turned to two of Vidocq's former colleagues, the highly talented Jean-Pierre Fossard and his friend Leganeur. Vidocq claims he was directing operations from La Force and believed that it was as a result of the ineptness of the police that Fossard, regarded as the more dangerous of the pair, was not picked up for a further fifteen months and then only when he took personal control of things.

One of the individuals Vidocq both helped and gave up in La Force was Barthélemy Lacour, known as Coco-Lacour, who would for a short period in the 1820s become his successor as head of the detective force. Criminologists searching for the reasons why people become criminals might profitably compare the early careers of Vidocq and Lacour. If Vidocq had been a lower-middle-class boy who had "gone wrong," then Lacour had never had a chance in life. His parents had died while he was young and he had been placed with a couple at the Palais-Royal arcades. From there he went to live with a brothel keeper, a woman named Maréchal. In prison regularly for minor thefts, he was taken under the wing of a known criminal, Muller, who both sodomized him and taught him to read. For a time Lacour was also protected by a young woman named Elisa, also known as Eliza the German, whose kindness to him, some say, he either abused, or, as others have it, he repaid by marrying her. His description is not altogether prepossessing. He stood around five feet two inches, with blond coloring and a bald head with a straight forehead and a slightly bent nose, which Vidocq describes as having a red tip. His eyes were blue and leaden. His hobby was fishing in the Seine for trinkets which he then sold to prostitutes.[12]

Now, in January 1810, he was awaiting trial on a charge of stealing silver from a police officer. So far so good, but in prison he was also suspected of being a spy for that same officer, something which would almost certainly have resulted in his death if Vidocq had not vouched for him. Vidocq, as was often the case, had his own reasons for showing this apparent clemency: he was watching Lacour on the orders of Henry. One thing all but the very best of criminals find impossible to do is to keep their mouths shut. They must have someone in whom to confide and one of Vidocq's great talents was that of being a good listener. Lacour told him that there was little danger of the police being able to pin the theft on him because the only witness was a street porter. He did not name the man but, foolishly, he did tell Vidocq in which street he lived. Two years.[13]

---

[12] Archives de la Préfecture de Police (APP), E/a 90 (16). Marie-Barthélemy Lacour was first given a month at La Force when he was found stealing lace. By the age of seventeen he was a noted pickpocket.

[13] Ibid. He received this sentence on January 18, 1810 and was then handed over to the marine department as a deserter. On January 22, he was again in Bicêtre as an incorrigible thief and was released on July 3, 1816.

Today it seems incredible that prisoners in what should have been a high security prison such as La Force should have access to funds and have visits from their wives and mistresses, but such was the case both in Paris and London. Messages were continually passed to Henry by Annette. There was little problem with this; female companions frequently spent their days with favored prisoners. In January 1792 Adelaide Freminot, an eighteen-year-old seamstress and possibly the mistress of a prisoner at the Abbaye, was accused of having had criminal correspondence with him. He had, it was alleged, passed her a note in a piece of bread. She claimed this was absurd since she had free access every day. She brought and cooked him meals and freely associated with him and his friends. He in turn bought her housecoats to wear in prison and gave her money.[14]

One early instance of Annette's help came when Legagneur, caught in flagrante executing a burglary in the rue de la Mortellerie with false keys, decided to have the money, which he had left with a receiver in the rue Sainte-Dominique, sent into the prison. Annette was dispatched to execute the commission but when she approached the man he threatened to have her arrested. Now Legagneur wanted some locks delivered to two friends, the celebrated criminals Marguerit and Victor Desbois. Annette took the locks to the rue des Deux Ponts where they were staying in a ground floor slum. She followed them, according to Vidocq, in various disguises, and was finally able to report that they lived in the rue St-Jean, in a small house with gardens behind it. The police were not as adroit as Vidocq's mistress and the men escaped out the back. It was some time later that they were arrested in the rue Hyacinthe St-Michel.

And so it went on. Vidocq's new cellmate, Robin, introduced him to another prisoner, an escapee from the galleys. He in turn introduced Vidocq to his old friends and in short order they all went back to the *bagnes*.

"Were I to relate half my successes in my new department, my readers' patience would be exhausted," Vidocq wrote, with becoming modesty. He would confine himself to the best cases, one of which was certainly the undoing of Blignon and Charpentier, the latter known as Chante à L'heure, who had killed an old woman in the rue de la Sonnerie.

---

[14] For her part, she spent six months in the Conciergerie. She complained that, as a woman of good morals, she should not be locked up with those of bad ones. Arch. Nat. Z/3 100, 110.

In La Force the convicts would walk a short paved strip for their exercise, particularly early on summer mornings. One morning a fight broke out between Blignon and Charpentier, who had the worst of it. It was then he said that, if he cared to talk, Blignon would go to the guillotine. Vidocq spoke with him and plied him with brandy and wine. It was only a matter of time before Charpentier told him of the robbery and another murder of a man in rue Planche-Mibray committed by the pair, along with two others who had not been caught. And that was the beginning of what led to an early end for them both.

Vidocq survived twenty-one months of this double life before, on the recommendations of Henry, he was released by baron Pasquier, who had replaced Dubois as Prefect.[15] From time to time another method of communication between Vidocq and Henry had been that Vidocq was brought out of La Force at regular intervals on the pretext of seeing an examining magistrate over his supposed murder case. Now on March 25, 1811, on one of these visits, he was allowed to escape back to Annette and his mother in the rue Neuve-Saint-François between the rue Vielle du Temple and the rue Saint-Louis in the Marais. He was, however, still expected to work for Henry and the Sûreté. At the news of his escape, the convicts in La Force foolishly celebrated.

Louis Canler, who as a young man joined the police some years later and himself became Prefect, disliked Vidocq intensely, and wrote sourly of the deal:

In 1809 the notorious Vidocq was in Bicêtre prison awaiting with other galley slaves the departure of the chain-gang with which he would return to the hulks whence he escaped. To this man, who was gifted with a vivid imagination and an ardent temperament, the thought of captivity was very painful, and as he had on several occasions acted as denunciator, in the baseness of his heart he hit on a method to improve his condition, even if it did not regain his liberty. He, therefore, offered to act as spy in the prisons, that is to say, gain the confidence of his comrades and make them confess

---

[15] Baron (later duc) Etienne-Denis Pasquier was born on April 22, 1767. His father was executed during the Terror, on April 21, 1794, along with twenty-two other advisers to or presidents of the Parlément. Pasquier hid in Paris. He entered the service of Napoleon in 1806 when nearly forty and became Prefect in place of the disgraced comte Dubois. A man for all seasons, he served the Empire, the Restoration, Louis XVIII, Charles X and Louis-Philippe. Offered a place in the Académie Française in 1842 he had only his *Mémoires* to claim as a literary achievement. He left office after the 1848 Revolution and died on July 5, 1862. It was said of him that he lacked both independent ideas and character. He had the qualities of a grand man of state but he lacked the best of them.

their crimes. At the same time he sent in a report about several convicts who had escaped or broken their bans and were detained at Bicêtre under false names. Lastly he gave such precise information about certain daring robbers, who had for a long time been infesting the capital, as led to their arrest.

At this period of time detective police did not exist or, more correctly speaking, existed under such conditions which rendered them almost of no effect. The police officers entirely independent of each other acted as they thought proper in their own district, and a robber who was hunted down in one quarter could carry on his trade with impunity in another. Vidocq's reports were examined and verified and the prefect of police thought that such a man would be invaluable as a spy; he was therefore employed in that capacity at Bicêtre and La Force, receiving pay proportioned to the importance of the captures which he helped to effect. M. Henry at length resolved to set him at liberty, on condition that he should act as denouncer, and each month supply the Préfecture with a settled minimum of criminals, under penalty of being sent back to Brest himself; he had a fixed salary of four pounds a month and a premium for each arrest.[16]

Whatever Canler may have thought, Vidocq's preferment in the police was rapid.

Michel Foucault sees his appointment in very dark terms:

Vidocq marks the moment when delinquency, detached from other illegalities, was invested by power and turned inside out. It was then that the direct, institutional coupling of police and delinquency took place: the disturbing moment when criminality became one of the mechanisms of power.[17]

---

[16] Louis Canler, *Mémoires de Canler.* The honest if somewhat prissy Canler had been a drummer boy and then a corporal in Napoleon's army. He fought at Waterloo before joining the police.

[17] Michel Foucault, *Surveiller et punir,* p. 283.

Part Two
Gamekeeper

Chapter 11

VIDOCQ
AGAINST *"SES AMIS*
D'ANTAN"

In which our hero is given an office and set to work – he is criticized
for betraying two old associates – avoids many temptations – and gives
chase to the Prince of Thieves, Jean-Pierre Fossard

IN FRANCE, the pre-Revolutionary system of policing was organized, financed and controlled by the Government, and its members were in effect the personal police of the King. The eighteenth-century citizen in Paris was far better served than his counterpart in London in the same period, which had at best the Bow Street Runners as a rudimentary police force. Control was under a *lieutenant-général de police,* appointed by the King and himself under the control of the minister of Paris. The lieutenant-general included in his remit the scrutiny of the social, political and economic activities of Paris as well as responsibility for controlling crime and maintaining order. Crime was low and there were roughly three police officers to every thousand inhabitants. The figure today is fifteen to every thousand.[1]

The principal weapon against crime was, however, the *mouchard,* or police spy, who obtained information from such sources as household servants and brothels, whose habituees were in the pay of the police. The Chief of Police Sartine once said to Louis XV, "Whenever three people speak to one another in the street, one of them will be mine." Reports went on a daily basis to the King and were then distributed through a *bulletin politique ou d'espionnage.* The King also had

---

[1] Claude Chariot, quoted by Eric Pincas, in "La Brigade de sûreté était payée sur des fonds secrets!," in *Historia mensuel,* September 1, 2001. For a full account of the workings of the police, see Philip Stead, *The Police of Paris.*

the power to issue the highly unpopular lettres de cachet which could order detention without trial.[2]

After the Revolution the police force in Paris was reconstructed and run by a number of committees. Unsurprisingly, this was not a success. The French Ministry of Police was created in 1796 with the specific authority to enforce the laws and defeat any counters to the Revolution. Three years later Joseph Fouché was appointed director. He had been teaching in a Jesuit college when the Revolution began and came to Paris in 1792. Stefan Zweig wrote of him:

> . . . in 1790 he was a priestly schoolmaster, by 1792 he was a plunderer of the Church, a year later he was a communist; five years later a millionaire and ten years after that the duc d'Otranto . . .
>
> This man during one of the most salient periods in history was the leader of every party in turn and was unique in surviving the destruction of them all.[3]

An outstanding intriguer, he was a part of the coup d'état which brought Napoleon to power.[4] It was he who divided the administrative powers of the police into four arrondissements, each with a *conseiller d'Etat*. It was Fouché who continued the pre-Revolutionary spy system, recruiting some three hundred spies, many of them ex-convicts. In 1800 control was placed in the hands of a Préfet de Police, a wholly administrative office. It was this network which Vidocq first joined and then, as his power grew, came to rule under the Préfet. On the way, however, he faced a good deal of hostility and suspicion.

Whatever the ambiguities, inaccuracies and downright lies which may be found in Vidocq's account of his life there is no doubt whatsoever that it was Vidocq's idea to establish the Brigade de Sûreté, a force of plainclothes undercover police which would not be trammelled by the parochial delineation which forbade gendarmes to pursue criminals across district boundaries without express permission. As a result criminals who committed a robbery in the Marais and then crossed the river would no longer be perfectly safe. In the autumn of 1811, within

---

[2] Lettres de cachet were often used by families to deal with their black sheep who were embarrassing them socially or politically. One well-known victim of a lettre de cachet was the politician Mirabeau (1749–91), who, after his release, played an active part in the early stages of the Revolution.

[3] Stefan Zweig, *Joseph Fouché*, p. xiii.

[4] Initially dismissed in 1810, after Waterloo Fouché transferred his loyalty to Louis XVIII with whom he had been negotiating for some years. He resigned shortly afterwards and retired to Prague. In 1818 he became an Austrian citizen and died in Trieste two years later.

six months of his arrival in the Sûreté, Vidocq's brigade was born. It was an almost perfect example of setting a thief to catch a thief.

It is both curious and alarming that, more than seventy years later, the Metropolitan Police had still not learned from Vidocq and the French. Writing in his autobiography, Frederick Wensley, who joined the police in 1888, told of the difficulties facing detectives:

> When I joined, an officer, except by definite instructions, was scarcely ever permitted to go outside his own division. The result was that criminals living in one district could, almost with impunity, commit crime in others.
>
> A divisional superintendent did not like officers leaving his district to operate in another; and a local detective–inspector resented detectives from other districts 'poaching' on his division. He would hint pretty broadly that if he wanted their aid he would apply for it.[5]

Pasquier provided funds and Henry provided offices at 6 Petite-rue-Sainte-Anne (now the rue Boileau) behind the Palais de Justice, where Vidocq was set to work. One of the first of his successes was the arrest of the forger Watrin, who had already escaped from the hands of customs officers.[6] Vidocq tracked him down to a house on the boulevard Montparnasse, where Watrin had left some property, and he rented an apartment in the building for himself and Annette, now together for some five years. A fortnight later he heard that Watrin, together with another man, had returned. By the time Vidocq was out of bed and had gone to the downstairs flat, Watrin was away again. He bullied the man's companion into telling him that they really lived at 4 rue des Mauvais Garçons and there tricked Watrin into coming out of his door by pretending he had gone down the stairs. They fought and naturally Vidocq won. Accompanied only by the faithful Annette, Vidocq took him to Henry at the Préfecture.

There was something of a sequel to the case. On the scaffold it became known that Watrin might inform on other members of the underworld. The execution was halted and he was led away. Either he gave thin milk or there was some other reason for the stay for within a few days Watrin was back on the block and this time there was no reprieve. He was executed on September 18, 1811.[7]

---

[5] Frederick Wensley, *Detective Days*, p. 39.

[6] The name is sometimes given as Vatrin and it may be from this that Balzac took the name Vautrin for his anti-hero introduced in *Le Père Goriof* (1834) and based on Vidocq.

[7] *Journal de Paris*, September 19, 1811.

Not every forger ended up on the scaffold. During the same period, in 1812, a singular discovery was made at the Banque de France, where several counterfeit notes had been presented to be exchanged for specie. The notes had been paid and they had then been passed to the police for investigation. Closer examination showed that Indian ink had been used and they had been made by hand. Watch was kept on gambling houses and within a fortnight a man, Allais, who was known to be a painter of miniatures, had been seen trying to pass a counterfeit note. The man's residence was not searched so as to allow him to manufacture another note and several days went by before the place was raided. Nothing was found, but then Vidocq saw the man glance at a stove in the middle of the room. In it the model used as a note was found. The fear was that if he were brought to trial there would have been great and adverse publicity as to how easy it was to forge and pass such notes and the man was treated as a prisoner of state and taken to Vincennes. Vidocq is said to have received a reward of 6,000 louis; if other grateful clients rewarded him with the same generosity, this would go some way in explaining how he amassed his fortune.[8]

Shortly afterwards Vidocq gained his revenge on Bouhin, the man whom he believed had informed on him two years earlier. On his information Bouhin and his coiner friend Dr. Terrier were arrested in flagrante counterfeiting five-franc pieces and were executed. Later there were suggestions that Vidocq had planted the evidence on him.

Although not naming him – for Vidocq was still then very much a public favorite and there were serious libel problems – the lawyer Antoine – Gérard Claveau, a critic of what he saw as a brutal and repressive police force, wrote:

France knows his work; unfortunates encouraged to commit crime, tools given them to do so, infamous betrayal with tranquillity, what a thought. Infernal traps laid to ensure success. I'll never forget in 1811 two unfortunates who had been given furnaces and crucibles and material to make false coinage and had been caught the moment the fire burned, going to the scaffold. I saw them upset and the naming of the unequalled monster they never dreamed would have betrayed them. I still hear the heart-rending cries. They didn't suffer long. Forty-eight hours later the executioner's axe put an end to their cries.

---

[8]E-D. Pasquier, *Memoirs of Chancellor Pasquier*, t. I, pp. 519–21.

He went on to ask the question posed by criminologists over the years:

> How do we discover the criminals if you do not employ scoundrels? It is a singular method. I'd rather call an arsonist to put out a fire or ask a known debaucher to guard the honor of my wife and daughter.[9]

Vidocq does not specifically deny the charge, saying:

> Let the reader remember the reply which this man made to me when, at Bouhin's house, I sought to persuade him to renounce his guilty industry, and he will judge whether Terrier was a man to allow himself to be drawn away.

The good doctor's answer had been:

> I see that you are one of those cowardly fellows of whom there are so great a number. Suppose we are detected, what then? There are many others who make their exit at the place de Grève and we are not there yet; for fifteen years I have used these 'chamber gentlemen' as my bankers and nobody has doubted me. It will do yet. And besides, my friend, attend to your own business.

All very fine, but Vidocq would not be the last police officer to plant evidence on a guilty man. Generally, Vidocq's detractors claim that he was not averse to setting up even those close to him. As an example of this, he is said to have loved a young woman, Henriette; feigning illness, when she went to steal medicine for him he had her arrested and saw her sentenced to ten years penal servitude.[10]

Vidocq, a one-man forerunner of the post–Second World War English Ghost Squad (a squad of detectives allowed to mix freely, and often in disguise, with criminals to thwart their plans), now began to haunt the brothels and taverns in one disguise or another. He had already set out his stall. In his *Dictionnaire universel de police* Desessart offers suggestions for the way a spy should conduct himself:

> In delicate and difficult missions an observer must be a veritable Proteus. His character, his speech, his bearing, even his face must have the greatest mobility. According to circumstances, he must be a man-of-the-world or

---

[9] A-G. Claveau, *De la police de Paris et ses abuses*.
[10] Jean Galtier-Boissière, *Mysteries of the French Secret Police*, p. 181

one of the people always insinuating, flexible, skillful, fertile in his methods and above all full of tricks. No dress should seem strange on him, or cause him to be remarked; his exterior must be ready to lend itself to all the forms which he desires to assume. He is ceaselessly occupied in inspiring confidence and he neglects nothing to divert suspicion.

A blueprint, indeed, for Vidocq, who perfected the art. On the publication of his memoirs *The Times* was enchanted with the accounts of his disguises:

> An Asmodeus as to place and a very Proteus as to person . . . the decorated Chevalier at the Café des Milles Colonnes, the quiet reader at the reading rooms in the rue de la Paix, the simple Bourgeois upon the boulevards or the wretched chiffonier in the streets picking up rags and waste papers.[11]

For the moment, though, to the thieves he was still Jules, a galley slave on the run, and so entitled to the protection of the underworld. By the same token, he says, they would not involve him in any activity which might compromise him. Most of them would not, that is. It was almost certain that sooner or later he would run into St-Germain and eventually he did in the company of a restaurateur from the rue des Provaires whom he calls Boudin. It was from St-Germain that he eventually learned that his former tormentors, Blondy and Deluc, had been executed at Beauvais. Some weeks later Vidocq, who was, he says, waging a one-man war against the criminal elements of Paris only hindered by the incompetence of the police, met St-Germain and Boudin again. This time they suggested he might like to help them with the murder of a pair of elderly men who lived in rue des Provaires.

He reported back to Henry, who was by no means convinced, thinking perhaps that his police officer was acting as an agent provocateur. He probably was. It was a subject about which Vidocq had his own ideas. To his mind such a role did not exist. Of another occasion he wrote:

> . . . in a robbery, I did not see how there can be any provocation possible. A man is honest or he is not; if he be honest, no consideration can be sufficiently powerful to determine him on committing a crime; if he be

---

[11] *The Times*, July 4, 1828. Asmodeus was the evil spirit in the apocryphal Book of Tobit (or Tobias) who lusted after the maiden Sara. In Greek mythology Proteus was one of the Old Men of the Sea, who guarded Poseidon's herd of seals and who constantly changed shape and form. He could also divine the future.

not, he only wants the opportunity, and is it not evident that it will offer itself sooner or later?

At the meeting with his chief, Vidocq successfully protested his innocence and was sent back out to continue spying on St-Germain. A day for the murder was finally fixed and Vidocq met them outside the city gates. There he was told that the deal was off but there was another on the stocks. There was also some bad news. St-Germain told him that he had heard the price of Vidocq's freedom had been that he was to work as a police spy. Vidocq's long suit was never modesty:

> My ever-ready genius quickly fled to my aid and without hesitation I replied that I was not much surprised at the charge and for the simple reason that I myself had been the first to set the rumour afloat.

St-Germain was convinced. The new job was at the house of a banker who lived at the corner of rue d'Enghien and rue Hautville. The banker was away and there were only two housekeepers. Best of all, there was a garden at the back. There was to be a fourth person but Vidocq was not told who it would be. It turned out to be a coach driver who had fallen on hard times and into bad ways. Vidocq managed to send a message to Annette who in turn contacted Henry. Boudin and St-Germain were captured and Vidocq staged his own death in the garden. This also convinced St-Germain who fell weeping on the corpse. For once Vidocq gives a description of the pair. Boudin was bow-legged,

> a deformity I have observed among several systematic assassins, as well as among many other individuals distinguished by their crimes.

In this single sentence Vidocq anticipates the findings of the Italian criminologist Cesare Lombroso by some forty years. It was Lombroso's theory that there were criminal types who could be recognized by their physical characteristics.

Possibly because of his great successes (and no doubt his arrogance), Vidocq was never popular with many of his colleagues who were jealous of the talented intruder, and one of his early problems was another secret agent, Gaffré, himself a former *galérien* whose criminal career far outshone that of Vidocq. His mother, said to be one of the most handsome Jewesses of her day, had been the mistress of Flambard, the Chief of Police at Rouen, but this had not saved her son, then aged eighteen, from a whipping and branding at the place du Vieux-Marché in the city, from which he was then banished. Under the name Caille he had been a *Chauffeur* and, says Vidocq, could turn his hand to assassination or pickpocketing as the occasion demanded. Despite the fact that, at the time, he was highly regarded he was also still working on the other side of the fence. It was Vidocq's belief that Gaffré, fearful he would be supplanted, intended to trap him in a compromising situation. For the moment, however, it was all smiles and bottles of wine and Vidocq played along. He had, after all, told Henry what was happening.

Gaffré received eight months for pickpocketing and, amazingly, on his release was re-employed. Ignorant of his betrayer, when he came out he suggested that he and Vidocq should try their hands at kirk-buzzing, stealing from people in church. The team was to be four-handed, with the agents Manigant and Compère making up the quartet. Again Vidocq sent out a message and a watch was found on Gaffré. This time he was not prosecuted but was sent to Bicêtre, and then exiled for a period from Paris, to which he returned before his death in 1822. But by then Vidocq had his feet well under the Sûreté's table.

Some former criminals turned out well, and for a time none better than André Goury, a former swindler, and Ronquetti, a onetime cardsharp, who seems to have lasted the course at the Sûréte. Goury had served two terms of imprisonment and, according to some accounts, became second in command there. According to Samuel Edwards, Vidocq apparently hoped he would take command after his retirement but this did not happen because Goury had never received a pardon. This cannot be correct because Vidocq was himself headlong before he was pardoned. More likely is Louis Guyon's version that Goury fell from grace when he stole some jewelry handed in to the police. There is also a story of Goury and his chief which contributed to the Vidocq legend, said to have occurred in the mid-1820s. When Goury's mistress, Marie, walked to Vidocq's house to dine with him and Goury, she was followed by a middle-aged man who mistook her for a prostitute. The man was inveigled into the house by Vidocq and Goury and taken to an upstairs bedroom where he was locked in with a singularly ugly maid. He was only released in the morning on payment of a large fee, which was, naturally – for it would spoil the story otherwise - given to the maid.[12]

---

[12] Samuel Edwards, *The Vidocq Dossier*, p. 85. Louis Guyon, *Biographie des commissaires de police et de la paix*, p. 234.

The Italian Ronquetti, who called himself the Duke of Modena, seems to have arrived in Paris, accompanied by an Italian mistress, a lady's maid and a tiny black servant, in the winter of 1816, a particular time of Republican plotting, and, as a foreigner, swam into Vidocq's view. Apart from his penchant for gaming clubs and his sleight of hand there seems to have been nothing against him and he was recruited into the Brigade de Sûreté. He is credited with saving Vidocq's life on one occasion when, in the spring of 1819, he saw a gang lying in wait for Vidocq as he walked home. He approached the chief and together they arrested the men. He is said to have stayed with the Sûreté for twenty-five years.

Another criminal who came good was the former forger Aubé, who was the general secretary of the Sûreté. In 1820 Vidocq left a stack of money he had collected from the Ministry of Finance to pay his agents in his office. Aubé saw the pile and stood guard until Vidocq returned. He would not, it is said, accept a reward but merely took a glass of wine.

Two instances early in his police career set Vidocq apart from other officers and earned him their enmity. The first was a raid on the suburb of Courtille of which it was said, "To see Paris without seeing Courtille is like seeing Rome without seeing the Pope." It was here the great thief Cartouche had been arrested in 1731.

A more or less lawless quartier, Courtille – in roughly the area where Belleville is today – was regarded as resistant to revolutions, changes of government, invasion and epidemics, and was at its height during the Restoration and for the next thirty years. It was full of *guinguettes* – dance-halls – such as Boeuf Rouge, Coq Hardi, Sauvage and L'Epée des Bois. One of its most celebrated bar owners was Jean Ramponeau who sold cheap wine.[13] He kept his costs down by selling his public house and then taking it back from the new owner. It was there that Vidocq, in the guise of Jules, spent much of his time.

In later years the pre-Lenten carnival of Courtille was positively bacchanalian, flourishing between 1840 and 1845. The cabarets disgorged their clients around 6 a.m. and the crowd made its way down from Courtille to Paris in their costumes in a slow-moving procession which took up to six hours before it reached the Marais. There the fashionable thing to do was sit in a carriage and watch the

---

[13] The spelling is sometimes given as Ramponeaux. In the argot of the time a truly astonishing thing was said to be *"une affaire à la Ramponeaux."*

sport. The shouting and excitement grew until the parade broke up around the corner of the faubourg du Temple and the boulevard du Temple.

Vicomte de Beaumont-Vassy described how Lord Seymour, known for his association with street arabs, the *titis,* of the theatre, as Milord l'Arsouille (or Blackguard) would throw gold coins from his carriage which he drew up outside the Vendages de Bourgogne.[14]

Shortly after Vidocq became an official police officer he led a raid on Courtille. His bête noire the Inspector Yvrier, one of the old guard, had suggested that such a raid would require a battalion of troops. Vidocq replied that he would manage with eight gendarmes. He took with him an additional two of his own men along with a sackful of handcuffs and some chalk.

At the time, the cabaret, run by a man named Desnoyers, was the height of fashion and villainy. Vidocq went straight into the dance-hall, demanded that the music and dancing stop and moved to the door. As each man filed past, he marked a cross on the back of those whom he knew to be wanted and the gendarmes outside arrested them. In all thirty-eight men were taken back to the Préfecture.[15]

After that Vidocq's cover was blown. There was no longer any point in pretending that he was not a police officer and he persuaded Henry to allow him to go to Bicêtre to watch the chains leaving for the *bagnes.* When he went to the *cour de fers* he was roundly abused by the convicts as a spy. In turn he rounded on them, reminding them that they would betray each other at the drop of a hat. In time things quieted down and one or two asked him to do favors for them, such as passing messages to their families. He complied and from then on was regarded as something of a friend to the succession of men who were to make their way across France in their chains.

The raid on Courtille was not an act which endeared him to the old guard and neither was his capture of Jean-Pierre Fossard. Vidocq always regarded Fossard as one of the great Parisian criminals of the time. Jean Savant, who was undoubtedly a great historian, was also

---

[14] Vicomte de Beaumont-Vassy, *Salons de Paris sous Louis-Philippe.* Born in 1805, Lord Henry Seymour, the brother of Lord Richard Seymour, the Marquis of Hertford, was one of the great English eccentrics who lived in Paris in the period. He died around 1860. The descent from Courtille is depicted in the last scene in *Les Enfants du Paradis*.

[15] In the 1930s the English racecourse gang, the Sabinis, did exactly the same thing, chalking the palms of their hands and slapping the backs of those rivals whom they wished to be identified by the police.

swept up with the romance of things. He considered Fossard the Prince of Thieves and offers a description of him:

> Medium height, brown hair and eyebrows, an oval face, a large and long aquiline nose, a dimpled chin. The whole produced fear. Yes, a frightening look.[16]

Born into a decent family and given a good education, Fossard looked set to become a career criminal from an early age. He learned his apprenticeship by stealing trifles and swiftly climbed the criminal ladder. His fellow convicts regarded him as among the *grinches de la haute pègre*, or a tip-top cracksman.

Among other things Fossard was a great and fearless climber as well as being a noted prison breaker and a man who could spot a policeman in disguise at a hundred paces. One of his escapes from Bicêtre had been over the rooftops. He was seen and fired on. Without speeding up or looking down he got to the side overlooking fields and slid down. "The fall was enough to have broken a hundred necks but he went unscathed," wrote Vidocq admiringly.

Jean-Pierre Fossard was sent to the *bagne* for twelve years with hard labor on June 24, 1808, and he escaped on March 24, 1810. He was next arrested at Nancy on a charge of possessing false keys and housebreaking. He had been working with Victor Desbois and a man called Noël the Spectacles, whose mother was a major receiver. Fossard committed a series of burglaries with Noël, who, as an accomplished musician, was invited to play at grand houses. Noël took impressions of keys which Fossard then replicated. It was an art in which he defied Georget and all the locksmiths in the world to surpass him. This time he got life imprisonment.

Fossard was sentenced on March 15, 1811, and was exposed the next day before being returned to the *bagne*. On May 31, Fossard, numbered 10183, was ready for the journey to the galley at Brest which took the traditional route of St-Cyr, Dreux, Alençon, Laval, Rennes and Morlaix, and he arrived at the port on June 21. It was only a matter of time before he escaped and all told he escaped four times from the galleys. Vidocq notes that Desbois and his colleague, Mongenet, were also regularly sent to the *bagnes* and just as regularly escaped.

---

[16] Jean Savant, "Le Cabinet de Médailles," in *Les Oeuvres Libres*, Vol. 81, February 1953.

There is little doubt that Fossard led the police in Paris a fairly merry dance with a series of accomplished burglaries. On one occasion his hideaway was discovered and it was decided that when he was out the police should gain entry and hide in the apartment. The plan worked well enough. Three agents hid in the flat and, three days later, when they heard the key in the door, they rushed him. Unfortunately they had left a knife on the table and Fossard grabbed it, threatened them, locked them up and was away. Recriminations followed and, if Vidocq is to be believed, the other officers, including his enemy Yvrier, were told that it was only he who would be able to lay hands on the man. They were not best pleased.

Vidocq, ever the showman, announced, to the annoyance of his colleagues, that he would arrest Fossard and deliver him up on New Year's Day as a present to the Prefect. The only information to hand was that Fossard was living somewhere in the Marais in a house with yellow silk and muslin curtains. Also in the house lived a hunchbacked tailoress who knew Fossard's mistress, Henriette Tonnaux.

It might be thought that yellow silk and muslin curtains would be easily identified but they were fashionable at the time. So it was a question of finding the hunchback without making it too obvious.

So it was now Vidocq, master of disguise, who padded the streets near Les Halles, passing himself off as a man of sixty walking with the aid of a gold-knobbed cane. To a great extent police work is common sense and, believing the woman would be out early in the morning shopping, on the second day he found her. Now he spun a tale that he was looking for his wife who had run off with an adventurer and gave a description of Fossard. Yes, Vidocq was told, he had been there with a fine-looking woman but had now gone. The hunchback did not know the new address, nor did the landlord. The next step in police work is the often tedious one of making person-to-person inquiries. Did the street porters know where they had gone? It was only a matter of time before Vidocq traced the man who had shifted the belongings. The pair had gone to live in rue Duphot. The porter was given a note to take to the Préfecture where he believed he was to be given a reward. Instead he was locked up as a material witness until the denouement was played out.

Now Vidocq changed his clothes and became a coalman. Fossard was sighted and an attempt was made to arrest him but when another agent signalled that the escapee actually had a pistol in his hand the attempt was abandoned. He was back in his apartment late on New Year's Eve and now it was a question of waiting for the best opportunity to recapture him without causing bloodshed. The idea was to ensure that the woman was out of the flat when Fossard was arrested. In the end a nephew of the owner of the wineshop on the ground floor of the building was enlisted to go and ask for some brandy for his sick aunt. Henriette Tonnaux was seized as she opened the door and the agents threw themselves on Fossard. When, on New Year's Day 1812, Vidocq brought him to Pasquier, the Prefect is said to have replied, "Here's what you call a New Year's gift."

For Fossard it was back to the *bagne*. At first there were reports that he was preparing to escape with the sole aim of killing Vidocq, but over the years that he remained there he apparently became docile and subservient. Henriette Tonnaux regularly sent him money and eventually he was allowed to work for a cabinetmaker. It was then that Henriette provided the necessary papers and Fossard escaped again on February 8, 1831, travelling to Paris by coach.

After Fossard's arrest Vidocq turned his attention to Victor Desbois and his colleague, known as Le Tambour. To find them he went to Noël's mother who lived in the rue Tiquetonne and who was known in the Marais and Saint-Denis as an accomplished piano player and was generally admired for her manners. She also had a thriving trade in forged passports and was well known for helping escaped galley slaves. At this time her son Noël was in the *bagne* and Vidocq passed himself off as a man called Germain, or Royer, also known as the Captain. Vidocq describes how he prepared his disguise:

> My haircut, *à la mode des bagnes*, was dyed black. As well as my beard, after it had attained a growth of eight days; to embrown my countenance I washed it with walnut liquor; and to perfect the imitation, I garnished my upper lip with a kind of coffee grounds which I plastered on by means of gum arabic and thus became as nasal in my twang as Germain himself. My feet were doctored with equal care. I made blisters on them by rubbing in a certain composition of which I had obtained the recipe at Brest. I also made the marks of the fetters and when all my toilet was finished, dressed myself in the suitable garb.

Noël's mother fed and watered him and when he asked of his former colleagues she told him they had been tipped off by an old police inspector, Joseph Longueville, that there was to be a search of the quartier.

Vidocq was not always fortunate in the agents whom he had not chosen himself. This time he was betrayed by one Manceau, still in his teens and effectively a probationary agent, who spilled the beans to Mme Noël. Fortunately Vidocq suspected him and, challenged, Manceau admitted that Desbois and Mongenet were lying in wait for him. For his sins he was sent back to the *bagnes*.[17] Desbois and Le Tambour never returned to the area but were arrested a short time later in another part of Paris and began yet again the long journey west. As for Mme Noël, she went to St-Lazare for six months as a receiver.

Noël, when at the *bagne*, was regarded as the best harpist in Brest. He and other convicts gave recitals to which the townspeople were invited. He led a small orchestra of convicts playing flutes and violins for the prison reformer Appert when he visited. Given that there was a constant flow of trade between town and *bagne*, with people being measured for suits and shoes, it is not surprising that there were opportunities for escape.[18]

---

[17] He received an additional six years and died following rough treatment while serving the sentence. Philip Stead, *Vidocq: Picaroon of Crime*, p. 66.

[18] Marcel LeClère, *La Vie dans les bagnes*, p. 370.

Chapter 12

VIDOCQ TRIUMPHANT

*In which our hero is accused of destroying the Emperor's
statue – arrests a legion of criminals – is involved in the Affair of
the Patriots – has his watch stolen – receives a pardon – denounces
the marquis de Chambreuil – arrests the comte de Pontis de
Sainte-Hélène – falls from a stage coach – and has countless
other adventures*

V IDOCQ MADE ENEMIES EASILY. He was a bully, arrogant, abrasive
and contemptuous of the police methods then extant. For their
part the existing peace officers might have had to rely on ex-convicts as
their spies but it was a totally different matter having one in charge of
them. Vidocq was, however, left untouched by the events of the 1814
exile and the return of Napoleon before his final defeat at Waterloo.
The new Préfet, Anglès, kept him in his position and did not regret it.
Without doubt this was on the advice of Henry, a civil servant of the
type impervious to political changes or to the overthrow of regimes
and who knew only their work. Henry's vocation was to combat crime,
and methods of government did not interest him. Under the Bourbons, just as under Napoleon, his job was to catch criminals. It was said
of him that if there were no criminals he would create some, rather
than deprive himself of the pleasures of the chase.

Before he begins his memoirs proper, Louis Canler, who could not
stand the sight or, no doubt, the smell, of Vidocq closer than a hundred
meters, had a few bad words to say about the origins of the detective
system in Paris and the part Vidocq played in setting it up. He also took
the opportunity to land a few blows on Vidocq and his reputation.

One of the acts which Vidocq's detractors attribute to him, faithfully
repeated by Canler, is his part in the destruction of the statue of

Napoleon wearing a toga that stands on top of the column of Austerlitz in the place Vendôme. On March 31, 1814, Vidocq, it was said, in his usual double-dealing way, and seeking to ingratiate himself with the Royalists, was seen leading a mob, including the comte de Maubreuil, which swarmed about the statue. Vidocq had managed to climb the column and smashed the statue of Napoleon about the ankles with a hammer, loosening it sufficiently to allow the mob to haul it down with a rope.

Canler had the story from both Yvrier and an inspector, appropriately named Bias, who had been there when he climbed the statue. They were so disgusted by this treachery that afterwards neither of them could bring themselves to mention Vidocq's name or see him without expressing indignation, something of which Canler heartily approved.[1]

Unfortunately the story is more or less completely untrue. It may be that Vidocq was in the crowd which attempted and failed to pull down the statue that day but he certainly neither smashed its ankles nor supervised the positioning of the rope. The statue came down in a far more civilized manner.[2]

On April 4 an application was made by Royalist supporters to General Sacken, the Russian commander, for permission to pull the statue down. It was pointed out to them that the work was protected, like all other monuments. Later an order was obtained by the comte de Semalle from Rocheouart, aide-de-camp to Emperor Alexander of Russia. This was then countersigned by baron Pasquier. The order for its removal was not wholly Royalist inspired; the founder, Launay, wanted both it and the column to be removed to a safe place and he arranged for them to be properly taken down.

The final exile of Napoleon the following year signalled the time for plots and counterplots, for Republican secret societies and intrigue against the restored Bourbons. Just what was Vidocq's involvement with the secret police during this period? In an interview his biographer Bruno Roy-Henry suggested that Vidocq then, and later, had been the keeper of state secrets, of the type that do not lie in the archives.[3]

---

[1] Louis Canler, *Mémoires de Canler*, p. 111. In another version of the story Maubreuil paid Vidocq, who shared the money with the crowd. L. F. and M. Saint-Hilaire, *Mémoires d'un forçat, ou Vidocq dévoilée*. Made from the twelve hundred cannons captured after Austerlitz and erected in 1810, the statue itself had a later checkered career. After its destruction the metal was used to fashion the statue of Henri IV on the Pont Neuf. Then, in 1833, a new statue was erected with Napoleon more modestly clad in a small hat and frock coat. In 1853 it was replaced by a grander version with him back in a toga. In 1871 it was pulled down by the commune on the demands of Courbet who was required to have it rebuilt the following year at his own expense.

[2] Jean Galtier-Boissière, in *Mysteries of the French Secret Police*, suggests he was seen in the crowd but no more.

[3] Catherine Decouan, "Vidocq un peu affabulateur" in *Historia mensuel*, September 1, 2001.

As for Vidocq he maintained he had no connection:

> I have always had a deep contempt for political *mouchards*, for two reasons:
> if they do not do their duty, they are rogues, and if they do, as soon as they
> become important, they are scoundrels. However, through my position,
> I found myself in contact with most of these paid spies; they were all known
> to me directly or indirectly . . . I played no part in their infamous work; only,
> I have seen both sides of them rather closer than other people . . .

Celui qui s'excuse . . . and Vidocq's detractors have also linked him to
the "Affair of the Patriots" in 1816. In the early days of the Restoration
one plot followed another and the police monitored them all. There
had been minor and easily suppressed uprisings in the Grenoble region
and in Paris three old members of the Federal Guard – Pleignier, a
builder, Carbonneau, a letter writer, and Tollern, a carver – had printed
and distributed to "patriots" cards bearing the legend, "Union, Honor,
Country." It was unfortunate that one of the cards should fall into the
hands of Scheltein, a former assistant executioner during the Terror
and a police spy under the Empire. Now largely redundant, he took the
card to the police and proposed that he be the one to follow things up.

He persuaded the men, who met in a cabaret called Abraham's Sacrifice,
to draw up and print a proclamation which would publicize their association.
Vidocq and another agent named Ricloky frequented the cabaret and it
was only a matter of time before the three men were being encouraged
to think of themselves as veterans of the Empire. Shortly afterwards, in
a classic agent provocateur strategy, Scheltein suggested a plot to blow
up the Tuileries by placing a mine in a sewer near the Pont Royal. Those
present at the meeting turned the proposal down saying they thought it
too dangerous. The next day twenty-six men who had been at the meeting were arrested. The trial, with a hostile President and no Scheltein to
be seen and cross-examined – "I am not aware he has been accused," said
the President – was a foregone conclusion. The jury, which consisted of
three solicitors, three householders, a barrister, a stockbroker, two bankers,
a Post Office official and a printer, found twenty of the twenty-six guilty of
"preparing an outrage." Eight were transported; others were sentenced to
terms of imprisonment ranging from six to ten years. The three principals,
if they can be called such, were each to have their right hands cut off and
then be executed. Scheltein became a sanitary inspector.[4]

---

[4] For an account of the case and some details of the trial, see Jean Galtier-Boissière, *Mysteries of the
French Secret Police*, pp. 184–7. In his memoirs Vidocq names the agent provocateur as Schilkin.

Of the affair Vidocq writes obliquely:

> In 1815 and 1816 there were in Paris a great number of music-halls known
> as *goguettes*. This kind of political mousetrap was formed to begin with
> under the auspices of the police, who filled them with agents. While drink-
> ing with the workmen they tried to involve them in false conspiracies.
> I have seen several of these so-called patriotic gatherings; the persons who
> appeared the most excited were always mouchards, and it was easy to rec-
> ognise them. They had no respect for anything in their songs, which were
> full of hatred and the most outrageous insults against the royal family, and
> these songs, paid for out of secret funds, were the work of the very authors
> of the hymns of Saint Louis and Saint Charles . . . The police have their
> troubadours and are very gay; unfortunately they are not always singing.
> Three heads fell, and the *goguettes* were closed; there was no further need
> for them, blood had flowed.

Although, over the years, Vidocq boasted quite wrongly that he had not
been let down by the former convicts, he was not always so fortunate
with others he chose to employ. Part of the job of the police was to
keep track of deserters from allied armies who were preying on the
people of Paris, and on the police files of 1816 there is an agonized
note from Vidocq instructing his men to arrest one Alexandre Vininski
on sight. He had been given bail on the condition that he would
become a police spy and promptly disappeared.[5]

Nor, if Vidocq's critics are to be believed, did all his prospective
agents behave well. Canler had his knife into Vidocq and was prepared
to twist it at every possible opportunity:

> In 1817 when the political excitement had grown calmer Vidocq was given
> a dozen agents of his own stamp to hunt down criminals and it was only
> from this date that he was chief of the detective staff. In 1821 the number
> of agents was increased to twenty-one and secret funds were placed at the
> disposal of the ex-galley slave, for which he did not account. What could be
> expected from men of this character?

He then went on to recount with some glee the story of how Vidocq
had attempted to recruit an agent called Jacquin. The man had said
he was a good bargainer and as a test he had been given ten francs
to buy some chickens. He returned with a brace of fowls and the ten

---

[5] APP. A/a 419.

francs unspent. Asked to explain himself, Jacquin demonstrated how he had picked the front pocket of the woman selling the chickens. Impressed, Vidocq recruited him but after Jacquin had left the room Vidocq found that his watch, chain and seals had been stolen. Jacquin never returned to take up the position and, Canler recounts happily, neither he nor the watch was ever seen again. Nor was Jacquin's name mentioned again in public.[6]

Canler also took pleasure in the fact that one of his own first successful cases as chief inspector was an investigation into theft from the house of the marquis de Faltans by a former Vidocq man, Valentin, who received twenty years hard labor. A 1,000-franc reward was paid to the Sûreté. The Chief of Police, Pierre Allard, kept half and gave the remainder to Canler and another officer.

Vidocq is sometimes wrongly given the credit for recognizing and exposing one of the great criminals and imposters of the time, Pierre Coignard, alias the comte André de Pontis de Sainte-Hélène. Theft and robberies had Coignard sent to the galleys in 1801 by the Tribunal de la Seine. After four years in the *bagne* at Toulon he escaped and the next year crossed the Pyrenees into Spain where, as head of a group of bandits, he looted the countryside. It was while he was in Catalonia during the Peninsular War that he met a Maria-Rosa, who had been in service with the late (and original) comte André de Pontis de Sainte-Hélène. Somehow she had acquired the papers of her late employer and so Coignard became the comte and she the comtesse. Now he claimed he was a Royalist officer who had escaped from one of Bonaparte's prisons and began fighting against the Napoleonic armies in Spain. Often wounded, after the first abdication of the Emperor he was given the Légion d'honneur in 1814.

Turning to the Bourbons after the second abdication of Napoleon, Coignard was awarded the title Lieutenant-Colonel of the Legion of

---

[6] Louis Canler, *Mémoires de Canler*, pp. 1–5. After his retirement Canler published his memoirs. By the time they reached the third edition they were suppressed on the grounds of a contravention both of public morals and, more realistically, breaking official secrets and there were suggestions that he should be prosecuted. This was rather hard, for the disgraced Gisquet had not been summoned after publishing his *Mémoires* in 1840. Nor had anyone taken offense to Canler's first two editions. On August 9, 1862, Canler wrote to Napoleon III protesting his loyalty. The examining magistrate closed the file on an undertaking not to publish reprints. Canler died three years later on October 24, 1865, in his modest home at 34 rue des Charbonniers-Saint-Antoine. He left a widow, Marie-Adelaide, and two adopted daughters, his wife's nieces. The Canler women started a basket-making business but his widow died on August 22, 1870, and the girls were not commercially minded. In short order the business collapsed and they hoped to live off the proceeds of the memoirs. They were disappointed and instead lived in penury, writing begging letters to the Préfecture. APP. E/a 88. *The Times*, July 26, 31, 1862; July 20, 1864.

the Seine, and he and the soi-disant comtesse were received at court. He had been living the life of the aristocracy for something like ten years when, in May 1819, he was recognized by an old companion of the *chaine* at a parade on the place Vendôme. The sign of a good blackmailer is his ability to place his victim between a rock and a hard place. Coignard was approached but he miscalculated. Instead of temporizing and then having the man killed, he simply refused to treat and was promptly denounced to the police. For a time Coignard brazened it out, offering to produce his papers. He was sent under escort to his hotel where the comtesse offered the accompanying officers wine while the comte went for his documents. Instead, he purloined a chef's outfit and was gone.

Unfortunately he made another mistake. He did not, as he should have done, leave Paris immediately. Instead he felt obliged to return to his old ways to survive and he set up in a summerhouse in the garden of 72 rue Saint-Maur, owned by a man named Lexcellent. Coignard left Paris for Toulouse with Lexcellent and two Italians, Saffieri and Carretti, and they were gone a fortnight. It was thought, but never proved, that they had robbed the stagecoach while they were away. On their return the team was caught following a failed robbery at Poissy. At the last minute the cashier gave the alarm and Lexcellent was arrested. He soon gave up Coignard who had escaped from the bank. Vidocq was given the task of bringing him in. It was a question of keeping a watch on the summerhouse, to which he was sure Coignard would return. Vidocq's *sous-chef*, Charles Fouché, took nine men with him to the rue Saint-Maur and waited. Return Coignard did. Fouché challenged him and, shot in the hand and shoulder, managed to hold on to him until the others came and arrested him along with Saffieri. Carretti was caught some days later.[7] Saffieri received ten years and Lexcellent and Carretti five each.

To the end Coignard protested he was the count but he was condemned to life in the *bagnes*. He ended his days in the galley at Brest in charge of the wine distribution there, reading the newspapers with gold-rimmed spectacles. It is rather pleasant to be able to record that

---

[7] Many versions have Vidocq as the arresting officer but in *La Police devoilée* Froment has Fouché, after receiving instructions from Vidocq, as actual head of the expedition to capture Coignard and lists the names of the men with him. It may be that by this stage in his career there was a certain amount of delegation by Vidocq. At the age of sixteen Fouché, who was no relation to Joseph Fouché, had served a sentence for armed robbery and had joined the police immediately on his release. He is described as a bull of a man who often led the police team when it was thought the criminals would put up a struggle. Samuel Edwards, *The Vidocq Dossier*, p. 85.

a deal was struck so that the countess avoided prosecution and she moved to Brest to be near the longtime, if soi-disant, count. He died in 1834.

Not that Vidocq was averse to peaching on his old companions, some of whom were succeeding in bettering themselves, socially and financially, with the help of forged papers. Four years earlier, in 1814, he had denounced the marquis de Chambreuil, then the Master of the King's Stables, as plain Chambreuil, the escaped *galérien*. Again the man denied his real identity but made the mistake of asking Vidocq to get rid of papers in a secret drawer. It was back to the galleys for him.

And in turn Vidocq was himself regularly denounced. A letter from the police librarian on May 20, 1813, reads:

Vidocq seller of eau-de-vie aged around 40 living in rue de Lorme, Saint Germain with a colossal constitution is a king of thieves, an escapee. He has only lived by crime. He is capable of going with whoever pays him most. Leave him in Paris where he will equally serve the police.[8]

That year had begun with his arrest of the Delzaive brothers, the younger of whom was known as the Shrimp, leaders of a twenty-two-strong band of thieves and housebreakers. Within three weeks the Shrimp had escaped with the help of other officers.[9] Two years later, in 1815, two agents, Consolin and Regnier, denounced him to the King's special police on September 28: "Here's Vidocq's gang which searches either for thieves or to steal themselves."[10] It did them no good. Vidocq's star was rising fast, and rightly so. He was cleaning up Paris.

These were the years, however, when generally Vidocq reigned supreme. He had seen off attempts by other convict agents such as Jean-Baptiste Goupil – who, years earlier, had taught him savate at Bicêtre – to inveigle him into theft or receiving. He had duly reported such approaches to Henry who, at least, regarded him as incorruptible.

One of the more entertaining of Vidocq's tales is his arrest in 1814 of the thief Sablin, described as a giant of a man, which, at five feet ten inches, in those days he would be. Vidocq traced him to Saint-Cloud where he met Sablin's wife on the stairs to the apartment. She tried to get back in to the rooms but Vidocq pushed her to one side, leaped on

---

[8] APP. E/a 90 (16).

[9] Arch. Nat. F⁸ 10353. Vidocq gives an account of the Delzaive brothers and their gang in *Les Vrai Mystères de Paris*.

[10] APP. E/a 90 (16).

Sablin and handcuffed him. It was then discovered that the woman was in the last stages of pregnancy and had been going for a midwife. Now, watched by Sablin, Vidocq assisted at the birth. In turn he was invited to become the child's godfather. Sablin served five years as the turnkey at La Force and made a good profit from it. Unfortunately, by the time he was released his wife had been sentenced to a term in St-Lazare. He turned to gaming, lost and hanged himself in the allée des Voleurs in the Bois de Boulogne. Vidocq does not say what became of his godson.[11]

In 1814 and 1815, with the release of prisoners of war, many of whom were criminals, there was an outbreak of robberies in the faubourg St-Germain, including ten in one night. Vidocq leaned on a thief whom he had arrested and within two months arrested a band of twenty-two thieves, one of twenty-eight and another of eighteen, along with smaller ones of eight and ten members, let alone receivers. As a result he was allowed four new agents and those he chose included Goreau, Florentin and Coco-Lacour, all long-term inhabitants of Bicêtre. Goreau and Florentin disgraced themselves, were sacked and ended in the *bagne* at Bordeaux while, for a time, Coco-Lacour did well, becoming Vidocq's secretary.

Why did Vidocq choose Coco-Lacour as his secretary? It cannot really have been that his conscience was troubling him about informing on the man nearly a decade earlier. It is unlikely that Vidocq had a conscience. Can there have been a homosexual relationship? Unlikely. At the time Vidocq was receiving visits from Annette and there is no suggestion, even by his enemies, that Vidocq was bisexual. Behavior in the closed *bagnes* may have been a different thing but in La Force and Bicêtre a liaison with Coco-Lacour seems extremely unlikely. Whatever the reason for the appointment, as the years went by it turned out to be a singularly unwise decision.

Vidocq may have prided himself on his choice of agents but his choice of secretaries left much to be desired. Desplanques was another who went to the bad. From a good family, Vidocq described him as a "robber with the soul of a pickpocket." He had served six years when he was recruited but was soon dismissed from the Brigade. Later he smashed the window of a money changer in the rue du Bac and stole a bowl of coins. Fleeing, he ran straight into the arms of two agents. He was sent to the galleys at Toulon for life.

---

[11] E-F. Vidocq, *Memoirs of Vidocq*, Vol III, Chapter XLI.

It was not only Vidocq who went about in disguise. He taught his men the art, too. Froment recalls that in 1816 the forger Dupaty was denounced by a man called Barloy, who hoped, as a result, to become an agent. Dupaty was arrested, gave a false address, maintained his innocence and was released. The loyal and experienced Fouché, disguised as a beggar, was sent after him. Dupaty went straight to the Hôtel de Strasbourg in rue Notre Dame-des-Victoires. He came out two hours later and paid for a number of goods with ten to fifty centime pieces. A warrant was obtained to search his lodgings and 180,000 francs in fifty-centime pieces were found. Dupaty maintained that they were for services rendered to the English Government which, with typical eccentricity, paid in coins of small denomination, but it did not help him. He received life imprisonment with forced labor and branding.

Vidocq trained his men with care. An agent should not disguise himself as a beggar if undertaking surveillance in a wealthy area, nor should he appear as a rich man if following a suspect in a working-class one. He should carry several brightly colored scarves to put on his hat, changing them regularly so the suspect should not notice he was being followed by a man with, say, a red scarf. If there was any indication that the criminal felt he was being watched, the surveillance should be called off at once. Better to come back another day than have the man change areas.

A good number of Vidocq's cases appear in Froment's *La Police dévoilée* and they show just how far ahead he was of the other officers of the time. Now with the gift of television and the cinema, some of his ruses appear simplistic but in those days his ideas must have been revelatory. Towards the end of 1816 there was a series of thefts in the quartier Saint-Honoré and the marché des Jacobins. Information came that the leaders were Pitron and Gaudet, makers of nightlights by day, who lived at 37 quartier du faubourg du Temple. Vidocq set up watch with Pierre Peltré and Fouché opposite their address. At 1 a.m. out came the pair with Gaudet's mother and his mistress. Peltré and Fouché wanted to follow them but Vidocq pointed out that as the moon was up they were sure to be seen. Better to wait for their return. They came back at 4 a.m. with the proceeds of a robbery of a spice merchant. Vidocq had no warrant but broke into their rooms nonetheless; each man received fifteen years forced labor and the women ten and eight years respectively. Elementary.

In 1817, the year Canler joined the police, Vidocq's twelve men made 811 arrests. These included 15 murderers, 341 thieves and 38 receivers to go with them. They had 14 escapees and 43 parole breakers along with 46 swindlers and confidence tricksters. There were now a good number of female agents as well, something far in advance of general police thought. Not that there were police of either sex in England or America in Vidocq's time. His critics have suggested the women were prostitutes whom he employed for their favors; given his sexual appetite, there is little doubt he combined business with pleasure. But, there again, there was little point in employing a countess to shadow a pickpocket in the Marais.

By now the faithful but enigmatic Annette had passed from Vidocq's life. There is no record of why she left him and his mother or to where she went. Indeed, we have only Vidocq's word that she ever existed in the form he relates in his memoirs. There are references to her by writers such as Alexandre Dumas père, but these are from comments Vidocq made rather than recordings of her being seen in the flesh. One reference by Dumas appears in a letter to Théophile Gautier. Dumas is recounting one of his own broken affairs and comments that he loved the girl "as much as Vidocq loved his Annette, but alas, like Annette she was married and her husband claimed her." It seems doubtful that such a free-spirited woman, who had been with Vidocq for something like ten years, would simply go off with her estranged husband, but he gives no explanation. It is possible that her husband was in fact not a merchant but another *galérien* who was eventually released but, if so, why leave the security and comfort of a life with Vidocq for one which was bound to be insecure?[12]

As for personal life, Vidocq's enemies seized on his remarks that he enjoyed the favors of women of all ranks from street walkers to a princess. One princess whom he certainly knew was Princess Bagration, the widow of the Russian general Prince Pierre-Ivanovich Bagration, who died on September 12, 1812, of injuries sustained at the Battle of Borodino. At the time of the Restoration she was known both as a political spy and for the numerous love affairs she conducted quite openly. Vidocq probably knew her during his first spell as chief and he renewed social relations with her in 1852.

---

[12] See Samuel Edwards, *The Vidocq Dossier*, pp. 43–5. Théophile Gautier (1811–72), journalist and novelist, is best remembered for his romantic 1835 novel, *Mademoiselle de Maupin*.

It was also said, with little supporting evidence, that Vidocq obtained sexual favors by fear rather than attraction. Certainly the wives of his colleagues were not regarded by him as being out of bounds. One bureau chief, Puteau, head of the Préfecture, killed himself because his wife, Anne-Rosalie, had become Vidocq's mistress.[13]

On November 6, 1820, Vidocq married for the second time. There has been great and inconclusive speculation as to the origin of his bride, Jeanne-Victoire Guérin, with suggestions that he married her for her money through a newspaper advertisement. This is almost certainly incorrect because he was, through his extracurricular dealings, well on the way to becoming a wealthy man, and a contract dated November 11 suggests he brought 30,000 francs to the marriage. There have also been suggestions that she was a high-class prostitute and that she was a young country girl whom he married to save from a life of crime. Whichever is the case she went to live in the house at 111 rue de l'Hirondelle, along with Vidocq's mother, for the duration of the marriage. Also living there was the delightful Fleuride-Albertine Maniez, the daughter of a cab driver and the twenty-seven-year-old niece of Mme Vidocq.

One of the problems Vidocq faced was that his conviction in the Boitel forgery case in 1796 still stood and so, technically, he remained a wanted man. From time to time inquiries were made of him, sometimes by the Procurator-General at Douai. These were generally ignored and then, in March 1817, a complaint lodged by a man named Ferey, describing himself as a civil servant from Versailles, prompted another letter from Vidocq.[14] This time a reply was sent to the effect that as more than twenty years had elapsed, nothing was to be done about it.[15] Vidocq was, however, still vulnerable. Finally comte Anglès, as Minister of Justice, wrote on Vidocq's behalf to obtain the King's pardon. Vidocq had submitted a petition which indicated, rather at odds with the facts, that after his last escape he had served in the navy as Brunel and in the 24th Cavalry as Blondel, under which name he had received a good conduct ticket. He wrote:

One mistake punished too severely, expired by lapse of years, wiped out by repentance and services to the public leads me to the feet of the throne to seek the clemency of your Royal Highness.[16]

---

[13] Jean Savant, *Le Procès de Vidocq*, pp. 54–6.
[14] Ferey had for some years been a public hangman. It is curious how hangmen liked to style themselves. The Victorian executioner William Marwood, who was by trade a shoemaker, had a sign 'Crown Agent' above the door of his shop in Horncastle, Lincs.
[15] Arch. Nat 1017 BB 18, Letters dated March 26, 8, April 23, 1817.
[16] Arch Nat. 1017 BB 18, Petition, January 31, 1818; letter, March 11, 1818.

The petition was granted and Anglès wrote to the Judiciary at Douai instructing them to note this in the court files. Samuel Edwards provides a footnote to the incident, suggesting that baron Pasquier had sent the petition and he and others were wined, dined and provided with prostitutes by Vidocq as a thank-you.[17] Although such a story contributes to the myth surrounding Vidocq, it is highly improbable. For a start Pasquier had been out of office for three years and within five years of the granting of the petition the austere baron wrote:

> [V] has even finished by becoming under M. Delavau the recognised head (which is most unfitting) at the Préfecture of part of the outside service. It is actually stated that he works directly for the magistrate. In my time he would never have crossed the threshold of my antechamber and he had no relations except with the Divisional Head who employed him. This confidence accorded publicly and with so little thought to a man with a criminal record, has had a bad effect and contributed much on several occasions to the discrediting of the police.[18]

It is most unlikely that this grand man would have been dining in these circumstances with such an underling.

One of the most famous, and certainly one of the most cited, of Vidocq's cases is his arrest of the attackers of a farmer in 1821. Helping him was his prodigious memory of the faces of criminals, the result of many hours spent in the Paris prisons.

The farmer, named Fontaine, had left his home in Courtille to go to the market in Corbeil to buy cattle. On the way he stopped at Essone and, falling in with two well-dressed and well-spoken travellers, mentioned the amount of money he had on him. They suggested he stay at the inn overnight but he wished to be early at the market and walk to Corbeil. The men suggested they should accompany him: three men together might deter highwaymen. As one of the men limped, he suggested a short cut to Corbeil. The farmer followed him and almost immediately took a blow to the back of the head. He was then stabbed nearly thirty times and passed out. When he recovered consciousness he found, to no great surprise, that his money was gone. Fortunately for him he was seen by a passer-by and taken to the hospital. He was interviewed by Vidocq who later went

---

[17] Samuel Edwards, *The Vidocq Dossier*, pp. 77–8.
[18] E-D. Pasquier, *Memoirs of Chancellor Pasquier*.

to the scene of the attack where he took rudimentary casts of the footprints. He also found two buttons in the mud and some fragments of a letter. One read, "Monsieur Rao, Wine Merchant, bar– Roche– Cli–," Vidocq reasonably deduced that the complete letter had been addressed to Monsieur Raoul, barrière Rochechouart, Clignacourt. Clair Raoul, known in the underworld as something of a cut above other thieves, ran a bar in the area. His wife was the sister of another ex-convict.

The bar was put under surveillance and the agent spotted a well-dressed man with a limp. He was followed to a room in the rue Coquenard and Vidocq was summoned at dawn the next day. When at 4 p.m. the man came out Vidocq recognized him as Court, a man he had previously arrested for robbery with violence. A search of his room, however, turned up nothing. He was nevertheless arrested again. Vidocq spent the next day in Raoul's bar talking to the barman in the absence of the proprietor. When Raoul returned Vidocq accused him of holding revolutionary meetings. The accusation was forcibly denied but Vidocq cajoled the man into allowing a search of the bar and also his room in Montmartre, without a warrant. In the room was a police court summons with the corner of the paper missing. It would match the paper Vidocq had already found. Realizing that the game was up, Raoul tried to snatch a pistol and was disarmed.

Now in prison Court confessed to the robbery/murder of a poulterer, carried out because his wife was starving. Vidocq asked him about the farmer and, again in another half remark, Court said the farmer would never give evidence against him. Told that the man was still alive, he at once signed a confession. It was standard police procedure. Only one suspect might benefit from a confession and that one was the first to make it. For a time Raoul held out but when again confronted, in turn he confessed. Bottles of wine were brought in to the prisoners in celebration, standard practice for the Paris detectives. Between them the pair named a third man, a retired revenue official named Pons Gérard who lived in a village near La Chapelle, as also being involved in the death of the poulterer.

Disguised as a horse dealer and with two men posing as his grooms, Vidocq went in search of Gérard, described as a Hercules with the pelt of a bear, found him and, claiming he knew Raoul and Court, discussed the possibility of horse smuggling. He then told him that the pair had been arrested by Vidocq. Gérard swore he was not afraid of Vidocq and in a little coup de théâtre Vidocq said, "You're sitting at the same table," as his men handcuffed him.

Vidocq attended the execution of Court and Raoul and, so it is said, persuaded the farmer not to attend. Unlike Canler and Lacenaire nearly two decades later, Vidocq, Court and Raoul embraced as the condemned man climbed up to the scaffold. Raoul had already given Vidocq his snuff box. Pons Gérard was sent to life imprisonment in the galleys.

Vidocq had considerable difficulty in getting his expenses of some 773 francs. The crime had occurred in the Department of Seine-et-Oise so why should the Préfecture of Police have to pay? It took until February 1823 before he was reimbursed. Overall, however, the authorities were pleased with their chief. In April 1822 Vidocq's annual salary was raised to 4,440 francs with an increase of 1,000 francs in April 1823.[19]

In 1824 another case garnered Vidocq even more publicity and became the subject of a number of woodcuts and engravings. In June that year a publican named Bertrand, down on his luck, met a wood-seller, one Rafflin, who bought him a meal and invited him to join a gang of smugglers. At first Bertrand declined, a good example of the fear of prison keeping men on the straight and narrow. He was persuaded when he was told that it was only a question of getting some 200,000 francs' worth of prohibited goods into Paris through the gate at Charenton. Crimes against the Government are often not considered real crimes.

And then, fortunately, he had what in the criminal trade is known as a touch of the seconds. He knew a police spy called Chignard and reported matters to him. He was given authorization to play along and, in turn, Chignard reported to Froment. Chignard was told to keep in touch with Bertrand but then things took a turn for the worse. When Bertrand joined the gang at Charenton he was told the job involved more than a bit of smuggling. They were going to hold up a stagecoach in the forest of Sénart. Bertrand seems to have kept his wits saying he had not brought any weapons. No problem: these were already hidden in the forest. Then what about an alibi and passports to aid a getaway if things went wrong? The job was postponed until the next day. Bertrand went to Froment who, in turn, went to see Vidocq.

---

[19] APP. E/a 90 (16).

Bertrand was given the money to go to the quai de la Féraille to buy a pistol which did not fire, and he later reported the proposed time and place to Vidocq whose plan was to fill the coach with agents. Curiously, the weak link was thought to be Chignard and Froment maintains it was he who decided that the agent should be taken out and made so drunk that he would not be able to come to work for two or three days. Chignard said he was hungry enough to eat a raw sheep and exactly that, along with the wine and liqueurs, was provided for him. By the end he was so drunk that Vidocq had to give him a fireman's lift into a cab to get him back home in the quai des Augustins.

On March 20 Vidocq and his agents caught the coach along with four regular passengers. The attack took place shortly before Lieursaint, at a spot where the road was blocked. Vidocq and the police jumped out firing and Bertrand, as he had been told, feigned being shot. The pictures of the attack depict Vidocq in his cloak at the door of the coach. Here, once again, legend takes over. As he climbed out of the coach, the great man fell into a ditch and dislocated his elbow.[20] In every other way the operation was a great success. Three men were sent to the scaffold. Rafflin was sentenced to the galleys for life. Another man, Raynaud, hanged himself in his cell leaving letters which confessed to other crimes. In all, fourteen men and seven women were arrested. Bertrand was offered a post with the police but, lacking the necessary nerve, he sensibly declined. He received the rather less than generous reward of fifty francs for his efforts. The robbers were executed by Henri Sanson in a triple execution on April 20 that year.[21]

Four years earlier Vidocq had, as it were, been leased out to deal with a new breed of *Chauffeur*. This particular case began as early as an evening in 1816 when an innkeeper was killed on a path leading through the Hurlu wood in the region of the Somme. The story went that an old woman in rags, walking with a stick and shivering with cold, asked him for help. The moment he produced his money she sprang at him and cut his throat. It was the beginning of a string of murders. In 1819, nineteen people had their throats cut in the Santerre wood. Although it was common knowledge that the killers were locals, the police received no information to help them. It was a case of the local people going in fear of reprisals from those who might not be swept up in any series of arrests. The leader of the gang was the

---

[20] Vidocq's detractors regard the fall as a sign of cowardice. "Real courage isn't found in the mud," wrote Louis Guyon, *Biographie des Commissaires de police et des officiers de La paix*, p. 236.
[21] Froment, "The Forest of Sénart," in *Mémoires*. H. Sanson, *Memoirs of the Sansons*.

seventy-two-year-old Prudence Pézé, known as *La Louve*, or the she-wolf. The simple-minded forty-five-year-old Fermin Capelier, known as Sabalair, described as being of Herculean build, was the one who actually led the attacks.

Their headquarters was an isolated inn with a clear view up and down the road and a back garden with woods behind. They behaved in exactly the same fashion as had those earlier *Chauffeurs* receiving information from peddlers.

In the autumn of 1819 the comte d'Allonville, Préfet of the Department of the Somme, wrote to Paris for help. He was invited to the capital in December and in the New Year plans were drawn up. It was a question of either the bandits becoming untouchable or, as Jean-Paul Lefebvre-Filleau puts it, the Minister of the Interior setting a trap.[22] That trap was Vidocq. He was to liaise with Edmé-Pierre de Vabre,[23] a senior officer in the gendarmerie.

In early January ten men and four women were seated around the table in the inn. The only picture on the walls was a lithograph of the duchesse de Berri and they were waiting for a peddler known as Bonnet Noir, who had contacted them some two weeks earlier and would be arriving that night. The peddler's name was Louis-Marie Frénot and observant readers will quickly recognize that this was Vidocq in disguise. He was late that evening because, some miles away, he had met up with Vabre, and had had to walk through the cold night to the inn. When he did arrive, naturally he charmed everyone, particularly Hortense the innkeeper's daughter. The only one not taken in was Pézé and she was right to be suspicious because Vidocq, who went to bed early apparently exhausted by the miles he had walked peddling his goods, was soon climbing out of the window of his room later that night and was off to pass messages to Vabre.

It became clear that Vidocq would have to participate in a raid, and, indeed, he went out with the band on three occasions. After the first foray he was deemed not to have sufficient steel to kill; he went out again on January 20 and February 2. On February 18 Vidocq left the

---

[22] J-P. Lefebvre-Filleau, *Vidocq contre "les chauffeurs" de la Somme*, p. 19.

[23] In 1823 and 1824 Edmé-Pierre de Vabre fought in the expedition to Spain to restore the Spanish despot Ferdinand VII, who had been threatened by a liberal rebellion based in Cadiz under the duc d'Angoulême. The expedition had the blessing of all the crowned heads of Europe except George IV. On his return, Vabre reassumed command of Mondidier, later taking command of Niort. On August 17, 1832, after thirty-six years and three months of service, with seven years in the field, he retired. He died just over two months later, on October 20, at Niort.

inn and met with Vabre. He was, he said, under increasing suspicion from Pézé but he believed for the moment that he had Sabalair's confidence. He would put an easy proposition to him – an attack on the house of an old man, Dégoutin, known as the Englishman because he had spent the Revolution across the Channel. Despite his age he lived alone in a house at Berny-en-Santerre and simply barricaded himself in at night. As for the grounds, they were surrounded by a two-and-a-half-meter-high wall. The raid was to take place on February 25 and on the 22nd one of Pézé's daughters reconnoitred the house and reported back with the news that the old man really did live alone.

La Louve, suspicious and also wanting to show who was in control, then announced that the raid would not take place until the 26th. Vidocq could get no further message to the gendarme and Vabre and his men assembled on the 25th to be taken to see Dégoutin by the local mayor to explain what was happening. That evening they took up positions in the house. They left the next morning at five o'clock after a wasted night.

The *Chauffeurs*, including Vidocq among them, left the inn at 10 p.m. on the 26th. Sabalair forced Dégoutin's door and they went to the old man's bedroom. As Sabalair went to shake Dégoutin awake, Vabre, in bed in place of the old man, shot at him. In the mêlée Sabalair tried to strangle a gendarme who blocked the way but was repeatedly stabbed in the back by another and was then shot.

Despite this, he apparently did not lose consciousness and Jean-Paul Lefebvre-Filleau says that, in a scene worthy of the best bodice ripper, he demanded: "Traitor, renegade, carrion, tell me your name."

inet Noir approached the criminal and uttered a single word: "Vidocq."

Sabalair's fury turned to delight. He had mixed it with the best police officer in France. He realized his defeat had been inevitable. It was possible to read in his eyes a certain pride in having been beaten by an opponent of such quality.

In the confusion, Pézé, although herself pinked in the backside, had managed to escape. Too old to think of serious flight she returned to her hovel where she was arrested with another of the thieves, Charles Lematte.

Sabalair died of his injuries on March 12, 1820, and the others were put on trial, which concluded on July 26. One woman, Françoise Bertin, the widow Bœuf, received a royal pardon and her sentence was commuted to one of life imprisonment, from which she was released after a few years. She went to Normandy where she took up a life of brigandage for a second time. When she was arrested once more she was well and truly executed. Three more of the gang, Pézé, Lematte and Rémy Germain, were sentenced to death, others to terms of imprisonment and to the galleys.

The three condemned remained in prison for eighty-two days. On October 17, 1820, the head warder appeared at the cells to tell each in turn:

> In a few hours the tomb in which you threw your victims will open for yourself. Before you face God give men the most touching proof of your repentance.

At eight o'clock Prudence Pézé, Charles Lamatte and Rémy Germain were taken from the prison under a horse guard. There was a stop for food and drink at the headquarters of the Rosiers gendarmerie where the three seem to have indulged themselves to stupefaction. At four o'clock the cortège arrived. It being a fine day, the crowd was in good spirits. Plenty of drink and food had been purchased and to pass the time there had been some community singing.

First to the guillotine was Lematte – "destroyed by the fear of dying he had no time to look around the crowd before his head was in the basket." Next up was Germain who, apart from what was described as an involuntary shrug of disgust as he saw the blood of his companion, maintained his sang froid and tried to address the crowd. As he died a shout rang out from the crowd, "Brave Germain." It was probably his father.

The third of the trio was *La Louve* from whom,

> at this moment, all illusions of egotism and greed fled. But the monster with a heart of steel remained stoic in front of the crowd. She refused the offer of the services of a young priest and then shamelessly relieved herself in front of the crowd. She then called out, "You may have my head but never my tail," stretched out her neck obligingly and died at 16:15 precisely.[24]

Hers appeared to be no idle boast, for, within two months, Germain's father had put together a second band. This time, however, the object was vengeance, firing a different village each night. It was not long

---

[24] Although there are records of the execution of the trio, the papers dealing with Vidocq's part in the arrests were destroyed in the First World War.

lived. Their last strike was to destroy five hayricks belonging to the mayor of Lamotte-en-Santerre. Germain père was arrested and peace returned to the area for the better part of a hundred years.

It is interesting to note how little had changed when, on January 12, 1909, the Pallet gang, a twentieth-century version of the *Chauffeurs*, including the brothers Abel and Auguste Pallet, Canut Vroman and Théophile Deroo, were guillotined before an excited crowd in Béthune. It was the first execution for three years and tickets for the inner circle around the guillotine were sold for the modern equivalent of between seventy-five cents and three dollars. Permission to film the proceedings had been refused but it was thought the film company might stage and film a mock execution. If so, said the Prefect, he would ban the display. Abel Pallet, who was the last to be guillotined, was defiant to the last calling out, "You pack of do-nothings. Down with the priests! Lead the social revolution."[25] It was thought this might be the last public execution because of the perceived bad behavior of the crowd and *Le Temps* suggested that if there had to be a headsman he should at least be kept out of sight. Other newspapers had some sympathy with the people of Béthune. Over a period of years the Pallet gang had perpetrated at least twenty-five murders or attempted murders and over one hundred robberies in the area; it was understandable that the locals should be just as happy and relieved as they had been when Vidocq broke the gang in 1820.

One murder which took place in Paris the year after the *Chauffeurs* were executed really should have been solved much earlier. Vidocq, like Homer, must have nodded and it was not until fifteen years later that the murderers of the seventy-year-old widow Houet, who disappeared on September 13, 1821, were discovered. At the time she had been living at 81 rue du Vaugirard.

On the day of her death a maid turned up late. The sprightly widow gave her a lecture on timekeeping and dispatched her on a series of errands. After the maid left someone clearly came to and after that no one saw Mme Houet again. She was known to be on poor terms with her son-in-law, Robert. She had a son but, although physically strong, he was feeble-minded and worked in a menial capacity earning two francs a day as a drudge. It was not for three years that Robert and another wine merchant son-in-law, Bastien, were arrested and released on the grounds that there was insufficient evidence against them. In due course her son-in-law rented out No. 81.

---

[25] *The Times*, January 11, 12, 13, 1909.

It was not until March 1833 that "C," a sort of man of affairs, ex-convict and one-time adviser to Bastien, told another old lag that for 500 francs he would both point out where to find the widow's body and name her killers. This was not difficult since, he said, Robert had contracted the killing and he and Bastien had carried it out. A dispute had then arisen when Robert refused to pay. Robert had fled to Bourbonne-les-Bains to keep out of their way.

Bastien was duly arrested and in his possession, quite amazingly, was a plan along with a letter which read, "I'm sending you a plan of your old garden where you made such progress in 1821."

In due course a letter was written to Robert in somewhat more cryptic terms:

> Do you remember the garden at 81 rue du Vaugirard? 15 steps from the end wall, 14 from the side. Deaths sometimes return.

The plan to lure Robert back to the garden was a success. The police borrowed an overlooking house, telling the owner they feared a burglary was being planned, and waited. Eventually he turned up. He was arrested and, as was practice, the police took him to what they believed to be the scene of the crime. He took up a position from which he was reluctant to move as the police dug the garden. He was actually standing on the grave when Inspector Laporte told him, "Move or do you want the old woman to grab your feet?" He was sentenced to life imprisonment. The real mysteries are what took the police so long and why the murderers kept incriminating papers for so many years.[26]

In truth Vidocq was probably not that interested in domestic murders. He was far keener on dealing with the fraudsmen and swindlers who had flooded Paris during the belle epoque. They included the financier Gabriel-Julien Ouvrard who was arrested at Vidocq's house at 2 p.m. on December 24, 1824, and the detective was well repaid for this arrest.[27] Ouvrard had a long and checkered career. He had helped Joseph Fouché negotiate peace with England and had been imprisoned under Napoleon. In 1817 the duc de Rovigo adopted his

---

[26] There are a number of accounts of the case. Canler deals with it in his memoirs and so does Rayner Heppenstall in *French Crime in the Romantic Age*. See also Jean Galtier-Boissière, "Mystères du police secret" in *Crapouillot*, May 1936.

[27] Louis Guyon, *Biographie des commissaires de police et de la paix*, pp. 235–6; *Supplément aux mémoires de Vidocq par L'Héritier I*, pp. 172–5. For an account of his career, see Jean Savant, *Tel fût Ouvrard*.

plans for financial reform. Ouvrard was released from Sainte-Pélagie but in 1823 he was compromised over a speculation supplying arms to the Spanish army. He was acquitted but he later received another five years in Sainte-Pélagie. During this sentence Ouvrard paid to have a bathroom installed at Sainte-Pélagie and while he was at the Conciergerie was able to put together a small garden. Another criminal to write his memoirs, he went to London where he died in 1846.[28]

However, in that year, 1824, there had been two significant developments in Vidocq's personal life. On June 18 his wife, the reclusive Jeanne-Victoire, died at a clinic on the rue de la Four. She had been in poor health throughout the marriage. Six weeks later on July 30, far more significantly, his mother died. It is arguable that women lost what voice they had during the Revolution with the advent of the notion of the ideal woman, one devoted to family life and the nurture of their progeny. Vidocq's mother easily fitted into the concept. The role of the *citoyen* was very different from that of the *citoyenne*. As late as 1872, Jules Simon asked, with little controversy, "What is a man's vocation? It is to be a good citizen. And the woman's? To be a good wife and mother." After the death of her husband, Vidocq's mother's place was in her son's home.[29]

There is no note of the funeral arrangements for Vidocq's wife but his mother was buried in style with condolences coming from politicians and a fine hearse with a cortege followed by a number of high-ranking officials. Quite when Fleuride-Albertine became her cousin's mistress is unknown; possibly even before the death of Jeanne-Victoire. It is impossible to believe she did not. Certainly she married him on January 28, 1830, at Saint-Mandé.

---

[28] There was a nice little tribute for him after his death: "He bore his acute sufferings with the firmness and resignation of a stoic and retained his self-possession and all his faculties till within half a minute of his dissolution." *The Times*, October 26, 1846.

[29] Arch. Nat. BB 18 744. I am most grateful to Annabel Thomas for her help in the assessment of the role – or perhaps subjugation is a better word – of many women in and immediately after the Revolution.

Chapter 13

VIDOCQ AT BAY

*In which a duke is assassinated – an unsolved murder is
cleared up – changes are made to the Bureau – allegations
are made – and our hero resigns*

I N A CURIOUS WAY THE DEATH of the duc de Berri altered
Vidocq's life; not immediately, but it led to changes in the police
hierarchy which inevitably affected him. Vidocq was, however, still in
the countryside chasing the *Chauffeurs* when Louis-Pierre Louvel,
a journeyman saddler, whose aim it was to eliminate the Bourbons
whom he believed had betrayed France, killed Charles-Ferdinand,
duc de Berri, the second son of Charles X. Since the duc de Berri
was thought to be the only remaining member capable of producing
children, he had become Louvel's target.

The duc, a formidable Anglophile with a number of mistresses from
the stage and ballet and a long-term English mistress, Amy Brown, by
whom he had two daughters, had been forced into a dynastic marriage
with the sixteen-year-old Marie-Caroline, Princess of the Two Sicilies.[1]
At the time of his death they had one daughter.

Now, on Sunday, February 13, 1820, on a day when Paris had giv-
en itself over to festivities prior to Lent, the duke and duchess had
been at the opera to see *Le Rossignol* and two ballets. Around 11

---

[1] For a time his cousin the prince de Condé, duc de Bourbon, was more fortunate. He had
remained in London with – prior to Queen Victoria – the Isle of Wight's most famous resident,
the prostitute Sophie Dawes. Thirty-three years younger than the prince, Sophie Dawes' greatest claim to fame was her almost certain involvement in his death when the prince de Condé
was found hanged on August 27, 1830. An official inquiry gave a verdict of suicide but it is much
more likely that the baronne de Feuchères, the title Sophie had acquired, murdered him. He
had won her in London in a game of cards some twenty years earlier and was threatening to
exclude her from his will. His family challenged the will extant at his death on the grounds of
undue influence and failed. Despite the scandal the baronne continued to be invited to the balls
given by Louis-Philippe. She died in 1840. It was the year that in Brussels photography was first
used for police purposes.

p.m., as he was escorting the duchess to their coach, he was stabbed from behind with such force that the point of the knife went through his blue moiré Riband of the Order of the Holy Spirit. Louvel, who had certainly acted alone, stood and admired his handiwork, waiting to be arrested.

The death of the duke was grand indeed:

He was carried into the private foyer of the Opera; and there, mingling with singers in their paint and ballet dancers in their tinsel were presently gathered all the members of the Royal Family, the Ministers and great officers of State. The King arrived from the Tuileries – old Louis XVIII, impotent in his feet, and hobbling painfully along, with his black gaiters, starched cravat, and powdered hair, which made him look like an old-fashioned notary. The Comte d'Artois was there too, his handsome face, usually so serene pinched with anguish; and so was the portly Duke of Orleans – afterwards Louis Philippe – who had a difficult part to play under the malevolent glances of courtiers seeking on his physiognomy for some sign of satisfaction at an event which appeared likely to establish the fortunes of his family. When all the illustrious company was assembled round the "property" mattress on which the Duke lay dying, the mild and polished duc de Quelqu, Archbishop of Paris – the last of the grand seigneur prelates, who wore diamonds and rubies like a Court beauty – walked in bearing the viaticum, and attended by choristers with incense.[2]

In attendance were also the English mistress and daughters to whom he spoke a few words, presenting them to the extremely good-natured duchess.[3]

Fortunately, or unfortunately, Louvel's attempt at extinguishing the Bourbons failed because the duchess was already pregnant at the time, something she revealed to her stricken husband. The dying, and ungranted, wish of de Berri was that the saddler should be pardoned. Instead he was guillotined by Sanson. Despite the pleadings of the

---

[2] *The Times*, August 25, 1883. It is suggested that the duc may have been returning to the ballet to see an actress known as Mlle Virginie and described as "pretty as an angel and stupid as a cabbage." Roger Langeron, *Decazes, minister du roi*, p. 147. For an account of the social and political repercussions of the murder, see Philip Mansel, *Paris Between the Empires, 1814–52*, Chapter V.

[3] There is some suggestion that he had actually married Amy Brown in London in 1806. On June 10, 1820 their two girls Charlotte-Marie-Augustine (b. July 13, 1808) and Louise-Marie-Charlotte (b. December 19, 1809) were created countesses of Issoudun and Vierzon respectively. Amy Brown died in Couffée at noon on May 7, 1876 aged ninety-three at the château of the baron de Charette. A. Castelot, *Le Duc de Berri et son Double Mariage*, C. Nauroy, *Le Premier Mariage du duc de Berry*.

Abbé Montès at the scaffold, Louvel adamantly refused to show any sign of repentance. Louvel was bald and, irrationally fearing he was going to catch a cold, begged the executioner to get a hat for him for the ride to the place de Grève. The hat story led some to believe that Louvel was in fact Louis XVII, the Dauphin, who had been imprisoned in the Temple during the Terror, and as a mark of respect his uncle had refused to allow him to go to the scaffold bareheaded. That part of the story has no credible basis.[4]

Matters did not end there. With the duchess enceinte, there was still the possibility of her having a miscarriage and so a plot was hatched to procure one. Bombs were to be exploded outside her bedroom window. The conspirators were Bouton, Gravier and Leydet, the last of whom was an associate of the police agent Rivoire. Leydet and Gravier went to the Tuileries on the night of April 29 and exploded a shell, which had no effect. Bouton and Gravier then decided to abandon the plan but Leydet persuaded them to try again. A second attempt was made on May 6. Leydet accompanied Gravier to the gate of the Tuileries in the rue de Rivoli but, like all good *agents provocateurs* he disappeared at the crucial moment and when Gravier bent down to place the bomb he was arrested. Leydet disappeared to Holland and the other two were condemned to death.[5]

The duchess seems, for the time being anyway, to have been imbued with good nature because she also sought the pardon of her would-be abortionists. In this case her wish was granted. Four months later, on September 29 at 2:35 in the morning, the duchess gave birth to a son who became the comte de Chambord, known as *"l'enfant du miracle,"* and baptized Henri-Dieudonné. There had been rumors that a changeling would be substituted in the event of a stillbirth and the leader of the Bonapartists in Paris, Maréchal Suchet, and the Maréchal de Coigny were chosen to be official witnesses. The birth was a rapid one and the duchess was particularly careful with her confinement, waiting until they were in place before "allowing the customary operation" of cutting the umbilical cord.[6]

---

[4] For accounts of more false Dauphins, see Chapter 19.

[5] When he returned to France, Leydet lived under an assumed name. Gravier died in June 1828 after a fall during some horseplay in the *bagne*. For a full account of the affair, see Froment, *La police dévoilée*. These were explosive times. There had been a previous attempt to blow up the palace of the duchesse d'Angoulême on January 29, 1821. Napoleon is said to have remarked that this most formidable woman was the only man in her family.

[6] *The Times*, September 30, 1879.

Urging Suchet, "Prenez, M. le Maréchal, tirez," the duchess invited him to make sure for himself that the child was attached to it. According to Sir Charles Stuart, Suchet proved a bit faint-hearted and she repeated, "Mais tirez donc, M. le Maréchal."[7]

The political fallout after the death of the duke was, of course, immense and the principal casualty among the police was the Préfet, comte Julien Anglès. He himself was at a ball and had appointed a police inspector, Joly, to guard the duke but at the moment Louvel struck Joly was off drinking coffee. Anglès was succeeded as Préfet by the Jesuitical Guy Delavau, who owed his position to Villèle, the King's Minister.[8] His appointment saw the marginalization of the Bonapartistes and Republicans in the police. The freethinkers were driven to church. Canler recounts that when he was once recommended for a reward he was sent for and told he could receive nothing until he produced a certificate of confession and promised to be a regular churchgoer. To his credit he refused and the reward was eventually paid anyway. There was also a good deal more spying on each other. The ingratiating Coco-Lacour took to going to mass at Notre Dame so as to be seen by the Préfet and his underling Duplessis, and for a month undertook the penance of walking barefoot at dawn to the rue Sainte-Anne au Calvaire. During this period he was not allowed to see his errant wife, who was undergoing similar chastisement, except when they met in church. His stock soared.

The other changes were partly due to events in the wider world outside the Sûreté. Louis XVIII died in 1824 and the throne passed to the ultra-reactionary Charles X, who promptly set about alienating as many people as he could in as short a period as possible. It was now a time for control of the press, and police officers were shifted from their regular duties to search out any lèse-majesté towards the

---

[7] Letter from Sir Charles Stuart to Lord Castlereagh, October 2, 1820. NLS MSS 6201. The story has to be second- if not third-hand. The duchess charmed all who met her, from the old roué Captain Rees Gronow, "At that time the fascinating Duchesse de Berri was the theme of admiration of every one" to the diarist Lady Clementina Davies, "Although an Italian, she had a beautifully fair complexion and in figure she was so slight that she almost a child . . . Sometimes on a wet day she would place a number of chairs in a row and amuse herself by jumping from one to the other." R. H. Gronow, *The Reminiscences and Recollections of Captain Gronow*, p. 105; Lady Clementina Davies, *Recollections of Society in France and England*, quoted in *The Times*, August 19, 1872.

[8] Delavau was presented by Fathers Loriquet and Rauzin. He and his aide Franchet were said to be under the orders of the "Congregation," a secret Jesuit society under the high patronage of the comte d'Artois, later Charles X. Henry Jagot, *Vidocq*, pp. 161–2. Guy Delavau served as Préfet from December 1821 to January 1828. On leaving the police he became a member of the Conseil d'Etat. After the July Revolution of 1830 he lost his position and from then on lived and died in obscurity.

Bourbons. Crime in Paris had been cut by up to 40 per cent under the Vidocq régime and at the time of Louis XVIII's death was fairly static. A random selection of the daily crime arrest reports for 1825 show no great changes throughout the year.[9]

January 3
Theft	6
Counterfeiting	1
Assaults	6
Minor offenses	3
Vagrancy	6
Prostitution	1

March 19
Theft arrests	4
Disorder	2
Street accident	1
Minor offenses	4
Lunacy	2
Vagrancy	6
Prostitution	8

May 13
Theft	1
Breach of release	2
Carrying pistol	1
Minor offenses	1
Vagrancy	5
Prostitution	16

June 25
Theft	3
Disorder	3
Lunacy	3
Adultery	1[10]

---

[9] Arch. Nat. F⁷ 3879.

[10] It was possible to have a wife arrested for adultery to be used as grounds in a divorce case. On the night of July 4, 1845, Victor Hugo and Mme Léonie Biard were taken in adultery, so to speak, in an apartment in the passage Saint-Roch. She had been trying to obtain a judicial separation and the intervention of the police was a pre-emptive strike by her husband. Hugo as

Breach of release	1
Abandoning child	1
Vagrancy	21
Prostitution	25[11]

August 29

Theft	3
Disorder	3
Lunacy	3
Adultery	1
Breach of conditions	1
Abandoning child	1
Aliens	1
Minor offenses	2
Vagrancy	2
Vagrancy	20
Prostitution	1[12]

November 1

Theft	8
Assault	11
Three-card trick	3
Lunacy	4
Vagrancy	16
Solicitation	2

December 15

Theft	7
Breach of conditions	1
Disorder	15
Attempted suicide	1
Vagrants	136
Prostitution	13

---

a *pair* - the rough equivalent of a life peer in Great Britain - was immune from prosecution but the unfortunate Mme Biard was taken to St-Lazare. For an account of that author's liaisons, see G. Robb, *Victor Hugo*. Years later the politician Clemenceau was able to secure the deporation of his wife following her adultery, even though they had been separated for many years.

[11] Sixteen women attended the public dispensary of whom two were sent for treatment.

[12] One hundred and twenty attended the dispensary but only one was referred for treatment.

December 24	
Disorder	2
Minor disorder	1
Bail offense	1
Aliens	1
Vagrancy	2
Prostitution	17

Vidocq's men had been making around 1,500 arrests annually but in 1826, with more time being devoted to political suppression, crime began to rise. Despite this there were only two executions in Paris that year. The French, after their bloodletting some thirty years earlier, were now far more squeamish than their English counterparts. On Tuesday, December 15, 1825, shortly before seven in the evening after his wife had left for the theatre, Joseph, one of the money dealers at the Palais Royal, was attacked and robbed of a quantity of gold. A cloth was stuffed into his mouth and he was stabbed three times in the head and once in the stomach but he survived and was able to report that one of his attackers spoke in Italian.

Virgilio Malaguti, who was thought to have committed a number of burglaries, and Gaetano Rata, both from Bologna, had been seen in the area and were under suspicion almost from the start. They had been watching Joseph for some time. Initially, there was not enough evidence on which to charge them. After the robbery Rata, covered in blood, had washed his trousers in the river while Malaguti changed some of the stolen gold coins near the Café Corrazza. They then hid the rest and Vidocq ordered a surveillance operation which lasted the better part of a month until they were seen in bitter weather carrying their hats like heavy packets under their arms. When searched the hats were found to be filled with the gold. Vidocq organized a rudimentary identification parade with police officers in plain clothes standing as foils for the suspects. Joseph picked out Rata and then fainted when he saw Malaguti before recovering and identifying him as well. Both confessed and were sentenced to death on April 25. They appealed and had a letter written to the Italian-born duchesse de Berri asking her to intercede for them, but they were executed on May 26. Curiously their victim died after the trial but before they were guillotined.[13]

---

[13] *Gazette des Tribuneaux*, December 15, 16, 17, 1835; February 3, April 18, 25; May 27, 1836.

In due course Vidocq's original employer, Henry, retired and his successor, Parisot, was discovered to have been a supporter of Napoleon during the Hundred Days. He was smartly replaced by an ambitious young man, Marc Duplessis, who had, somewhat spuriously, obtained the Knight's Cross of the Order of St. Ferdinand of Spain. Now he liked to be addressed by his correct title, Chevalier, something guaranteed to provoke a clash with Vidocq. A former *mouchard*, Jacques Peurot described Duplessis as a "ridiculous agent and a callow despot." Relations were not helped by the fact that both Vidocq and his superior drove smart tilburys and that Vidocq's diamond studs were superior to Duplessis'.[14]

Nor was Vidocq's position helped by an incident involving a cloak belonging to Delavau's wife, which disappeared one evening. Vidocq was ordered to find it. When his men failed to turn it up, it was suggested that he was losing his grip. Eventually the cloak was returned either by a servant who had carried it away by mistake or by Coco-Lacour, but the relationship was further soured.[15]

There was more trouble about the way in which Vidocq's agents comported themselves. They were frequently to be seen in low cabarets, wine shops and brothels. Many might think, given they were meant to be gathering information, that that was exactly where they should have been but it was something that did not please the prim Chevalier.

There were also suggestions that Drissen and Ripaud, two members of Vidocq's squad, had been running a long-standing game of Find the Lady (a version of the three-card trick in which the mark believes he cannot fail to find the Queen of Spades from three cards shuffled by the dealer – and fails to do so every time), bringing a complaint on January 13, 1823, from Delavau that they were taking money from honest workers. Not only were the sharps themselves members of the squad but there were at least six other players who were members, in one form or another, of the police. It was said that in a two-week period in the summer of 1823 the game had taken 4,364 francs.[16]

In his memoirs Vidocq defended his men:

> They robbed no more. As to the rest they were always debauched; addicted to wine, women and play; many of them lost their monthly pay

---

[14] For the relatively independent Froment's disparaging remarks on the man, see the chapter "M. Duplessis" in *La police dévoilée*. J. Peuchet, *Mémoires tiré des Archives de la Police*, Chapter LXXX.

[15] Philip Stead, *Vidocq*, pp. 114–15 and also Froment.

[16] J. Peuchet, *Mémoires tiré des Archives de la Police*, Chapter LXII.

at gaming instead of paying their lodging or the tailor who provided them with clothes. In vain did I devise means of giving them the least possible leisure, they always continued to indulge their various habits. Compelled to devote 18 hours per day to the police they were less debauched than if they had been entirely at leisure but yet they committed various follies which, when they were but trifling, I usually overlooked.[17]

What was never explained was the word "trifling" and it is also tempting to ask where they found the money to replace that lost at the gaming tables.

There were other allegations being made against Vidocq. The ungrateful turncoat Lacour and another agent, Descustor, claimed that money given by the Banque de France to trap the swindler Collet had found its way into the chief's pockets. There was another suggestion that he had organized the looting of a boutique after which the police took their share. He was described as "soiling the city with his presence." The allegations were dismissed.

What was undoubtedly correct was that:

Unemployed thieves came to 6 rue Sainte-Anne where Vidocq held court from 11 a.m. until midday . . . The cream of the cut-throats were lodged with him where he clothed and fed them and where the wife of one of them did the cooking.[18]

Others take the more charitable view that these were the cream of the brigade, on hand at a moment's notice to spring into action, but there is little doubt Vidocq was under siege.

Nor can it have helped that one of his men, Moureau, received a one-month sentence for assault in June 1826. Vidocq was sent a reprimand by Duplessis which he ignored but when a second one arrived, on June 20, 1827, he wrote a flowery letter of resignation:

For 18 years I have served the police with distinction. I have never received a single reproach from your predecessors: I must therefore think that I have never deserved one. Since your nomination to the Second Division this is the second time you have done me the honour to address one to me complaining of the agents. Am I their master in their spare time? No. To save you, Monsieur, the inconvenience of addressing me any similar

---

[17] Chapter XXXVIII.
[18] Louis Guyon, *Biographie des commissaires de police et des officiers de la paix*, p. 234.

complaints in future, and myself the trouble of receiving them, I have the honour to ask you to be good enough to accept my resignation.

Vidocq was able to make such gestures. He retired a rich man at the age of fifty-two. Incredibly Duplessis' choice of his successor was the new *religieu*, the weak Coco-Lacour. Vidocq had always believed in what is today called proactive policing – the prevention rather than merely the solution of crime – but by the following year offenses had increased to such an extent that the newspapers suggested:

Murders, robberies and suicides are becoming so frequent in Paris that the French police must soon lose its reputation as a preventative power.[19]

---

[19] *The Times*, September 6, 1828, quoting *Le Journal des voyageurs*.

Chapter 14

VIDOCQ
AT SAINT-MANDÉ

In which our hero survives a reported hanging for trying to kill a
"baby eagle" – displays genuine altruism – faces questions as to how he
amassed his fortune – builds a house and opens a business – encounters
local opposition – and finally gives up in the face of difficulty

OVER THE YEARS there were regular reports of Vidocq's premature death. The first of these came in August 1827 when a remark that Vidocq, "Chef des Mouchards de Paris," had been hanged in Vienna over his failed attempted assassination of Napoleon's son, Napoleon II – better known as the duc de Reichstadt and called l'Aiglon – was overheard in a cabaret in St-Malo.[1] Had it been true few would have been particularly surprised. Throughout his short life the duke was a continuing trouble to the Bourbons.

François-Charles-Joseph Napoleon Bonaparte was born on March 20, 1811, after a difficult birth for his mother, Marie-Louise of Austria, who the Emperor had married on April 1, 1810.[2] For a time his life was in danger but he survived and his birth was greeted with the firing of cannons in the Tuileries. Roads were closed in the area to give the boy and his mother some peace but Parisians were later ordered to light up the façades of their houses. Honors flowed. He was created King of Rome and Grand Eagle of the Légion d'honneur, a non-hereditary order instituted by his father while still First Consul. He was also awarded the Grand Cross of the Crown of Steel, to which honors was added the Golden Fleece. As might be expected, François-Charles was painted in his cradle by Gérard with a scepter and a globe as his toys.

---

[1] Letter from Cabinet du Préfet, Rennes, August 24, 1827. Letter from Préfecture de la Somme, September 6, 1827. Arch. Nat. F⁷ 6989, dossiers 13752, 13764.
[2] Napoleon divorced Josephine Tascher de la Pagerie in 1809 after a childless marriage.

Napoleon only saw his son twice. The first time was on his return from Berezina and again after Leipzig when, on New Year's Day 1814, the boy was presented to loyal officers in one of the theatrical scenes so beloved of the Emperor.

When Paris was threatened by the Allies, François-Charles was sent with his mother to the safety of the countryside south of the Loire. Escorted by a small group of cavalry, they arrived at Blois at the same time as the Allies entered Paris. It was then on to Orléans where for a time they lodged with the bishop. Now came one of the less agreeable episodes of family loyalty. Jérôme, Napoleon's brother and King of Westphalia, who was accompanying the party, decided to abandon the Empress and abscond with a *coffre* of diamonds. He crushed the skull of a guard but was caught before he was able to escape. Perhaps it was a case of the devil you know because, amazingly, he was released and allowed to continue the journey. The travellers doubled back on their tracks and there were no further incidents before they reached safety when they crossed the Rhine at the end of April.[3]

When Napoleon abdicated he retained the throne of Rome for François-Charles. The Allies would not, however, allow his son to accompany him to Elba and the boy was sent to his grandfather the Emperor of Austria. On June 11, 1817, the Dukedom of Parma was granted to Marie-Louise with reversion to François-Charles but the reversion was cancelled by the Bourbons. The abiding fear was that the child could unify the disparate interests of Republicans and Bonapartists against them. After his father's death in 1821 his name became a rallying cry but he did not survive long into adulthood.

Once in Austria at the castle of Schönbrunn with his grandfather, François-Charles was effectively a prisoner. He may have been created the duc de Reichstadt but in practice it did him no good at all. He was surrounded by foreigners, watched continually and his correspondence was censored and suppressed. He was never permitted to receive news of his father and was rarely seen in public. Described as good-looking and tall with fair hair, and a good horseman, he seems to have borne his troubles reasonably well, only complaining, "What do they want of me? Do they think I have the head of my father?" He died on July 22, 1832, either from phthisis or from cancer of the

---

[3] Jérôme died in Paris in 1860. His kingship was short-lived: he reigned only from 1807 to 1813. His son, Prince Napoleon, nicknamed Plon-Plon, was for a time the French Ambassador to Madrid.

stomach, something of a family complaint, and was buried in the cathedral at Vienna.[4]

It is a measure of opinion regarding Vidocq that he should be thought capable of political assassination. The story came from a man called Guillemin who had it from his son, a carpenter working in Paris. It was reported on August 24, 1827, and it was taken seriously enough for the Prefect at Rennes to write to the Minister of Justice who denied it four days later. It was not the only story in circulation at the time. A variation was that it was Charles X himself who had sent Vidocq to Bavaria.[5] The story was taken up. Now it was put about that the Jesuits had paid Vidocq 100,000 francs; that he had not gone to Vienna himself but had sent an Italian named Sparzi, whom he had furnished with a passport in his own name and that he was the one who had been hanged. The story that the Jesuits had paid Vidocq this huge sum undoubtedly stemmed from the fact of Charles' pro-Catholicism.[6]

In fact our hero was alive, well, rich and busying himself with a factory at SaintMandé, then a village near the Bois de Vincennes to the northeast of Paris, and certainly a walkable distance from the center.

It was more or less a wholly altruistic enterprise. There was little work available to ex-convicts. Balzac's criminal Vautrin, echoing Vidocq, comments to the Procurator-General Granville, "Being a fugitive between two games, one called the *bagne* and the other the police is a life where triumph is an endless labor, a struggle where peace seems to me to be impossible." The celebrated convict Fossard said he thought that France was one great *bagne* for the released prisoner.

First, there was the question of exclusions. As part of a sentence a convict could be banned from returning to his home after his release

---

[4] The duc does seem to have had some slight consolation. He was the acknowledged admirer of Fanny Essler, described by Captain Gronow as "of delicate and graceful proportions. Her hair was auburn, her eyes blue and large, and her face wore an expression of great tenderness." *The Reminiscences and Recollections of Captain Gronow*, p. 106. His body was later moved to the Invalides. His death was the subject of an ode by Victor Hugo. In 1900 Edmund Rostand wrote the hugely popular verse drama *L'Aiglon*, representing him as a man tortured by dreams of unrealisable glory. Formerly and frequently played by Sarah Bernhardt, it is still the subject of regular revivals.

[5] Charles X, the brother of Louis XVI and Louis XVIII, had returned from England after the Revolution and led the Ultras, the extreme Royalist party. On the death of Louis XVIII he ascended the throne. See Chapter 15.

[6] Arch. Nat. F⁷ 6989, Dossiers 13752, 13764; M. F. Raban and M. Saint-Hilaire, *Mémoires d'un forçat, ou Vidocq dévoilé*, t. IV, pp. 285–6.

from prison. Secondly, released criminals might be given a yellow passport, a sure indication to prospective employees of where they had spent the previous years. So more or less all that was legitimately open to them was in the white-lead industry, itself a killer. It meant isolation from other workers who would not risk drinking from a glass, even when washed, which had been used by a white-lead worker. As a result the men had their own cafés.

Vidocq had already built a house and now added workshops, possibly with financial assistance from the social reformer Benjamin Appert, with the express intent of employing former convicts of both sexes in a paper mill. The former prisoners were to have their keep for six months while they learned the trade and would then be paid a living wage. For the moment, machinery was acquired and cardboard, from which the paper would be made, was purchased. As he had done with his agents, so Vidocq championed his workers. Of course, some were dismissed for drunkenness and petty theft but, overall, he believed former prisoners could be reformed.

Sadly, the venture did not meet with the success for which he hoped. To begin with, questions were being asked as to how, on a salary of around 5,000 francs, he had acquired the money to build himself such a fine place, staff and run it. It is a question which is asked of many a police officer. He had certainly acquired a mass of property and investments. As far back as 1815 there had been a tavern in the rue de l'Orme-Saint-Gervais, which was a regular haunt of thieves. Over the years he was thought to have acquired others in the rue de la Juiverie and behind the place de Grève. There were his houses in the rue de l'Hirondelle and another on the quai Saint-Michel. He was a moneylender and there was a thriving, and perfectly legal, business of providing substitutes for those who wished to avoid conscription. He had, after all, a ready supply of substitutes – thieves to whom he could offer the choice of prison or the army.[7]

There were legitimate rewards, such as the one given by Pasquier for his arrest of one of the Delzaive brothers, the Shrimp, but there remains the suggestion that he had, under the protective cloak of the Sûreté, continued his Wild-like double career as thief-taker and – if not thief himself – then putter up and receiver. There was also said to be money from criminals in the form of protection:

---

[7] APP. E/a 90. Report to duc de Rovigo, May 20, 1813. Philip Stead, *Vidocq*, pp. 118–19. It was standard practice in Europe at the time, as it was during the American Civil War, to provide substitutes for conscription.

These agents were very numerous and it was not the promised bounty that increased their numbers, but the crowd of swindlers, forgers and thieves of every kind who joined only to ensure themselves some kind of immunity. Once enrolled in this famous band they could ply their trade without fear, so long as they gave Vidocq a share of their profits.[8]

Froment claims that at the time there was a licensing system. Thieves had to obtain permission to steal as did prostitutes to work. On the eve of public holidays the tolerated thieves were mustered by circular letter and went to prison for thirty-six hours, something they did with good humor. Prostitutes paid a tax of three francs a day to Vidocq and his agents.

Particularly, it was suggested that in the early 1820s the fraudsmen Joseph Meihac and his colleagues Martin, Chamon, Renault and Travers had given Vidocq gold snuff boxes and money for his protection. The diamond studs and smart trap driven by Vidocq certainly did not come from his salary. Vidocq, as has many another officer after him, explained his wealth as coming from gifts from people grateful for the return of their jewelry and wallets which he had secured.[9]

According to *Mémoires d'un forçat, ou Vidocq dévoilé*, Vidocq had his château built with stones from the old bridge of Charenton which had been destroyed by the Allied armies. The stones were in the middle of the Seine, and Vidocq, who had the ear of the Préfet, persuaded him first that it was dangerous to navigation and secondly that he should oversee the clearance, which was how they ended up free of charge at Saint-Mandé. Nonsense, it was a modest house, said Vidocq's great champion, Barthélemy Maurice, adding that it was difficult to imagine how many untruths there were in a few short paragraphs.[10]

The authors of the *Mémoires d'un forçat* had certainly no love for Vidocq. They described him at the time as having a coach regularly driven by an ex-convict and "he never goes out without a pair of pistols and a long dagger with a large golden blade and a handle garnished with stones." There were loaded pistols in his bedroom and he was guarded by two mastiffs.

---

[8] See J. Galtier-Boissière, *Mysteries of the French Secret Police*.

[9] It would not be the last time that allegations of corruption by a detective were parried in this manner. Thomas Byrnes, the Chief of Detectives in New York in the 1890s, turned aside allegations of bribery saying he had been privately rewarded by bankers for keeping thieves out of the Wall Street area.

[10] Barthélemy Maurice, *Vidocq, vie et aventures*, pp. 159–60. The *forçat* (convict) was supposed to have been Malgaret, an officer of the *armée roulante*, who had known Vidocq in the *bagne*.

The Saint-Mandé experiment was doomed to failure. For a start there was an early example of the "not in my back yard" attitude which has in recent times swelled in England and elsewhere whenever a prison or reform home has been scheduled to be built in a genteel locality.

Then there was the question of undercapitalization. The machines cost 100,000 francs each, the workers produced nothing for the first six months but they still had to be fed and clothed and throughout the experiment there was increasing hostility from neighbors. Finally, retailers refused to pay the market price, arguing that he was employing convict labor and therefore they should be able to buy more cheaply. Vidocq could not sustain the drain on his capital. The factory at Saint-Mandé was closed and now he needed new employment.

Chapter 15

VIDOCQ
RESTORED

*In which our hero possibly acts as a police spy – possibly finds some
medals – certainly arrests some burglars – with the help of an arms
dealer gets his old job back at an increased salary – helps to break up an
insurrection and, for his pains, is criticized – hides one of his men from
view and ultimately suffers for it*

DISCONTENT WITH THE Government of Charles X came
to a head in 1829 when the King dissolved the Chamber of
Deputies for protesting against his anti-liberal pro-Catholic reaction-
ary policy. Born in 1757 the younger brother of both Louis XVI and
Louis XVIII, an émigré in 1789, he spent several years in England
before returning at the Restoration to lead the Ultras, the extreme
Royalist party. He succeeded to the throne in 1824 on the death of
Louis XVIII. His coronation at Reims on May 29, 1825, was an occasion of great pomp with considerable religious emphasis, something
which disturbed many.

With the July Revolution of 1830 the elder branch of the
Bourbons which had been restored in 1814 was overthrown and
Louis-Philippe, duc d'Orléans, now became King.[1] The revolution
of July 28, 1830, lasted a bare three days. The previous year, when
the King had dissolved the Chamber of Deputies for protesting
against his policies, the reply was swift. A new chamber was returned
with a much larger opposition party. On July 26, 1830, the King
then issued ordinances which once more dissolved the chamber
and changed the electoral law. In doing so he violated the Charter

---

[1] After his overthrow Charles X spent his life in exile, part of the time in Holyrood, Edinburgh,
and partly in Prague. He died in Gorizia in 1836.

of 1814.[2] His act was seen as a small-scale coup d'état and was roundly condemned. Street fighting broke out on July 27 and lasted for the three days known as *les trois glorieuses,* before Charles abdicated in favor of his grandson, the ten-year-old duc de Bordeaux, son of the duc de Berri. Some thought that if the ever-popular duchesse de Berri had actually appeared with her son and said, "This is your King" the crowd would have risen to acclaim him.[3] She did not, however, and the Orléanist faction then successfully engineered the establishment of a constitutional monarchy. On August 7 Louis-Philippe was proclaimed King. The same day a new charter replaced the one of 1814.

There is no record of Vidocq taking an active part in the Revolution. He had, however, been caught up in an earlier street disturbance when, on May 10, 1830, he was near the Commissariat of Police when an ex-convict and ex-police spy, Renaud, recognized him and began to incite the crowd against him. Taken in to the Commissariat he changed clothes with a man, Valcour, who then left in a cab. Vidocq, now unrecognized, slipped away in the crowd.

Always one with an eye for the main chance, he remained at Saint-Mandé during the three days of the Revolution where, at seven on the morning of July 28, he hoisted the tricolore. He declined to lower it on the instructions of both the gendarmerie and the Commandant of the troop at Vincennes. No one seems to have been prepared to argue with him.

Apart from hoisting flags it is not at all clear what Vidocq was up to politically at the time. Things had changed dramatically in the police during the three years since his resignation and the detective division had fared badly. Coco-Lacour had certainly done nothing for the position. He had curried favor with the despised Delavau and had also spent much of his time indulging his passion for fishing; now and then he had to be retrieved from the banks of the Seine to attend to police business. One of his less shining moments came in the police-inspired riots of November 1827 after the elections had proved a triumph for the liberals. Canler discovered that a ringleader in the rioting in the rue Saint-Denis was one of Coco-Lacour's men. He fell

---

[2] On June 4, 1814, Louis XVIII granted La Charte Constitutionelle which upheld social and administrative order and provided for Government by a constitutional monarchy with a largely hereditary House of Peers nominated by the King, and an elected House of Deputies. In theory there was a free press but in practice it was restricted by law.

[3] *The Times*, November 1, 1843.

from grace, and view, and, it is said, became a small-time money-lender and secondhand clothes dealer while retaining his connection with the Bureau, working as an informer. Delavau had resigned in 1828 and was replaced by de Belleyme. The tiresome Duplessis also went. From 1830 until the appointment of Henri Gisquet in the autumn of 1831 there were no less than seven Préfets.

It is highly probable that Vidocq worked in the background, thinking of his own restoration. Although he always denied that he had been a political spy, others are by no means as convinced. At the time he had certainly been very close to the secret police and, indeed, in England his name and that of Fouché were almost interchangeable.[4] Although, in theory, he had been away from the police since his resignation in 1827 there is little doubt that he was being used as a spy or was acting as one on his own behalf. There were suggestions that he had been using the name Laurent, something he denied, and that he had been known to disguise himself as a workman and do battle with rioters in 1831.[5] He was certainly basking in the success of his memoirs but he also had an office in the rue Pavée, not a stone's throw from the Sûreté.

It is easy to see how the rogue in Vidocq may have appealed to Gisquet. Born the son of a customs official, at Vezins in the Department of the Moselle in 1792, the new Préfet worked first as a clerk in a banking house owned by Casimir Périer. In 1819 he was made a partner and in 1825 he founded his own bank. He was also the owner of a large sugar refinery at Saint-Denis. In 1830 he went to London to purchase 300,000 muskets on behalf of the Government. Nearly a third were bought in very poor condition and he resold them to the state at a substantial profit. It was on this deal that his reputation would later founder.[6]

A man of equable temper, he is alleged to have told his wife after a gun accident blew off one of his hands that at least he would be able to save 50 percent on gloves. Périer, now First Minister, appointed him Secretary-General of the Préfecture in September 1831 and a month later he was appointed Préfet. It was written of him:

He was the official the most reviled by the opposition Press, whether Legitimist, Bonapartist, or Republican. He was accused of having taken

---

[4] *The Times*, January 14, 1865.
[5] Philip Stead, *Vidocq*, p. 130. He was almost certainly using the name for secret reports to Gisquet.
[6] *The Times*, January 14, 1865.

and given bribes on the occasion of the purchase of rifles in England, faking attempts against the King, and staging hoaxes alleged to be political conspiracies, and the epithet "ignoble" was commonly applied to his police service, which was guilty of persecuting honest patriots.[7]

Gisquet's appointment coincided with a hoped-for resurgence of the Carlists and the activities of the high-spirited duchesse de Berri. The monarchy may have wished that a decade earlier Louvel and the others had been more successful, for now Her Grace led a hopeless Bourbon rebellion in the Vendée.

After the 1830 abdication of Charles X in favor of Louis-Philippe the Bourbon court had moved to Edinburgh and then to Prague. Two years later, it was decided that the duchess, the idol of the Royalists, should start for France and after her arrival in the Vendée should revive the old Breton loyalty in favor of her son, the comte de Chambord. In theory it was a perfectly acceptable argument but, unfortunately, there had been a miscalculation. Had there been a Republic in Paris the Vendéeans might have understood the issues. Instead the Crown had been transmitted with comparative quietness and, to the peasantry, one king seemed much like another. It was certainly nothing to get excited about.[8]

As a by-product Vidocq may have enjoyed one of his greatest successes and on the back of it returned to the Sûreté as its head. It was a piece of theatre which included an unlikely cast, all treading the boards at the same time. In the wings was the duchess but center stage was the vicomtesse de Nays-Candau, born Delphine de Jacquot d'Andelarre, who must rank as one of the most high-spirited if not reckless fillies of her time. In supporting roles were her valet, Drouillet, a former convict and a notable locksmith, for whom her lobbying had obtained a reprieve. There was also one of those princes of thieves who turn up every few years: in this case it was Vidocq's old friend Jean-Pierre Fossard, currently on the run after his last escape from the *bagne*.[9]

Known as the l'Affaire du Cabinet de Médailles, the incident resulted in the theft of coins and medals from the Bibliothèque

---

[7] Jean Galtier-Boissière, *Mysteries of the French Secret Police*, p. 195.

[8] In Paris, however, passions ran high and a duel was fought over the duchess by Armand Carel of *La National* and Roux Laborie, editor of *La Revenant*. Laborie was run through the arm and Carel the stomach. Neither man was able to continue and their seconds were about to take their places when the police intervened. J. C. Milligan, *The History of Duelling*, p. 251.

[9] Arch. Nat. F^2 10364. See also Chapter 12.

royale on November 6, 1831, nine months after Fossard's escape. The haul included Greek and Roman medals, jewels found in the tomb of Childerac, the golden scepter of Louis XII and a fine gold medal belonging to Louis XVI, as well as a quantity of gold. The robbery, it was suggested with some force, was carried out to help the duchesse de Berri finance her revolt.[10]

When Gisquet received news of the theft he went at once to the Bibliothèque, taking with him the most capable employees in the Préfecture. At any given time in any country there are only a limited number of criminals with sufficient expertise and contacts to undertake certain high-class jobs and almost without exception their names are known to the police already. It is therefore genuinely a case of rounding up the usual suspects. In the frame were Fossard, Drouillet and a man named Touprinat. Touprinat was, however, thought to be in England. Asked his views immediately after the theft, Coco-Lacour said it could only be Fossard but for the fact he was in the *bagne*.[11] He had not yet heard of the escape and, given that Fossard was known to be out and about, there was a high possibility of his involvement. But how could he get into the Bibliothèque in the first place? The answer was with the considerable help of the vicomtesse de Nays-Candau.

After Fossard had made his escape from the *bagne* he had gone to Paris to see his former mistress, Henriette Tonnaux, and there received a shock. Unfortunately, while she might provide for him she no longer wanted to be with him. He wanted her to accompany him to America but she was now perfectly comfortable with a man named Hazart, who had been her companion since Fossard's capture sixteen years earlier. The *galérien* now made his way to one of his brothers, Jean-Baptiste, a jeweller in Palaiseau. The vicomtesse purchased jewelry from Jean-Baptiste and it was at his shop that she had met Drouillet, through whom she heard of Fossard's escape. Her supposed maid was, in fact, the wife of another criminal, Drouhin.

On November 7, 1831, the day after the robbery, Vidocq, no doubt with officers in tow, arrested Fossard and Drouillet carrying the

---

[10] For a full account of the affair, see Jean Savant, "Le Cabinet de Médailles" in *Les Oeuvres Libres*, "Les Trente-six incarnations d'un policier," in *Lectures pour tous*, 7th year, Book 4. It was not the first time the Bibliothèque had been looted. There had been a previous burglary in 1804. Before that in September 1792 a daring raid had been made on the *garde-meuble national* when 17 million "francs" worth of Louis d'or and jewelry were stolen. The thieves, Deschamps, Salles and Dacosta, were sent to the *bagne* at Toulon from which they escaped a short time after Vidocq. Caught after another theft at Auteuil they were subsequently executed.

[11] *Gazette des Tribunaux*, February 11, 1832.

equivalent of two million francs. Vidocq, of course, knew Fossard's brother and, visiting him in the disguise of a beggar, had tricked him into giving information of his whereabouts. Then, however, came word that Fossard had political protection and that he should simply be returned to the *bagne*. For the moment he was taken to Bicêtre to await the chain. Once again, it is amazing how criminals cannot keep their mouths shut. Time and again they will let slip what could be regarded as a half remark. Fossard was one such. "Someone helped me," he said, "but it's a secret which will die with me." For a Vidocq, in search of his own restoration, there was no such thing as a secret. Little by little he learned of the vicomtesse's visits to prisons and her efforts to secure the release of some career criminals. The vicomtesse was also asking for the return of the money Vidocq had seized when he arrested Fossard, explaining her interest by saying he was the brother of her clockmaker. She also presented herself to Gisquet pleading on his behalf. In turn she was watched and was spotted coming out of Drouhin's wife's home in the rue des Mauvais Garçons carrying a money bag. Still no one would believe Vidocq. Premature arrest would cause far too much scandal.

Then on July 28, 1832, at 5 p.m., a woman with numerous bags and a handsome wardrobe arrived at Brest from Paris and stayed at the Hôtel de Provence. It was the vicomtesse herself accompanied by Drouhin. She, along with Drouhin's wife, was arrested. The vicomtesse spent the night at the town hall and was taken the next day, as befitted her station, to a nearby château. Now the authorities adopted a different attitude. A Bourbon plot could not be excluded and so orders came to assist Vidocq. In her valise were found not only the medals and bullion but also – the shame of it – love letters from Fossard. Interrogated by Vidocq she at first claimed the protection of the Queen but then confessed and gave up the names of her co-conspirators. When Vidocq arrested Drouillet the entire story came out. He had long been a beneficiary of the vicomtesse's favors, something he did not mind sharing with Fossard in later months. Fossard's brother was willing to explain his part in receiving the goods. The Queen seems to have done what she could for the erring vicomtesse. A month later came the order for her release. In the words spoken of many an acquitted person, "This is a complete vindication of Mme la V. de Nays." It may have been because of his habit of fishing in the Seine for trinkets that Coco-Lacour got some of the credit – for some of the jewelry was retrieved from the river. Certainly Gisquet praised him for his part in the resolution of the affair. There is no mention of Vidocq in Gisquet's memoirs in relation to this incident. Gisquet maintains that it was Coco-Lacour – who had been out of a job for the last three years – who saw Fossard and followed him.[12] Nor does Vidocq mention the incident in his own books. His champion is Jean Savant. It is not, however, impossible that he was involved. He certainly had more common sense and better contacts than Coco-Lacour and there is also no doubt he was treating with Gisquet, who had just become Minister, at the time.

Fossard remained staunch. He was offered a pardon, a substantial sum of money and a passport to a country of his choice if he would disclose the whereabouts of the remainder of the jewelry. He declined and later also refused a passage to Switzerland.

When the trial opened in February 1833 there was the vicomtesse as a witness. Only after the court dissolved with laughter after she claimed that she had only been trying to help an unfortunate was the session held behind closed doors, both to silence the press and to hush up the scandal. The trick had been worked when she had taken Drouillet to the Bibliothèque as her servant on a private visit and he had taken impressions of the keys to be cut by Fossard.

As is often the case it was the poor who got the blame. Fossard's brother received ten years and Drouillet twenty years with hard labor. In the end, however, the chambre de conseil took the view there was not sufficient evidence against either man and they were released. For Vidocq it was another step on the road back to the Sûreté.

After Fossard's escape on February 8, 1831, he had intended to go to Marseilles and then on to Algeria. Unfortunately he had been recognized in the city by an old convict working with the police and fled to Lyons. He had, he said, taken the medals in the hope of ransoming them in exchange for a pardon.[13]

Fossard was exposed in the place de Grève on April 3 and he was given a further three years for his escape. It hardly mattered, nor did the forty years for his part in the theft; he was already serving life imprisonment. He did not last long. He was transferred to the *bagne* at Rochefort, arriving there on August 14, 1833. He was taken ill in the autumn of the next year and on November 18 died in the cholera epidemic which also claimed the lives of twenty-three other convicts.

---

[12] H-J. Gisquet, *Mémoires de M. Gisquet*, Chapter XVIII.
[13] E-F. Vidocq, *Les Voleurs*, p. 79.

The duchesse de Berri's revolutionary expedition was probably doomed from the outset. Nevertheless she retained considerable support. For example, the politician and writer Chateaubriand, who had been her supporter since his book about the duc, produced a pamphlet after her arrest, *"Madame, votre fils est mon roi!,"* which sold in its thousands.

She had chartered the steamship *Carlo Alberto* and, after landing at Marseilles, wandered west under a variety of disguises, generally as a young peasant, Petit Pierre, raising an army. A number of her followers on the boat were promptly arrested.[14] For a time there was some success and in one skirmish the Chouans captured eighty muskets. The duchess announced that she expected the early defection of several regiments of the line in her favor but she was disappointed.[15] Her army was defeated in a brief skirmish and she tried to flee, again disguised as a peasant, sabots and all. She made her way across France, undertaking a good deal of the journey on foot. In October she had reportedly left Dieppe and was on her way to Boulogne. "The 'notorious' Vidocq arrived only 22 hours after the departure of the Duchess."[16] Inspector Joly, who had failed to prevent the killing of her husband a decade earlier and who was now reinstated, was also sent off after her.

She was finally betrayed by Simon Deutz, baron de Gonzague, who operated under the name Hyacinthe,[17] and is said to have netted £40,000 for his treachery. He discovered the house where she was hiding and she was arrested on February 7, 1833. When ordered to hand over the reward money to Deutz, Colonel de Géry told his young son, "Sit in the room and you will witness a scene you will never forget." Géry handed the money over using fire tongs saying, *"Voilà – va-t'en."*[18]

---

[14] *Gazette des Tribunaux*, August 20, September 7, 1832.

[15] *The Times*, June 11, 1832, April 20, 1870.

[16] *The Times*, October 19, 1832, quoting the *Brighton Gazette*.

[17] Anon., *Relation fidèle et detailée de l'arrestation de S.A.R. Madame, Duchesse de Berry.*

[18] "The Orléanists" in *The Times*, February 15, 1883. Deutz, the son of the chief rabbi of the Jewish consistory in Paris, was the godson of the duchess, who lavished affection and attention on him. After his betrayal Deutz ran through his reward money with a mixture of that unhealthy triumvirate of gambling, drink and women and became a pariah begging sums off the police. On October 21, 1842, he did, however, write a self-exculpatory letter to *The Times*. At one time he was given 3,000 francs to live abroad but he was back in Paris within the year. He probably died in poverty in the rue Meslay. In her romantic biographical study of the duchess, Baroness Orczy, author of *The Scarlet Pimpernel*, suggests Deutz either went to England or was killed in the rioting of 1851.

Unfortunately then the duchess rather blotted her copybook and fell from grace. During her imprisonment it was discovered she was again pregnant and she was obliged to admit to a secret marriage with the Italian count Lucchesi-Palli. Charles X never forgave her. The young comte de Chambord had been smuggled out of France by the duc de Blacas and placed in the care of the masculine duchesse d'Angoulême, who had survived the attempt to blow up her palace a decade earlier. His mother was never permitted to see him again in his infancy. She was repatriated to Sicily on July 8, 1833. She outlived both her husband and Ann Marie Rosalie, her daughter by him, dying in Holy Week 1870. The comte de Chambord attended her funeral.[19]

Just how much he had been acting behind the scenes and for how long is not clear but Vidocq's second official stint in the Sûreté lasted less than a year and its brevity was largely his own fault. Its roots lay in an incident which happened before his appointment – a failed burglary at Fontainebleau.

His detractors claimed he played a major part in the whole game, suggesting that the idea was to show his indispensability and so win reappointment. Laurent Léger, one-time cook, baker and now police secret agent, had been employed by a restaurateur called Schmidt who had premises at the *barrière* at Fontainebleau. He told Vidocq of a conspiracy to burgle the premises. In turn Vidocq told the mayor and when the burglars, the Desplantes brothers, along with two women and two other men, Lenoir and Séguin, went to the first floor they were watched by a gendarme through a hole drilled through the wall as they broke open the secretaire and crushed the silverware. One of them, Séguin, was rifling the safe and the others pouring themselves some wine when they were surprised. In all, eight arrests were made in the sweep.

Vidocq had his early reward. Gisquet appointed him Chef de Brigade de Sûreté, replacing Hébert. His salary, with effect from April 1, was to be 6,000 francs, 1,800 more than the transferred Hébert would receive in his new position with the Municipal Police. Vidocq moved to the small office in the rue Sainte-Anne and recruited twenty-eight agents from his collection of criminal acquaintances. This was certainly an instance of regrouping to jump higher because it had been reported that both he and Coco-Lacour had been named in an order posted in the bureau on February 10 forbidding police agents to associate with them.[20]

---

[19] The comte died on August 24, 1883. *The Times*, August 25, 1883.

[20] *Gazette des Tribunaux*, February 11, 1832, This seems difficult to understand because Gisquet was certainly treating with Vidocq at the time.

L. M. Moreau-Christophe, an Inspector of Prisons, wrote of Vidocq at the time as:

> . . . common of language, vulgar looking, was fine of spirit and "distingué de sentiment." His voice was hoarse. His eyes were round, small, green and sparkling. He was generous to the point of prodigality. He had small feet, short arms with hairy hands, flared nostrils, round stomach, squashed nose, large shoulders; his once firm cheeks became jowly in his old age.

He also had bad body odor:

> He walked fast and, although tireless, perspired freely. The odor he exhaled took one not so much by the nose as by the throat. The office of M. le Crosnier, Head of the Division concerned with the prison service in which I often encountered him in 1832, needed herbal fumigation every time he left it.[21]

Perhaps it was the smell of the galleys he carried with him. Vidocq himself would say he could recognize a former *galérien* from his smell. In fairness Moreau-Christophe seems to have been the only person to record this. Of course, others may merely have been more polite.

The months that followed saw, first, Vidocq's finest hours and, second, the signs of the disfavor into which he would fall with officialdom. The first sign of trouble was the cholera epidemic from which, nine days after his appointment, more than eight hundred people died in one day.[22] There was considerable public disquiet and the police were accused of poisoning public drinking fountains as well as fruit and vegetables in order to spread the disease.

The cholera epidemic had broken out in the swamps of the Ganges in 1817 before making its way to Bombay the next year. From there it spread through India and travelled east to Peking in 1820. It arrived in Persia the following year; Siberia five years later and Moscow in 1831. It broke out again in Calais on March 15, 1831. As with many similar epidemics, unpopular groups were blamed for its spread. In Poland it was believed the Jews were responsible; in Hungary people thought that bismuth, which the government prescribed as an

---

[21] L. M. Moreau-Christophe, *Le Monde des Coquins*, p. 229.

[22] By May the total death toll was 18,402 and on May 16 it included Vidocq's patron Casimir Périer. He is buried in a fine mausoleum topped by a life-size statue of him dressed in a toga at the *rond point* Casimir Périer in the Père Lachaise cemetery.

unquestionable remedy, was instituted by them and the aristocracy to destroy the working class. In Russia people, believing that they were being poisoned, would not go to the hospital for treatment.[23]

The touchstone for a very short-lived uprising came with the funeral of General Maximilien Lamarque on June 5, 1832.[24] As the coffin passed along the boulevards there were cries of "Down with Louis-Philippe, down with the soft pear." The marquis de Lafayette made an inflammatory speech, a shot was fired and the fuse was lit near the place du Pont d'Austerlitz.[25] Things were not of course, spontaneous. Some three thousand insurgents took a section of Paris between the Châtelet and the faubourg St-Antoine. This was the old pre-Haussmann Paris and, with the barricades up, it was possible for a relatively small group of men to hold a street against a cavalry charge; a few snipers could do infinite damage to loyal troops. But, just as they were better organized than their 1830 counterparts, so was Maréchal de Lobau who controlled the National Guard. In turn Louis-Philippe displayed more courage than many a soft pear. He rode out of the Tuileries to survey and thank his troops who, after a brief waver, had stayed loyal. By the evening of the next day the fighting was over. The city was firmly in royal control and already there were tribunals in place to administer summary justice to rebels.[26]

And what was Vidocq's part in all this? Again, it depends on whom you believe. There is no doubt that he and his men had been mingling with the crowds at Lamarque's funeral and had reported back to Gisquet when the situation degenerated. It was now his men who arrested placard and arms carriers. He ran messages between the Sûreté and the Hôtel de Ville to which one of his men had accompanied the comte de Bondy. It was he, himself who, dressed in a workingman's smock, accompanied Gisquet when the Prefect went to the Tuileries, persuading the crowd to let them through. He and his men in plainclothes – to the annoyance of the Republicans – ran skirmishes against pockets of insurgents as well as the criminals who were taking advantage of the situation. During the night

---

[23] See Dr. Sophianopoulo, *Relative des épidémies du choléra en Hongroie*.

[24] Comte Jean-Maximilien Lamarque had served with distinction in Spain and during the Hundred Days put down an uprising in the Vendée. Exiled in 1815 he returned three years later and in 1828 was elected Deputy for the Landes. His talent for oratory made him one of the leaders of the Opposition.

[25] The bridge roughly links the Jardin des Plantes with the road leading to the Bastille.

[26] For an account of the insurrection, see e.g., Heinrich Heine, *De la France*. For a wonderfully readable account of the period generally, see Philip Mansel, *Paris Between the Empires, 1814–1852*.

he patrolled the streets. One of the particular pockets controlled by the criminals was the Ile de la Cité and Vidocq persuaded Gisquet to allow him to lead an attack against a group commanded by Edouard Colombat. Some accounts have Vidocq seizing him at the corner of rue de la Juiverie and rue de Calandre and with that another pocket of resistance crumbling.[27] It may be that Vidocq and his men broke up that particular barricade along with five others but they did not seize Colombat there and then. In fact, he was arrested at his home later that night and, at his trial, produced an alibi in the shape of his girlfriend, Sophie Harmond. It was not accepted and Colombat was sentenced to death. The conviction was later quashed and, after a second trial, on August 11 he was sentenced to deportation.[28]

In due course Vidocq wrote a report of the affair in suitably immodest style but for once there is independent evidence in support of his actions. Gisquet may not care to mention him too often in his *Mémoires* but in the immediate aftermath of the revolt, when things were still going well with Vidocq, he wrote to the Minister:

> Amongst the agents of my administration who displayed the greatest zeal, courage and devotion in suppressing the revolt of those two days of the 5th and 6th of June, I must distinguish the Sieur Vidocq, Head of the brigade de Sûreté.
>
> This report, a copy of which I have the honour to address to your excellency will bear witness to the presence of mind and intrepidity shown by this agent at a critical time and the dangers he ran in defence of public order and the law.

Vidocq ends his report with the request that his sole reward shall be that the King shall know of his conduct.

The old fawner. Gisquet concluded that it was, of course, for the King to decide "whether this desire, in itself commendable, can be granted."[29]

There is another story that Vidocq, disguised as a duchess, presented himself to Gisquet and carried on the pretense of giving information about Legitimist malcontents for some time. Gisquet

[27] Philip Stead, *Vidocq*, pp. 136–7.
[28] Gisquet, *Mémoires de M. Gisquet; La Tribune*, August 14, 1832; *Gazette des Tribunaux*, June 22, July 1, August 2, 14, September 20, 1832.
[29] BHVP, MS 1041, 2928, fols. 10, 11; APP. A/a 421.

was so delighted that he summoned his carriage and drove to Neuilly to present the duchess to the King, who in turn was delighted and introduced him to members of the Royal Family who were also delighted, etc. Ben trovato. If Gisquet had to address matters through his Minister it is extremely unlikely he would have had direct access to the throne.

There was also a tribute to Vidocq's brigade in the Chamber of Deputies when M. Thiers told the members:

> The Préfecture of Police was obliged to send the Municipal Guards to the places where the insurgents fired most briskly; he could not send them into the narrow streets of the city, where malefactors had fled for refuge. The inhabitants of the city asked for help; the Brigade de Sûreté ran to that place with fire-arms, and seized the criminals whose only desire was to plunder; indeed two of them were condemned for that act. The Brigade de Sûreté delivered that quarter of this gang; and the inhabitants of the city (I have the proof of what I advance) thanked the Prefect of Police for the great services he had just rendered to them.[30]

But, by the time of that encomium, Vidocq was gone.

Meanwhile, the Republican press went on the attack. *La Tribune* which earlier had written, "The presence of mind, and the courage of Vidocq, saved the royalty,"[31] now claimed that he was acting as an agent provocateur, but for once the insurrectionists seem to have managed without his help. There were also allegations of police brutality and the use of agents to stir up the crowd against captured Republicans, in one instance urging the mob to push a police wagon containing prisoners into the Seine.[32] A continuing stream of criticism was now directed against him. "The Gisquet police is the most unspeakably foul . . . Vidocq and his like . . ." and more in the same vein.[33]

For a time he was able to defend himself against the attacks in the press but the continuing criticism would not help him in the forthcoming trial of the Fontainebleau burglars. Before that, however, there had been another unfortunate episode. In the summer the somewhat dubious marquis de Crouy, born in Russia and of the Hungarian aristocracy, was charged with an attempt to raise money on false banknotes. He had been at Holyrood (where the Bourbon court

---

[30] November 29, 1832.
[31] *La Tribune,* July 6, 1843.
[32] Adolphe Chenu, *Les Conspirateurs,* p. 13.
[33] *La Tribune,* July 3, 1832.

was in exile) and it was claimed that this was part of a Carlist conspiracy
to flood France with forgeries. After all, there was the duchesse de
Berri still stirring up trouble in the Vendée. Crouy's defense was that
he had been given the forged notes by a police officer in disguise and
the case had then been whipped up by Vidocq. To great acclaim he was
found not guilty.[34]

Overall, it was not a good time for the police. At 5 a.m. on August 2
a duel was fought between M. Jacques Coste, editor of *Le Temps,* and
M. Bénoit, a Commissary of Police, who took exception to an article on
how orders had been distributed among commissaries. In the Bois de
Boulogne Bénoit asked Coste to fire first but he declined. Both fired
together, Bénoit was hit and died soon afterwards.[35]

At the trial of the Fontainebleau burglars, which began on September
20, 1832, the defense claimed that Léger's behavior provided a classic
example of the agent provocateur at work. Léger had given them the
essential details of the layout of the premises and Vidocq had set it up.
The allegations were that Léger had not only egged them on but had
actually provided an impression of Schmidt's key for them. Now Léger
had been added as a defendant and the case quickly became a trial of
the head of the Sûreté. For a start, for some time there had been no
sign of Léger.

Over the months Vidocq had helped neither things in general nor
himself in particular. His detractors say this was just another example
of the man's duplicity. Others, his champions, say there is no proof
of his involvement and what followed was an example of an officer
protecting his men. This is probably a charitable view of the affair
because, when a warrant for Léger was issued, Vidocq reported to the
court that he had disappeared from Paris. Four months later it became
clear that he had not gone at all but was working for Vidocq under the
name of Auguste. A new order was issued for Vidocq to surrender him
and this time he complied.

At the trial Léger was keen to point out he had been acting under
supervision. Vidocq had, himself, been watching the criminals
plotting; M. Froment had been there when he received his orders
from Vidocq. No, he had not seen Vidocq since his arrest but, yes, he
had written to him.

---

[34] *Gazette des Tribunaux,* August 24; September 7, 1832; *The Times,* September 8, 1832.
[35] *Gazette des Tribunaux,* August 3, 1832; *The Times,* August 6, 1832.

It was a trial full of allegations and counter allegations. Vidocq, who was the figure of greatest interest to the press and public, wandered in and out of court at will, and claimed counsel was trying to intimidate witnesses. For his part he maintained he believed in Léger's innocence and that, far from his being on the run, the agent was working in the provinces on a mission the details of which he could not disclose. The allegations against him were part of a plot cooked up in La Force by men who had been dismissed from the Sûreté and, in particular, by one Barthélemy. One of the defendants, Moureau, alleged that Vidocq had offered him 500 francs to confess but not to implicate Léger. It was all plot and counterplot and it sounds very much like some of the trials of today. Barthélemy, who seems to have played both sides off against each other, gave evidence that he had told Vidocq he had heard that Léger had confessed to an examining magistrate, saying it was the chief who had ruined him. Vidocq had replied in that case Léger could go and fuck himself. If Léger had confessed, it certainly was not in the papers before the court. What really told against him was the fact that he had already worked for Schmidt. That weakened the suggestions of a plot by the prisoners.

In the end the jury took four hours to find the men guilty. Moureau, Lenoir and Cloquemain, who had taken the impression of the key, each received twenty years. Séguin and one of the Desplantes brothers received five years but the crunch was that Léger was sentenced to two years.

Now it became standard defense practice in the courts to claim that the prosecution witnesses were old *bagne* acquaintances and had set things up. With it Vidocq's position became untenable. He had to go. In fact he jumped before he was pushed, writing on November 15, 1832, to Gisquet offering his resignation, saying that his wife was ill and he was needed at Saint-Mandé. It was a fiction everyone accepted. Vidocq received 500 francs a month pension which unfortunately stopped after six months.

Later he would say that he had made his mind up after the June troubles:

I handed in my resignation after the June business. The higher up administration thought they should restructure the agents who worked under my orders. I thought that I could not work efficiently against criminals without the aid of people who knew them and had lived with them. My agents whatever their background had served faithfully and loyally. Deprived of these useful tools I believed myself struck with powerlessness. I refused to sacrifice them and myself. I handed in my resignation.[36]

Technically he did hand in his resignation after June but it was more likely to have been at the end of September. It might also be asked – if the newspaper reports were correct, which is by no means guaranteed – what he was doing chasing the duchesse de Berri across France the previous October.

On the day of Vidocq's letter the Brigade de Sûreté was dissolved and a new one established. In the new articles setting up the force it was written that no one with a previous conviction, however minor, should be allowed in the service. Pierre Allard was appointed Head and Louis Canler became his Chief Inspector. Members of the Sûreté were now given the title of inspector of police, a rough equivalent of detective constable. New offices were found in 5 rue de Jérusalem.

Canler may have been a new broom but he still used the tried and tested Vidocq methods:

I resolved to form a squad of informers . . . I recruited newly convicted criminals and put them under regular discipline. Each of them was well rewarded.

He also maintained a "secret police composed of ex-convicts on parole who had broken it to come to Paris." They had the option of returning to prison or joining the detective force as auxiliaries and there is no doubt which most chose.[37] Additionally, there was the problem of Vidocq's men who, it was feared, would return to their old ways. To solve this they were offered a room, a salary of fifty francs a month and a reward for every arrest made through their endeavors. Only fourteen accepted the offer. Neither they nor his new recruits served Canler as well as had those employed by the old fox. Crime control dipped alarmingly.

By 1840, when he wrote his memoirs, Gisquet was now quite happy to distance himself from Vidocq:

---

[36] *Gazette des Tribunaux,* May 4, 1843.
[37] Louis Canler, *Mémoires de Canler.*

A man M. Vidocq who had acquired a sort of celebrity under the Restoration was the founder of the brigade de Sûreté. Vidocq in the shackles of old liaisons surrounded himself almost entirely with men branded by justice. He chose them himself, arbitrarily fixed their salaries, was always the intermediary between them and the administration over their remuneration, and placed them as he saw fit.

After the *affaire de Fontainebleau* on March 23, 1832, I decided because he had been using tainted agents to sack him and dismiss them.[38]

In other words, Gisquet was perfectly happy with Vidocq until he was found out and then he had to go. It is difficult to see, however, just how Gisquet did not know of his employee's practices. Traditionally in the French police no one really minded about provocation and worse if it produced results, but on this occasion it did not and hands could only be thrown up in horror.

As for Gisquet, he had never had entirely clean hands. After his appointment as Prefect of Police he used his position to give contracts to his friends and over the years he relentlessly suppressed any press criticism. In 1838 he sued *Le Messager* for libel over the accusations they had made regarding the *Fusils Gisquet*. On December 28 the court awarded him the minimum possible sum of 100 louis. He won the action but lost his position. On January 3, 1839, it was announced that Gisquet had ceased to be a state councillor. He was effectively ruined. He died in January 1866.[39]

Vidocq moved on to pastures new. From then on, however, for the next sixteen years he fought a long-running war with his former colleagues at the Sûreté. It was one which, if he did not actually lose, certainly contained some pyrrhic victories.

[38] H-J. Gisquet, *Mémoires de M. Gisquet,* Chapter V.
[39] *The Times,* January 31, 1866.

Chapter 16

VIDOCQ
AND HIS AGENCY

*In which our hero sets up a detective agency – is accused of
bribing government officials – expands the agency – goes to
prison before being acquitted – goes to prison a second time and
this time is acquitted on appeal*

V IDOCQ NOW LOST NO TIME in setting up his detective
agency, the first in the world. Paris of the 1830s was ready for
one. Just as it had been immediately after the Terror of 1793 so once
again money was the keyword in the era of Louis-Philippe. This was
the time for the sharps, the swindlers, the mountebanks to emerge
into the sunlight. Much of his work as a police officer had been devoted to them; now Vidocq had the opportunity to benefit even more
from their depredations. It was a logical and financially astute step to
open a detective agency.

So, twenty years before Allan Pinkerton had even left Scotland
for America, Vidocq set up his *Bureau des Renseignements* at
12 rue Cloche-Perche. Out went the publicity material. An annual
subscription of twenty francs or five francs per interview would gain
the great man's services. And, of course, such money as he recovered
would be subject to a percentage charge.[1]

The bureau was run on strict terms with employees knowing where
they stood or sat from the moment of their employment. From April 1
until October 1 all office staff had to be in place at 8 a.m. There was a half-
hour lunch break from 10:30 and a dinner break at 5:30 p.m., from which
they must return by 7 p.m. Work continued until 10 p.m. In winter work
began and ended a half-hour later. The bureau had to be manned at the

---

[1] *The Times*, February 5, 1833.

weekend but Sunday work ceased at 3 p.m. Anyone who worked after the office closed would receive overtime.

For the agents themselves there were no set hours. They were expected to be on the job as long as required but if they began before 9 a.m. or finished after midnight they would be paid by the hour.[2] The agents, who at the peak of the agency's popularity numbered around forty, had nicknames: the Cyclops, because he had only one eye, a dandy known as the Man About Town, the Satyr. Vidocq's personal office was decorated with paintings of dubious taste. There was Damiens being quartered and John the Baptist losing his head; Ravaillac being tortured.[3] They were set alongside portraits of former police administrators – Fouché, Gisquet and so on. Vidocq also instilled in his agents rudimentary manners – to spit on the floor only as a matter of last resort; to remove their hat when entering a building, not to pass a letter in front of a young lady. Then there were a number of axioms and pieces of advice. "In the underworld two and two do not make four. Two and two make twenty-two." "The best way to tail someone without being seen is to walk in front of them."

Hiring seems to have been fairly ad hoc. Léo Lespès, later a well-known journalist who wrote as Timothée Trimm in the *Petit Journal*, said of his first meeting and subsequent employment with Vidocq, "I saw a short, thickset man with blue eyes, wide lips and thick graying hair." What clearly impressed Lespès was Vidocq throwing whole *pains au chocolat to* a bulldog.

Vidocq gave him some dictation and employed him on the spot without asking for references. Lespès says he worked for the great man for a fortnight without knowing who he was. This is hard to believe since in the office there was a big red shield emblazoned with Vidocq's name.[4]

In 1833, when Vidocq appeared in the Chamber of the Correctional Police of Paris, the description of him was hardly flattering:

> The appearance of one of the prisoners at the bar was that of a fat gentleman dressed in full black, with a sharp eye, a huge mouth and a bag of pastilles in his hand which he used repeatedly.[5]

---

[2] ABVP, MS 2928, Dossier 8.

[3] In 1610 François Ravaillac assassinated Henry IV. Robert-François Damiens attempted to assassinate Louis XV in 1757.

[4] Léo Lespès, "F-J. Vidocq, Breveté de Gouvernement." in *Le Figaro*, May 21, 1843.

[5] *The Times*, June 28, 1833. The *habit noir* in which Vidocq appeared had, over the years, blurred the dress style of the aristocracy and the bourgeoisie but distinguished its wearer from the working classes who wore blousons and smocks.

Much of the work undertaken was debt collecting, and a letter from the agency – at first handwritten then, as the business grew, in later years printed with blanks to be filled in – started proceedings. Headed grandly *"Ex-chef de la police particulière de Sûreté qu'il a dirigé pendant 20 ans avec un succès incontestable,"* it was intended to, and no doubt did, inspire some fear or at least attention. A typical example is a letter to a Mme Pêche at 67 rue de Provence, dated April 11, 1845:

> I have the honor to ask you to trouble yourself to come to my offices on receipt of my letter before you enter into an affair which concerns you and which will cause you trouble and expense if you choose to ignore my invitation.
>
> While awaiting your visit, I have the honor to sign myself, The Director.[6]

Translated in simple terms it meant "Come and discuss how you're going to pay." And come and discuss it they did in droves.

Other headings on his notepaper included a suggestion that he had a royal patent. He did but this referred to the type of paper he had designed to avoid fraud rather than to the agency. It was a heading which would cause comment and redound not to the credit of the ex-Chef.

But once again Vidocq was hoist with his own success coupled with his inability not to crow over others less successful. "Vidocq is a man gifted with intelligence and character; only a little troubled by the need to speak of himself," wrote Gisquet.[7] It was perfectly all right to write of the downfall of rival agencies which were setting up all over the city, some of which – The Tocsin, The Lighthouse, The Illuminator among them – were mere vehicles for blackmailers, but it was foolish to brandish his triumphs in the face of the police, however justified it might be.

Some of the agency's troubles undoubtedly came about from a lack of direct supervision. At the height of its popularity Vidocq was seeing more than forty clients a day but some of the agents – including the Satyr – were not behaving as well as they might.

Nor was he above suspicion even from the early days. In June 1833 "the Terror of Thieves" was in the dock along with a young man, Lebas, accused of swindling on his own account:

> This was none other than Sieur Vidocq of famous memory as ex-chef of the Secret Police... Several witnesses were called one of whom was examined

---

[6] ABVP, MS 2928, Dossier 26.
[7] H-J. Gisquet, *Mémoires de M. Gisquet,* Chapter V.

by Vidocq. Vidocq (in an authoritative tone) "Silence, sir. You are telling a falsehood – You are a false witness." Confusion in Court.

Vidocq was found not guilty and awarded his costs. In reporting the case the *Gazette des Tribunaux*, which noted that Vidocq "left in an elegant tilbury which took him to his numerous clients at 12 rue Cloche Perche," also took the opportunity to comment on the dangers inherent in such an agency.[8]

In November 1835 there was another minor scandal. It concerned one of his agents, Maurice, employed to watch the shop of a wine merchant named Sauvelet. By accident or design Maurice made a poor showing and was spotted by Sauvelet, who challenged him. Maurice immediately changed sides, offering to stop the surveillance and also to tell him the name of his employer for a sum of 100 francs, reduced the next day to forty. Sauvelet went to the police and Vidocq was obliged to appear in court to explain that Maurice was a rogue agent.[9]

Controversy dogged him that year and the next. Four months later he was under fire – which he successfully withstood – from two chemists, Debraine and Kersselaers, who claimed that they were the true inventors of the unfalsifiable paper used in the agency.[10]

There was another court case in 1836 when he declined to pay an artist named William 100 francs for a portrait to be included in *Les Voleurs*, his book published that year. He claimed it was not a good likeness and that William was lucky to have the commission which was payment in itself. He was ordered to pay half the fee. When it came to it a portrait by Achille Devéria was used for the frontispiece.[11]

On the other hand, the year produced one of the great triumphs for the agency when it broke the Duhaim père et fils organization run by a former *galérien*, Rupp. His bank was another version of the long-firm fraud but worked with false drafts instead of goods. Rupp moved out of Paris to Boulogne but Vidocq, matching correspondence, traced him there and Rupp returned to prison. Vidocq on this occasion was displaying signs of petulance. A crowd gathered to see the great detective when he attended court and he was not

---

[8] *Gazette des Tribunaux*, June 23, 1833; *The Times*, June 28, 1833.
[9] *Gazette des Tribunaux*, 24 November 1835.
[10] *Le Sens commun*, October 6, 1833; *Gazette des Tribunaux*, October 23, 1833.
[11] *Gazette des Tribunaux*, December 24, 1836.

pleased, first trying to get out by a back door and then turning on his admirers.[12]

It is absolutely true to say that post-Vidocq the police leaders lacked both the drive and technique of the great man. One case which summed this up was that of a businessman, Carton, who in 1836 had a great deal of money stolen from him and was reduced to poverty. He had given the police the names of those who had robbed him but they had done nothing. Nine years later the men were sentenced for other crimes.[13]

The first really serious blow to the agency came on Saturday, November 24, 1837, when the police, under the direction of Allard, arrested four employees of the Ministry of War and charged them with misappropriating official documents. A search was made of their homes and of secondhand dealers and a quantity of the missing papers were found. It had been a long, ongoing series of thefts. Four days later Vidocq's offices, now in rue Neuve Saint-Eustache, were raided and some 3,500 files and documents were seized. It was leaked that half of them were related to the inquiry into the clerks at the Ministry of War. The newspapers also reported Vidocq as a man long suspected of having sinister links to various government departments. Such reports were quickly denied and the *Gazette des Tribunaux* wrote that Vidocq was still at large and could be seen wandering about the Palais de Justice.

The worries of the authorities were twofold. First, there was the power base Vidocq was building, and, second, there were his money-lending activities. A good deal of the business was with government employees and in return there were fears that he was obtaining secrets in addition to the interest payments. There was also speculation that he might be selling on the secrets:

> This affair is becoming daily more intricate assuming a more serious turn than was at first supposed. The former chief of the safety police had formed, in Paris, an extensive establishment, to which the dupes of swindlers, well known to Vidocq, were in the habit of applying for the recovery of their lost property. By providing him with a certain percentage, they were sure, if not of getting back their money at least of securing their debtor. Vidocq derived a very handsome income from his undertaking;

---

[12] *Gazette des Tribunaux*, June 23, November 23, 1835.
[13] APP. E/a 90 (16).

he kept up a regular intercourse with men placed in situations to be well informed on various subjects; he had, in short, organised in the capital a sort of private police. He likewise undertook some money transactions and by accommodating officers of the Administration with sums they wanted he contrived to be informed by them in a variety of secret details. At a moment when several foreign Governments are known to keep up in France a numerous and active police, the facilities thus afforded Vidocq to come at important information are not without danger. We hope the conduct of the late chief of the safety police will be mightily investigated. The Government must show no weakness. We do not suppose that foreign agents care for anything in the affair until they might be concerned and the bare possibility thereof imposes on the Government imperious obligations.[14]

The confiscated papers should have been sealed in his presence and handed to the Ministry of Justice. In an effort to remedy the omission Vidocq was ordered to report to the Préfecture but he refused. On this occasion he knew what he was doing. He lodged a series of complaints against the Commissaires and followed them up on December 18 with another complaint, one against the Prefect Delessert. He had, however, committed one serious error of judgement. When approached by a Palais-Royal jeweller, one Tugot, to try to retrieve the proceeds of a theft, he asked for his 15 percent recovery fee up front. On December 19, 1837, a count of fraud was added to the allegations against Vidocq. Now, in a brilliant stroke, he retained the young and contentious barrister Charles Ledru who had appeared for the defense in a number of cases arising out of the 1832 troubles in which Vidocq and his police officers had featured.

Ledru, a committed Republican and a devout Roman Catholic, a noted swordsman and a fine advocate, disliked Vidocq and all he stood for. He had appeared for Louis Alibaud, executed the previous year for his attempt on the life of Louis-Philippe.[15] Nine years later, in 1845, he ran into considerable trouble with his whole-hearted and continuing defense of the Abbé Contrafatto, a possible victim of one of the many miscarriages of justice of the period. He unfortunately overextended himself on this occasion, writing a letter to the Abbé which suggested that witnesses had been

---

[14] *Le Commerce*, quoted in *The Times*, December 7, 1837.
[15] On June 25, 1936, near the Tuileries, the twenty-six-year-old Alibaud fired at Louis-Philippe at almost point-blank range. Incredibly, the King was unharmed. See Chapter 19.

got at. A newspaper published the letter, as a result of which he was disbarred.[16]

When Vidocq approached him in late 1837 he was inclined to refuse the brief. Years later he would explain his initial refusal, saying that he would only accept the case if Vidocq made a donation of 1,000 francs to the Sisters of St. Vincent de Paul. On December 12, Vidocq wrote to Ledru saying:

> I chose you to defend me because you are one of the advocates who attacked my actions when in office most firmly.
>
> I recall that not only to ask for your support; I want my counsel to be my first judge, and my severest. I need only tell you that I have nothing to fear.[17]

Vidocq said he would call on Ledru between three and five in the afternoon and, when he did so, he produced a receipt signed by a Sister Henriette on behalf of the Mother Superior. It was the beginning of a friendship which would last until the end of Vidocq's life.

On December 13 the magistrate, Fleury, signed a warrant for Vidocq's arrest and it was executed by Jenneson, the Commissaire of Police, with Allard and Louis Canler in attendance. Vidocq went to Sainte-Pélagie prison, where he spent Christmas and the New Year awaiting the investigation of the examining magistrate, M. Legonidec. There were in effect three charges laid against him. The first was obtaining money by false pretenses; the second was corrupting members of the Civil Service; and the third accused him of usurping public functions. It was a deliberate blow aimed at Vidocq's agency.

---

[16] The Sicilian-born, twenty-eight-year-old Abbé Joseph Contrafatto was convicted in October 1828 of indecently assaulting Hortense Lebon, the five-year-old daughter of the widow of a former Colonel of the Empire. The Abbé, who seems to have been something of a rake, denied the charges, saying the child had come to his room of her own accord and he had merely given her sugar. There was much prejudicial evidence about the women in his rooms to whom he was, he said, giving overnight Italian lessons. Although there was some medical evidence there is also suspicion that the case was one of anti-clericism and there was, seemingly, a deathbed recantation of her evidence by the *veuve* Lebon. Ledru spent a good deal of effort trying to have the conviction overturned. Remarkably Contrafatto seems to have been quite well treated by other prisoners during his sentence. He took prayers in his cell and had a statue of Our Lady of Loreto by his bed which was in one of the best rooms at Bicêtre before his transfer to the galley. Contrafatto's sentence of life with hard labor was gradually reduced and he was released after seventeen years although the conviction was never quashed. See *Gazette des Tribunaux*, October 16, 1827; Froment, "Contrafato et Molitor," in *La Police dévoilée;* Charles Ledru, *Mystères de procès de l'Abbé Contrafatto.*

[17] Charles Ledru, *La Vie, la mort et les derniers moments du Vidocq après sa confession à l'heure suprême,* p. 5.

On January 4, Vidocq wrote a defense to Legonidec setting out his stall. The affair was, he wrote, principally because of the work he had done bringing twenty-thousand criminals to the courts. The police were jealous. He had also been concentrating on the swindlers who were now infesting Paris. He had denounced false counts and marquises, cheats who had awarded themselves honors. In turn these men had pushed false stories about him into the newspapers.

The hearings before Legonidec often included violent quarrels between Ledru and Vidocq, one of which ended with a handsome flowery written apology:

> Diogenes, philosopher of cynic memory, lantern in hand sought an honest man throughout Athens and found him not.
>
> Happier than he, I have found one in the Modern Babylon whom I love and respect. That man is you Charles Ledru.
>
> Please, monsieur, do not forget that the respect of Vidocq is a cross of merit which very few people possess.[18]

Three hundred and fifty witnesses were examined by the magistrate, including those called by Ledru. Vidocq's witnesses included the magistrate Zangiacomi, who had conducted the investigations against the Republicans in 1832 and against the Corsican-born assassin Joseph Fieschi four years later.[19] He was heavily in favor of the ex-Chef de Sûreté, as was the Procurator-General, Franck-Carré. In February 1837 Legonidec ruled there was no case for Vidocq to answer and he was released. Never a man to sit on his hands Vidocq responded with a poster:

Liberté !!!

de

Vidocq

"Hatred of rogues! Boundless devotion to trade"

and so forth.

There was, however, one concession to caution. In future every Vidocq agent would carry a signed commission.[20] There were also counter-attacks on the press complaining about the excesses of

---

[18] Ibid.
[19] See Chapter 19.
[20] BHVP, MS 2928, Dossier 18.

journalism which, he believed, had brought about his imprisonment. He sent letters to three newspapers publicly thanking Zangiacomi for his support and saying the world would be hearing from him soon.[21]

Vidocq was now in his sixties but his energy remained boundless. In November 1839 the agency was moved to bigger and better premises at 13 galerie Vivienne. Even in his sixties Vidocq was a formidable man to cross physically, as one of his employees, Lobstein, discovered. On February 2, 1841, he brought an action against the great man saying that he had been hit on the head, in the stomach and on the chest when trying to make a report which clearly displeased Vidocq. Poor Lobstein had been knocked through a window, breaking three panes of glass. Now he claimed 600 francs as compensation for having to take to his bed. Not so, said Vidocq. He had only thumped him once; and besides, the report had been so ill-produced that it had been well deserved. The Sixth Chamber took a lenient view of Vidocq's conduct. Lobstein's claim was reduced to sixty francs and Vidocq was fined an additional fifty francs.[22]

Overall the agency prospered mightily but Vidocq was careless in the way he made enemies. He always had Canler to contend with and he needlessly made an enemy out of Delessert while not helping his cause with Allard either. Delessert's brother had been robbed and the police had failed to retrieve the stolen goods. Delessert's brother wrote under an assumed name and address, asking for Vidocq's help. The property was recovered by Vidocq who, knowing full well the identity of his client, was unable to resist tweaking noses and sent it to him at his real address.

The opportunity for the authorities finally to put paid to Vidocq came in the case of Champaix, a swindler who worked a version of what, in modern terms, is known as a long-firm fraud. Acting through an intermediary, Landier, Champaix obtained trade references, bought goods on credit and sold them at a considerable discount to the tradesmen who had so kindly supplied him with the references. The suppliers offered Vidocq 45 percent of any money recovered. Vidocq let it be known he was interested in the case and on August 11, 1842, the intermediary Landier came to the offices at galerie Vivienne to ask for 25 percent of Vidocq's share if he could find Champaix for him. Perhaps unwisely Vidocq agreed.

[21] BHVP, MS 2928, Dossiers 21, 22; *Galignani's Messenger,* March 7, 1838.
[22] *Gazette des Tribunaux,* February 3, 1841; *L'Estafette,* February 4, 1841.

On information received, as the police would say, early the next morning Vidocq and one of his agents, Gouffé, were waiting at the corner of the rue du Bac opposite the Pont Royal. Landier's information was correct, for there was Champaix. Vidocq went to one side, Gouffé to the other, and Vidocq showed Champaix some notes of hand signed by the swindler, indicating that these needed to be discussed. A cab was taken to the offices where Champaix signed papers acknowledging his debts and gave Vidocq a draft for 2,200 francs. In return Champaix was given five francs for his supper. To all appearances the matter was satisfactorily resolved from the point of view of all parties.

Not so. Five days later, on August 17, seventy-five officers, led by Canler and Eloin, Commissaire at the Préfecture, swooped on the bureau and arrested Vidocq and Gouffé on charges of false pretences, false arrest and sequestration of property. Files were seized and his business plate was removed from the door. Vidocq went to the Conciergerie to await his trial. Regarded as the worst of the Parisian prisons at the time, life there was particularly daunting. There was a wait of a fortnight for a room with a bed and a prisoner paid eighteen francs a month for the privilege. When the river rose it reached the level of the prison floor and every wall streamed with humidity. Vidocq's wife, the faithful Fleuride, who throughout his months on remand was endeavoring to manage the bureau, wrote to the Prefect asking permission to see her husband. Permission was refused.

That October Vidocq wrote complaining that the damp was affecting his health. Now he had both catarrh and rheumatism. He was, after all, now sixty-seven. A medical report by the police doctor said there was no need for him to be moved. It was only after Fleuride's third petition that she was even allowed to see him.

The hearings before the examining magistrate continued throughout the winter. Ledru recommended that Vidocq be defended by Jules Favre, one of the senior members of the Bar. Finally the hearing was set for May 3, 1843.[23] The Advocate General would be Vidocq's old enemy Joël Anspach, who had been successful in the defense in November 1839 of the case Vidocq had personally brought against

---

[23] Captain Gronow said of Favre, "[He] is a great favourite; an acute and intellectual pleader, he is employed by all parties; but his ultra-liberal views are not always relished. He is a fluent speaker, and has the tact of making juries attentive to him; for he has a plain straightforward manner of speaking, and his language is pure and correct." *The Reminiscences and Recollections of Caption Gronow*, p. 292.

Prince Charles-Louis-Gaspard de Rohan-Rochefort for recovery of debt.[24]

The case against Vidocq, Gouffé, Landier and, in his absence, Tartière, on whom the draft signed by Champaix had been drawn, was heard by M. Barbou in what was the equivalent of the police court rather than the assizes. In theory this was a victory for Favre but the court still had far greater powers of sentencing than the English equivalent. The courtroom was packed for Vidocq's appearance, with counsel having trouble finding room on the benches because of the number of witnesses in court, let alone the spectators. Vidocq appeared dressed entirely in black except for a white cravat; even his gloves were black. He carried a green briefcase, and a young man, described as his secretary, was allowed to sit next to him to assist with the papers.

The case, at least against Vidocq and Gouffé, was simple. Vidocq had arrested Champaix in the rue du Bac, "In the name of the law." He had also seized him by the coat. Champaix had, according to the prosecution, then asked to be taken to the King's Procurator and had been told it was nothing to do with the man. He had been put in a cab and driven to the galerie Vivienne where he had been searched from head to toe. His day had been spent in effective custody until six in the evening when, to secure his release, he had signed the draft and other papers – false arrest, false imprisonment, and sequestration. Even allowing that Champaix would put the best possible construction on things in his own favor, it does have the ring of truth to it. And many people would not blame Vidocq in the slightest.

Champaix had been arrested for fraud two days later and had at once told all, to the horror, indignation and joy of the police. The case had also expanded. Now it was no longer a simple matter of Vidocq against Champaix. There had been an investigation into the general conduct of the agency and with it allegations against Vidocq of overcharging, abduction of young women on instructions from their parents and placing them in convents, and the purchase of decorations on a client's

---

[24] Earlier, a member of the Prince's family had been involved in the *affaire* of Marie-Antoinette's necklace, an out-and-out swindle by "Countess" Jeanne de la Motte. Boehmer, the court jeweller, had made the piece as a speculation and needed to sell it. Cardinal Louis de Rohan wanted to win the approval of Marie-Antoinette and the countess and her associates persuaded the pair that Marie-Antoinette did indeed want the piece. The Cardinal signed a contract on the Queen's behalf and de la Motte made off with the necklace. Later de la Motte escaped from prison and made her way to England where she wrote her memoirs. See Thomas Carlyle, *The Diamond Necklace*. Joël Anspach, also known as Paul-Léon, was born around 1800 in Metz. Later he became the only Jewish magistrate in Paris. He wrote the highly regarded *De la Procédure devant les Cours d'Assizes*.

behalf. In fact, all the things which make the newspapers worth reading. Favre was, however, confident of an acquittal.

A French criminal procedure is conducted on an inquisitorial basis, unlike the English accusatorial one. Questions are put by the court and if advocates wish to cross-examine then their questions must also be put through the judge. Consequently, instead of the prosecution calling its witnesses, Vidocq was the first to give evidence, explaining himself from the time he was employed by Henry until his arrest. And everything which could be held against him was. His dismissal in 1828 from the Sûreté was an early point. No, he had not been dismissed; his resignation was on file. What about the *brevet* on the notepaper of his agency? That was to do with the unfalsifiable paper. Vidocq was ever a chancer. No one had told him he couldn't put that on the detective agency notepaper. Surely someone should have done so.

As for the arrest of Champaix, as might be expected his explanation differed. He had merely said, "Good morning M. Champaix. Have you any money for your creditors?" Nothing at all had been said about the "name of the law." Champaix had asked who he was and Vidocq had properly given his name. It was Champaix who suggested going to the galerie Vivienne. He had been under no obligation at all. Before they took a cab they had passed a police post. Champaix could have run in for help. Once in the cab Champaix had begun to weep. At the office he could have left at any time he wished. Favre produced witnesses to say that Champaix was left unguarded in a large room looking onto a terrace. Another witness, Pichon, said that he had in fact met Champaix the next day and he had been well pleased with the way Vidocq had sorted things out. Barbou was not impressed. "He was under the sway of the terror your name and unexpected appearance had inspired in him." And possibly he was right.

Vidocq, as the ex-police chief, explained from long experience on both sides of the fence what he surmised had happened when Champaix had been arrested. He had been pressured into giving evidence against Vidocq in return for favorable treatment. Unfortunately, one of his own agents, Ulysse Perrenoud, then gave evidence that he had been put to guard the unfortunate swindler while Vidocq had him at the agency. For his pains he was accused of being a police spy. Now things went off at a tangent; witnesses were called on this diversionary point and it was not always clear who had got at whom. One woman, Mme Bonnefoy, was expected to say that she had heard a bet struck in her bar that Perrenoud was a police spy. She knew nothing of anything, an ignorance she announced in advance of being asked a first question. Another witness was called to say he had heard Perrenoud boast in the bar that he was indeed a spy, something which seems a foolish thing to do. Another witness said Perrenoud had boasted that he had stolen papers from Vidocq's office. The agency seems to have had its own suspicion of the man because he was followed and seen to go into the Préfecture. When questioned, Perrenoud denied he was a spy and said that, aware of the surveillance, he had used this as a diversionary tactic.

Champaix was forgotten and things turned to the much more interesting subject of the kidnapping of young women and placing them in convents. The allegation had been that the first girl had been lured from the theatre by one of his female agents and imprisoned for forty-eight hours. Nonsense. Vidocq had a ready explanation. She had been placed in the convent not by him but by her parents. She had escaped and was now appearing nightly on the stage and living quite openly with her lover, the comte de Sarda.

And the second girl? There was nothing really sinister in it at all. The lady in question had been married to a brutal husband. She had left him to live with a much kinder man. Overcome by remorse and shame she had abandoned this second man and her children and placed herself in a convent. Vidocq had merely been asked to trace her, which he did. She was now happily reunited with her lover.

But there were other cases which Anspach had in mind. What about the postmaster who had hired Vidocq to kidnap a young girl? Vidocq had delayed things and raised such apparent difficulties that the post-master had given up. And a jealous woman from Argenteuil? This was a woman who saw mistresses behind every flowerpot. Vidocq had been retained to watch her husband and was able to provide him with such a clean bill of amatory health that the mania had been cured and they were happy again.

Now it was the question of the purchase of honors. The suggestion was that a marquis Duvivier wished to be awarded the Légion d'honneur but had done nothing to merit it. He approached Vidocq's office, which came up with the Order of the Spur and the Sultane d'Eldi. For this Vidocq had charged 3,000 francs and the prosecution's case was that this was a fraud. In the event the marquis returned both awards. Vidocq explained that there was little money left after he had paid the insiders in the honors office. The marquis had in fact paid 8,000 francs but Vidocq had returned 5,000. This was certainly a weak strand in Vidocq's defence. Even with the most favorable explanation put upon things it was extremely dodgy behavior.

In fact, while it may have been easy to explain each individual case the cumulative effect was wearing on the defense. A criminal can explain how he was found with the stolen goods, how he was identifed by three witness to the robbery, how he made admissions to the police, how his photograph appeared on the bank's camera. To each of these he may have a perfectly acceptable answer – innocently minding things for a friend, mistaken identity, lying police, he was a customer of the bank and so on – but what he cannot do is to get over them all together.

Then came a string of witnesses for Vidocq, all expressing their satisfaction with Vidocq and the agency and the generosity afforded them. There had been an interest-free loan to Antoine Braud of the Opéra Comique; Vidocq had collected money for Chatel, another theatre manager; and other grateful individuals included an expert from the Commercial Tribunal, as well as Vidocq's doctor, Dornier, who would be with him for the next fifteen years. Ledru himself gave evidence, relating the story of Sisters of Charity, and also another about how Vidocq had personally guarded Franck-Carré, the Procurator-General, in the riots of 1838. Vidocq had himself stood sentry when he heard that an attack was to be made on the Franck-Carré household. The story had not, in fact, come from an unusually modest Vidocq but from two of Ledru's other clients. There was also the story of how he had "saved" the singer Julia Grisi.

Quite how he had done this was never fully explained but she was certainly a woman who needed saving. Described as a beauty with a voice to match, she was the star of the London and Paris opera of the 1820s to the end of the 1850s. She appeared in London in all 925 nights singing *Norma* 79 times, *Lucrezia Borgia* 100 and making 92 appearances in *I Puritani*. She married the impoverished vicomte Gérard de Melcy, and so bought herself a title at what would prove to be great emotional and financial cost. The service Vidocq provided may have been to prevent a duel between the count Giovanni Mateo de Candia, who sang as Mario, and her estranged husband. Or it may have been in one of her many court battles with de Melcy.

There had been an earlier duel and from it stemmed many of her problems. It came about because of the interception in London in

June 1838 of a letter to Grisi from Lord Castlereagh, the nephew of the former British Prime Minister. From then, until her death in 1869 in Berlin the pair fought a series of financial court cases, almost all of which were won by de Melcy.[25]

Anspach urged the court to find Vidocq guilty on all charges. Here was a charlatan, he said, a vain man who would take work, however dubious, and who by his conduct was a menace to family life. Favre, of course, took a wholly different view. The court had the evidence of dozens of witnesses as to Vidocq's worth. The only real complainant was Champaix. Everything else was a replay of the 1837 case. No single person had come to the court claiming Vidocq had robbed him. On the contrary, he had spent thirty years devoting himself to justice. He was confident, he said – breaking an accepted rule of at least English advocacy – that Vidocq was not a man capable of knowingly doing evil. He was also confident that the court would judge him only on the facts.

His confidence in Vidocq himself may have been justified. His confidence in the court, however, was misplaced. A verdict of guilty on the major counts was returned and, given his previous conviction for forgery – despite the pardon – Vidocq was sentenced to five years' imprisonment and fined 3,000 francs. Lantier was sentenced to two years and Gouffé was acquitted. Vidocq nodded to the judge and left court without a word.

Vidocq appealed. Now his political friends were prepared to weigh in. Lamartine, also a friend of Balzac, intervened and new counsel was obtained. Now with the advocate Landrin retained for the case it was a very different story. Landrin's argument was that the judges had been wrong in listening to the story of Vidocq the convict and legend, rather than the Vidocq of reality. In Landrin's words, Vidocq was the saviour of the weak and put upon; of girls threatened by seduction and worse; of those being blackmailed; in fact, he was a living saint by any other name. It is easy to believe that the whole thing had been pre-arranged. It was a question of "The Court is with you M. Landrin." In a matter of minutes and, by the time he turned his attention to Champaix, he

---

[25] On June 15, 1838, de Melcy sought out Castlereagh for a duel and it was arranged for 4 a.m. at Wormwood Scrubs. The parties arrived but an argument broke out over the pistols to be used. It was felt that if the duellists had their own there might be an unfair advantage. A brace was bought and the duel took place at 10 a.m. when Castlereagh was hit in the arm above the wrist. In turn he fired in the air. He had by then handed a letter to his second exonerating the diva and saying that this was the first time he had communicated with her. De Melcy indicated he was satisfied. It was without doubt, however, the end of the marriage. See *The Times*, June 21, 1842; for an account of Grisis' life see Elizabeth Forbes, *Mario and Grisi*.

had persuaded the judges that the convictions should be quashed.[26] Vidocq was released from the Conciergerie on July 22, 1843. He would only return to prison on one further occasion. Vidocq plastered the streets of Paris with another series of posters this time headed "Resurrection!" Now he needed some favorable publicity. Despite the efforts of his wife, Vidocq's stay in the Conciergerie had badly damaged the agency. Having Vidocq in charge was one thing, having his wife in charge was a completely different matter. Financially, he was no longer in the shape he had been. His had been an expensive trial and in addition to his own he paid the costs of his fellow accused.

Overall, publicity had not been good and now the number of clients started steadily to decline. It had not helped that the public had been reminded of the allegations relating to the investigation into a particular divorce case. On August 18 a Mme G. petitioned for a judicial separation and told the court how, when she had been in a convent at Versailles, Vidocq, calling himself de St-Firmin and describing himself as a friend of the family, tried to trick her out of documents which supported her case. She was granted the separation and Vidocq wrote to the newspapers the following week saying that while he had indeed called on her it had been under his own name and he had taken no papers.[27]

Then, in the autumn of 1843, Gouffé, described as Vidocq's secretary and who had, with Fleuride, kept the agency afloat for the previous year, was prosecuted for obtaining money by false pretenses. Vidocq had sacked him on September 1.

Possibly because of these cases the authorities were not yet done with Vidocq. On September 21 Louis Fresne, the Commissaire of the Police, ordered Vidocq to report to the Préfecture as he was illegally in Paris in breach of an order of July 7, 1806. So far as the Préfecture was concerned the letters he had obtained to help his 1818 pardon were false. This did smack somewhat of persecution and Vidocq had no intention of taking it lying down. Vidocq was in fine form, firing off another pamphlet:

> An act of iniquitous persecution emanating from the administration of the police has just hit me anew in the middle of my works and at the breast of my family.

---

[26] The conviction against Lantier was also quashed. See *Gazette des Tribunaux,* April 29, May 4, 5, 6, 11, 14, July 23, 1843.

[27] *Gazette des Tribunaux,* September 19, 26, 1843. Bruno Roy-Henri gives her name as Guérin. *Vidocq du bagne à la préfecture,* p. 301.

Released a few days ago from the punishment of prison where I had been detained for eleven months, detention which a recent judgement declared without foundation and justice, I have not lifted a single recrimination. I was seeking to rebuild the ruins of my business, which has been odiously broken up; I was trying to reassure my clients whose interests by my long absence have been compromised and to restore them my help which my persecutors have vainly tried to hamper. When all of a sudden M. le préfet de police resurrecting against me a conviction of more than forty-six years believed it was possible to interrupt my business, my family, my home, to try – despite the judgement which set me free – to make me walk to his whim at the age of seventy without resources, support, money in the corners of France where the spite of an authority, spiteful and pestering, may torment me at its ease.[28]

Vidocq, like Fossard and other released convicts, had the right to be bitter. Along with their yellow passports they could not live in Paris or in certain other major towns or within twelve kilometres of the coast or a frontier. A released convict could not change his residence without the consent of the local Prefect. It was a regime thought to be a prime cause of recidivism.

On September 23 he went to the Salle des Pas Perdus at the Palais de Justice where he told journalists that he would not obey the order and was seeking a declaration that the measures taken against him were illegal. Ledru, Landrin and others rallied round and drew up a memorandum of their opinions on the illegality of the order. For once Vidocq had the sympathy of both the Bar and the public. The matter never came to court. The Procurator-General intervened and the order was withdrawn. On November 28 Gouffé was acquitted of the last of the charges but more damage had been done.[29]

By 1846 Vidocq was toying with the idea of selling the agency. Unfortunately there were few reputable buyers about. Alexander Pierie, of 237 rue St-Jacques, who ran another debt-collecting agency, was willing to pay 19,000 francs by installments but sadly he was himself arrested for fraud shortly after making the offer. Another potential purchaser was D'haine, a former police officer of 5 rue Bailleul, who approached Vidocq on February 1, 1847. That bid also came to nothing and the agency closed that year.[30]

---

[28] BHVP MS 2928, Dossier 33.

[29] *Gazette des Tribunaux,* November 29, 1843.

[30] BHVP, MS 2928, Dossiers 56, 57. Many detective agencies in Paris in that era were clearly built on shifting sands. Another owned by a lawyer, Maître Plique, closed when he was obliged to flee his creditors.

Chapter 17

VIDOCQ
IN POLITE SOCIETY

*In which our hero writes his memoirs and other books – meets
great men of letters and social reformers as well as
the public hangman*

MEANWHILE, ALREADY something of what would today be called a "B" list celebrity, with the publication of his *Mémoires* in 1828 Vidocq moved into the life of the literati. Vidocq may not have liked his memoirs but others certainly did. They were an immediate success: "The book must have already moved down from the drawing room to the servants' hall, from the reading rooms to every shop counter in town," enthused the *Nouveaux Journal de Paris*.[1] Suddenly, the argot of the underworld was spreading throughout polite society.[2] Within a year it had been translated into English. The next year the police officer Froment produced another version as well as his own *Mémoires* which recounted some of the later incidents from his viewpoint. The year 1829 also saw an anti-Vidocq tract, *Mémoires d'un forçat ou Vidocq dévoilé*, allegedly by the former convict Malgaret but in reality by two journalists. Other versions of the manuscript flowed thick and fast. In 1830 came *Le Paravoleur* for which Vidocq's name was simply stolen, probably by a man called Laumier. In theory a warning to country and suburban bumpkins of the dangers of city life, it was little more than erotica. Although Vidocq tried to have it suppressed it ran to several editions before a court case in 1831, by which time the publisher was long gone.[3]

---

[1] October 28, 1828.
[2] See, for example, Prosper Mérimée, *Correspondance générale*, t. I p. 34, in which he writes of a duchess telling a peeress about "nicked" earrings.
[3] Samuel Edwards, *The Vidocq Dossier*, p. 105.

In 1836 Vidocq published *Les Voleurs*, possibly a rather more realistic book than his actual memoirs. Nowadays all Vidocq's books would be called faction. *Les Voleurs* profited from the concept of *Le Paravoleur* because the general drift of its theme can be taken from the book's fashionably long subtitle, which translates as *Physiology of their lives and language. A work which unveils the ruses of all rogues, destined to become the vade-mecum of all honest men.* After the introduction the first section is a dictionary of current criminal slang which in some cases was expanded into ten or more pages of the exploits of criminals and what Vidocq and his agency were doing to clamp down on them. The entry *Faisans* ran the better part of twenty-five pages in the original, much of it a puff for Vidocq's agency along with a tariff of his fees. Then came a classification of criminals and their methods coupled with diatribes against the penal and judicial systems.

There is little doubt that Vidocq had help with *Les Voleurs* and there are suggestions that he did not write any of it at all. He must, however, have provided the basics, probably to the ghostwriter Alfred Lucas.[4] The book was, again, a great success. He did not trouble himself with a publisher; he had had sufficient problems with Tenon and L'Héritier over the *Mémoires. Les Voleurs* came in two octavo volumes sold at a stiff fifteen francs. It sold extremely well and went into a second edition. Some of its success was perhaps due to Vidocq's practice of insisting that any borrower from his money-lending business purchase five or more copies of the work as part of the advanced money.

By the 1830s Vidocq was cutting a dash in Paris and it was then that he met Benjamin Appert, the social reformer, who on the accession of Louis-Philippe had grown in stature as a courtier. Vidocq was a regular guest at the dinners he gave at his homes on the quai d'Orsay and Neuilly and on one occasion suggested a somewhat unusual man be invited to dine. Appert concurred and the invitation for Monsieur de Paris, the hangman Charles-Henri Sanson, was to be for Good Friday.[5]

It is unimaginable that the chief hangman in England at the time would have been received into any sort of society, polite or otherwise.

---

[4] J. M. Quérard, *Les Supercheries littéraires dévoilées.*

[5] Benjamin-Nicolas-Marie Appert (1797–1847), a philanthropist and prison reformer, was a member of the Société Royale des Prisons de France. He started life as a teacher of soldiers and then of prisoners. Unfortunately, two of his pupils escaped and it was into La Force for him, where he experienced the degradation of prison life for himself. He appears under his own name in Stendhal's *Le Rouge et le Noir* (1830).

He was William Chalcraft who lived in Devizes Street, Hoxton, east London, and whose hobbies were skittles and breeding rabbits. He owned a pony which followed him around like a dog. He appears to have had none of the demeanor of Charles-Henri Sanson, but at the close of the Sheriff's dinner on the last day of Sessions he was allowed into the dining room where he was given a glass of wine with which he toasted his patrons and "expressed with becoming modesty his gratitude for past favours and his hopes for favours to come." Despite forty-five years in the job he was not unduly talented and a number of his clients met agonizing deaths as they strangled simply because he had failed to calculate properly the length of the drop.[6]

Even in France such an invitation was unusual. The day before the dinner Appert was working in his study when his secretary announced a man who would not give his name. He was dressed in black with an old-fashioned lace jabot and a heavy gold watch chain. The secretary thought he might be a suburban mayor. Appert had him shown into the drawing room and asked his name. The words came rushing out:

> Monsieur, I have respected you for many years, but if I had not been assured that you had been so extremely kind as to invite me to dinner on Friday, I should never have permitted myself to come to your house. I am the Public Executioner.

Adding that:

> On account of my duties I lead a family life and receive no one but my colleagues and assistants, who are relatives of mine for the most part.

His reticence was in no way unsurprising. The Sansons and other public executioners lived very much a closeted life in France. A son took over from his father, and a daughter would be expected to marry into another executioner's family or for her husband to take over duties

---

[6] William Ballantine, *Some Experiences of a Barrister's Life*, p. 88. Nor, in fairness, did Sanson and other French executioners always display great talent. One execution Charles-Henri's father botched was that of the comte de Lally-Tollendal who, after the capture of Pondicherry, was accused of misappropriating public funds and was sentenced to death in the summer of 1766. The man's hair had not been cut properly and it deflected the blade. Lally got up and glared at Sanson. Barbara Levy, *Legacy of Death*.

On another occasion at Saint-Flour, Gabriel Mique was not bound properly and escaped. He barricaded himself in a courtyard and pelted the hangmen and others with paving stones until gendarmes were ordered in to shoot him. *Gazette des Tribunaux*, March 23, 1832.

if there was no son. Charles Jean-Baptiste, the great-grandfather of the last incumbent, was so young when he succeeded his father on October 2, 1726, that he was given an assistant, Prudhomme, but the presence of the child even at the age of seven was required to sanction, if not sanctify, the proceedings.

In the provinces a hangman was not expected to live in the town in which he worked, for he would find difficulty in obtaining lodgings or even a baker prepared to sell him bread. He was, however, entitled to a *droit de havage*, a toll on corn, fruit and other merchandise sold in the markets. He was also required to administer floggings. Other duties included branding, fitting neck pillories and scolds' bridles, iron cages placed on a woman's head with a metal plate which held down the tongue. The most feared punishment was breaking on the wheel, in which the culprit was spread over the wheel, with arms and legs attached to the spokes. Each limb was broken in turn with a heavy iron bar. If the court decreed, after a period he could be killed either by strangulation with a thin cord or a blow to the heart. This was known as the *retentum*.

Appert, whose manners were considered impeccable, reassured Sanson that he was expected. It seems that the old man feared Vidocq had played a joke on him when he invited him and he wanted to make sure he would be welcome.

The dinner was a huge success. Sanson was seated on Appert's right hand and Vidocq on the left. Other guests included Lord Durham and Sir John Bowring, the linguist and explorer. Durham asked how many heads Sanson had cut off to date and he replied, "About three hundred and sixty, milord." One of his clients had been Marie-Antoinette. Bowring wanted to know the gruesome details:

My assistants secure the patient, cut his hair and prepare the baskets to receive his head and body. I am simply present to see that all goes well and swiftly. My work is confined to releasing the cord holding the blade which cuts off the head.

Vidocq seems to have enjoyed himself, mildly teasing Sanson at the dinner table, commenting that, while the executioner was a good fellow, he found it odd to be dining at the same table and telling the man that as Head of the Sûreté he had given him plenty of work. Sanson, for his part, was happy to explain some of the mysteries of the profession. He believed there was sometimes still suffering after decapitation. "The face is convulsed, the eyes roll, the head is as if it were enraged."[7]

Naturally, the guests, and in particular Lord Durham, wished to see the machine in all its glory. Sanson lived in seclusion with his family in the rue des Marais du Temple and their Lordships visited him one Saturday. It was another great success. Durham had been so enthusiastic and told so many people that half the English colony followed Durham and Appert in their carriages. On the way Appert had some difficulty in persuading Durham that it would not be appropriate to buy a sheep for a working demonstration. Instead some bales of straw were used. Vidocq was on hand to help Sanson and his son explain the intricacies of the machine.[8]

The last in the Sanson line, Henri-Clément, fell from the high standard of his ancestors. He was constitutionally unfit for the job and would stand and watch the spectacle, rarely taking part, sometimes crying and his face simultaneously ashen and blotched. Fortunately for him between 1840 and 1847 there were only eighteen executions. In his memoirs he recounts how he was relieved to have been given the sack on March 18, 1847. For the April 1846 execution of Lecomte, the head ranger of the forest at Fontainbleau, guillotined for the attempted assassination of the Royal Family, Sanson's equipment had been redeemed from his creditors to enable him to carry out his work. Now separated from his wife, he became a great gambler, often in the company of the actor Frédéric Lemaître. There were also suggestions that he was sacked because of his homosexuality: "He liked young men and gambling. The two penchants cost him dearly." He died on January 25, 1889, and is buried in the family grave in Montmartre cemetery.[9]

For the rest of Vidocq's life Charles Ledru continued to dine him, when he would regale the other guests with stories from his past. "He spoke of his prowess," said Ledru, "as a general might have recounted his battles." It was Ledru who wrote that whenever the wealthy Sir

---

[7] Benjamin Appert, "Un diner chez M. Appert," in *Le Figaro*, June 1, 1857. The dinner must have been painful for Sanson. The life of an executioner was a solitary one. When James Rousseau, the editor of the *Gazette des Tribunaux*, visited Henri-Clément Sanson in 1844, Sanson did not offer him snuff. Rousseau took out his own *tabatière* but Sanson drew back. A *bourreau* could not touch another man's possessions. At the end of the interview Rousseau held out his hand and again Sanson flinched. An executioner could not touch the flesh of any but his own family and his victims.

[8] For the Sansons' family life see Barbara Levy, *Legacy of Death*.

[9] C. Gury, *L'Honneur professionel d'un bourreau homosexuel en 1847*. There were eighteen applicants for the job of executioner after his dismissal and Charles-André Ferey was appointed.

Francis Burdett went to Paris he made a point of dining with Vidocq at the Frères Proveçeaux in the rue Palais Royale. They were very much kindred spirits for Burdett was a champion of abolishing corporal punishment.[10] Vidocq also continued to see Appert, who rather used him as a guide to the underworld of Paris and went with him to see the Shrove Tuesday debaucheries of Courtille.

Lawyers and policemen have always been welcome guests at dinner tables for the stories they can tell. Vidocq may not have been the best writer in the world but he was certainly an engaging raconteur. One of the stories Vidocq told came about as a result of a complaint by Balzac, with whom he had been dining, and who lamented that, although people brought him plots, they were never complete. Vidocq claimed he had a perfectly rounded and finished plot for him.

The journalist Léon Gozlan recorded the story Vidocq then told, which in essence has him at the Préfecture on a writer's night eating chestnuts and drinking rum and white wine – apparently a regular occurrence – when around 1 a.m. a lady appeared with her maid. She wished to see the Prefect and bandied the name of Louis-Philippe. Her husband was in Bordeaux on business and she had been entertaining a Hungarian officer when he had dropped dead in her bed in the appropriately named rue de Bellechasse. She and her maid had dressed the body and had managed to put it into a cab which was waiting outside the Préfecture. Her husband, the count, was due back within the hour. The Prefect told Vidocq, who suggested it would be best if the man were found dead in the street, his money and jewelry taken. The lady apparently had qualms about this; nor was she in favor of burying the body. Vidocq said he would get the body back to the officer's lodgings.

The cab driver was asleep, huddled on his box, as Vidocq and another agent bundled the body out of the cab. The driver was woken up and told to take the women home, while Vidocq and his colleague more or less dragged the body from the quai des Orfèvres to the Pont Neuf, where they put it into another cab and told the driver to go to the officer's house on the rue Florentin. When the second driver reached

---

[10] Born in 1770, in 1806 Sir Francis Burdett, before his election to Parliament, fought a duel and later spent some time in the Tower of London after he had been accused of a breach of parliamentary privilege. He was sentenced to three months' imprisonment at Leicester Assizes and fined £2,000 following his support for the victims of the Peterloo massacre. In the *Dictionary of National Biography* he is described as having made free speech possible and being the perfect type of English gentleman. A fox-hunting squire, whose purse was open to good causes, he died in 1844.

the house and got down from his box he found the man dead and called out the servants. The death was attributed, possibly correctly, to apoplexy, and there was a fashionable funeral at the Madeleine. The countess reached home before her husband and sent Vidocq a diamond ring in gratitude. Later the count fought a duel in Zara and, although far the better swordsman, after twice disarming his opponent he allowed himself to be killed.

Balzac complained that the story was not complete but outside was the second cab driver, the man who had driven Vidocq to Balzac's home. Vidocq maintained it was the driver from the night of the death and they began to question him. He recalled that some time later he had found a letter in a leather wallet in the cab addressed to the countess. He drove round and gave it to a man and woman getting into another carriage. The man had read the letter, blanched and told the valet to give the cab driver two francs.

The story is full of basic improbabilities but there is a certain truth in it. Gozlan set the story in the winter of 1834–5 but by then Vidocq had left the police and Vidocq had reminded the cabman the incident occurred some twelve years earlier. The writer and editor Francis Lacassin places the incident as happening after the publication of the *Mémoires*. Jean Savant believed the man in question was not a Hungarian officer but possibly the man-about-Paris Charles Kinnaird Sheridan. The story has passed into literature as Guy de Maupassant's celebrated short story *L'Affaire* and has become a standard "body in the wrong bed" scenario.[11]

---

[11] E.g. *Le Rideau Cramoisie*. Léon Gozlan; "Une 'pêche de Montreuil' ou Vidocq à la table de Balzac" in *Balzac Chez Lui*; Jean Savant, *Le Procès de Vidocq*.

Chapter 18

VIDOCQ
AT THE THEATRE

*In which our hero becomes a patron of the stage – a great silent actor is
charged with murder and dies – art imitates life – Vidocq is taken up by
Balzac and the King takes umbrage – and plays are written about him*

NOT ALL VIDOCQ'S ADVENTURES with the stage were
great successes. Theatrical debtors tended to disappear without repaying loans. One transaction gives an insight into Vidocq's loan
arrangments. In 1841 the actor-impresario Joseph-Antoine Couderec,
who appeared in a number of highly popular pieces by Aubert, including
The Black Domino and *Crown Diamonds*, borrowed 2,000 francs,
repayable by July 6. Interest for the six months was to be 49 francs
but additionally there was a fixed fee of 110 francs to be added. By
July, Couderec had only managed to repay 150 francs and the loan was
extended, with the addition of another 120 francs interest. Now 2,129
was required to be paid in installments of 100 francs. He seems to
have defaulted again in April 1842 at the time he left France to appear
in Belgium and England. He did not return home until 1850, when
he appeared as Shakespeare in *Song of a Summer Night*, a serious
role which one critic thought "showed the breadth of his abilities," by
which time Vidocq seems to have let the matter slide.

Nor was Vidocq much luckier with Hippolyte-André-Jean-Baptiste,
whose great success was a piece entitled *Le Combat de Herman* and
who skipped off to Augsberg from where he wrote a piteous note
saying that the theatre to which he was contracted had gone bankrupt. Baptiste then moved to Weimar where he was in charge of
the orchestra until the arrival of Franz Liszt put him in the shade.
No more payments seem to have been forthcoming from him either.

An indirect involvement with the Ambigu Theatre at first proved no more financially successful. The file does, however, give a description of the agency's methods in tracing erring women. Vidocq was retained by a financier, one Bouglé, to produce a report on his mistress, Aimée Charles, whom he maintained at her address at 31 Notre-Dame de Lorrette, near what is now the Bourse, and who persuaded him that he was the father of her small boy. Now he suspected she was being unfaithful to him when he took his family to the countryside of a Sunday afternoon. He was right. Vidocq employed the agent known as the Satyr to follow her from her home. The Satyr was most impressed, reporting first that "She will need great care. She is like a snake you can't take your eyes off." Once she threw him off the trail by going straight to church but he was able to report that, more usually, she was going straight to the Ambigu at its new home on the boulevard St-Martin, where she was conducting a liaison with the producer-director Pierre-Etienne Cormon.[1] All this was duly reported back to Bouglé who clearly did not like what he had heard because he steadfastly ignored Vidocq's bills. The last of Vidocq's letters to him is a barely veiled threat of exposure in court proceedings.[2] The original Ambigu on the boulevard du Temple, which opened in 1769, burned down in 1827.

He fared rather better in his dealings with the poet, novelist and man of letters, the comte de Vigny. Regarded as having a secure marriage to a rich Englishwoman, nevertheless by 1835 Alfred de Vigny had a mistress, the celebrated actress Marie Dorval, with whom his relationship was deteriorating. On June 18 he employed Vidocq to spy on her and the great man discovered she was seeing Jules Sandeau, the one-time lover of George Sand, at his home on the rue du Bac on the Left Bank. Reconciliation followed quarrel followed reconciliation until the pair finally separated at the end of August. This time, however, Vidocq was paid and de Vigny used his services over the next three years.[3]

Vidocq was, of course, something of an actor manqué. Role-playing was mother's milk to him. Apart from his more workaday performances, in his time he appeared as a horse dealer, an archbishop, a duchess (possibly), a colonel of the Hussars and a Russian general.[4] Given his

---

[1] Born in Lyons on May 5, 1811, Cormon's greatest success was *Paris la Nuit*, which played with the actress Marie Boutin in the starring role.
[2] BHUP, MS 2982, Dossier 25.
[3] *Correspondence d'Alfred de Vigny*, t. III (1994) P.U.F., pp. 284–8 and 333.
[4] Jean Savant, *Les Voleurs*, p. 9.

enthusiasm for disguise it is not surprising that Vidocq was a patron of the theatre. When the players at the Ambigu went on strike for the payment of back wages it was he who advanced three million francs interest free so that performances could go ahead. He submitted a play but it was never produced and he also wanted to appear on the stage. He had, after all, proved himself a master of disguise; why not tread the boards? Throughout his life he mixed with actors and particularly actresses and one of his friends was the great Frédéric Lemaître, "The French Kean," who began his stage career with Jean Gaspard Deburau in what was called the Funambules. It was to Lemaître that he confided his ambition. Lemaître wrote in his diary, "Vidocq! His confidence! He consults me. He wants to go on the stage!"

The Théâtre des Funambules was situated on the old boulevard du Temple in Paris, known as the Boulevard du Crime because of the numbers of seductions, murders and deaths which seemed to occur nightly on stage.[5] The Funambules itself was created in 1816 by Michel Bertrand for tightrope walkers and acrobats but from around 1825 it began to play pantomines and light comedies with puppets, such as *The Red Egg and the White Egg* and the *Toys of Bric à Brac*. One peculiarity was that as each person came on stage he or she was required to perform a cartwheel or somersault. Another requirement was that, while the actors could sing, they were not allowed to speak. In this way they would not pose a threat to genuine theatre.[6]

In 1830 it achieved great fame with Jean Gaspard Deburau, who signed a contract in 1828, which tied him to the Théâtre des Funambules, for whom a number of writers such as Charles Nodier (*The Golden Dream*) and Champfleury (*Pierrot Marquis*) provided material.[7] Thanks to Deburau the theatre became immensely popular. Grand ladies mingled happily with criminals, and writers and artists mixed with *Les Enfants du Paradis*, the Children of the Gods,

---

[5] The theatre was situated at the eastern end of the boulevard near what is now République. It was destroyed in the reconstruction of Paris under the supervision of Haussmann. Sometimes, if rarely, the subject matter was considered too strong. Antoine Mingrat was a priest of fanatic austerity and violent lust who was found guilty of the murder of one of his young female penitents. He was condemned in 1822 but pardoned; he died in Fenestrelle in Sardinia three years later. Ferdinand Laloué and Henri Villemot wrote *Le Curé Mingrat* for the Cirque Olympique where it was produced in October 1830. It was regarded as too strong even for the Boulevard du Crime, where it provoked a critical response. It was not revived after its third performance.

[6] There was a similar requirement in the penny gaffs of late Victorian England where the performers could sing and sign, but if the action was too complicated they were obliged to hold up a banner describing the next moves. See James Greenwood, *The Wilds of London*.

[7] "Deburau," in *L'Histoire*, October 1998.

in the cheap balcony seats, all there to admire him. And, for that matter, to admire the stage effects which were often astonishing. The pantomimes and the fairy plays were staged with great care and cloth was not cut – there was no need. The theatre was a great financial success. Two performances were given on Sundays and holidays. The first two directors, the father and son MM. Bertrand, became millionaires.

When, on April 18, 1836, Jean Gaspard Deburau and his family were on an outing, he was approached by a man, his wife and an apprentice named Nicolas Florent Vielin. It seems the man could not believe his luck in seeing Deburau but the apprentice, who had been drinking, began calling the Pierrot names and some hours later, when they met again by chance, began abusing Deburau and shouting out, "Look at the Pierrot from the Funambules with his whore' and calling him "dummy" and "scarecrow." Deburau hit him on the head with his cane and Vielin died an hour later in the hospital. There was much sympathy for the actor if not for the fact that he received a speedy trial. Deburau was acquitted after a month in prison whereas a case of this kind would normally take at least a year. He had been a member of the National Guard and the officers and men of his company to a man wrote testimonials of his unfailing good humor. In fact this may have been somewhat misplaced for whatever he was on stage he was moody and uncommunicative by day. It was said of him that he only smiled at night. Subsequently he refused to play the Pierrot in Cot d'Orlan's pantomime *Chand d'habits* because it contained a murder.[8]

Deburau died at 3 a.m. during the night of June 16–17, 1846. The previous February he had had a fall on the stage during a benefit performance for him. A trap door initially failed to open but when he stamped his foot impatiently it opened suddenly and he fell, hitting his head on the stage. It was announced that he had been injured and

---

[8] Deburau and the Funambules were recalled in *Deburau* by Sacha Guitry, translated by Granville Barker with Robert Loraine as the Pierrot, which opened at the Ambassadors in London on November 3, 1921. It closed three weeks later after poor reviews. It is notable now perhaps only for an early appearance by Ivor Novello in a small role as The Young Man. Far more successful was Marcel Carné's loving cinematic reconstruction of the Boulevard du Crime, *Les Enfants du Paradis*, which featured the cream of the French stage of the period including Jean-Louis Barrault as Deburau, Arletty, Pierre Brasseur as Lemaître, Marcel Herrand and Maria Casares. In one version of the script Deburau kills Jericho, the Old Clothes man, played by Pierre Renoir, who has been shouting similar insults at him. It was never shot. The last scene of the film, in which Barrault chases unsuccessfully after Arletty, depicts the descent from Courtille.

the audience called out for him to leave but he indicated they had come to see him and he would continue. The fall undoubtedly affected his health.[9] On his last appearance in *Les Noces de Pierrot* he was so exhausted that he asked to be excused some of the dances particularly a *chahut*. At first the audience wanted him to go on but, seeing his physical distress, they called out, "No *chahut*." It is said he left the theatre at midnight carrying the bouquet of flowers from the performance. "A bouquet of his wedding with Death," said Champfleury.[10] Deburau is buried at Père Lachaise cemetery.

Larousse provides an elegant little obituary to the Funambules:

Today there is no more Funambules, no more pantomimes, no more Pierrot, no more blows with a stick, no more flour-covered clowns. Pierrot is dead or relegated to the fair at Saint Cloud which is worse than death.[11]

The Funambules was never regarded as the real métier of Lemaître, the Lion of the Boulevards, whom Vidocq knew the better. Lemaître appeared as him on the stage – well, actually as Balzac's Vautrin – if only for one performance.

On April 25, 1833, Lemaître appeared again as Robert Macaire in a revival of the hugely popular *L'Auberge des Adrets*, this time at the Porte-Saint-Martin. For the production there was a new one-act epilogue by Benjamin Antier and Maurice Alhoy called The Last Three Quarters of an Hour, Les trois derniers quarts d'heure, purporting to analyze the feelings of Macaire and Bertrand while they awaited the guillotine.[12] It was not well received but after the execution came what was described as a fantastic apotheosis in which the two rogues were seen in places of honor in a thieves' heaven.

The large backdrop which consisted of the great robbers of the past, including Dick Turpin and Cartouche, and naturally including Vidocq as well as minor scoundrels such as lawyers and wine merchants,

---

[9] George Sand in *Le Constitutionel*, February 8, 1846. He was also suffering from asthma. It is suggested that the fall was the incident which triggers the danouement of Edmond de Goncourt's circus novel, *Les Frères Zemganno*.

[10] Champfleury was the nom-de-plume of Jules Husson, or Fleury. Born in 1821, in 1857 he wrote one of the first studies of the Realistic movement in literature. He wrote for the Funambules and also novels which included *Les Aventures de Mademoiselle Mariette*, a rather tougher version of Murger's *La Vie bohème*. Later he became director of the state porcelain factory at Sèvres and died in 1889.

[11] P. Larousse, *Grand dictionnaire du XIX siècle*.

[12] Macaire, who was immortalized in the drawings by Daumier in the 1830s, appears to have been based on a semi-mythological French criminal. After murdering his master Macaire was set on by a dog. An arrangement was made for a formal fight and, after the dog had seized Macaire by the throat, he was questioned and confessed. Anon, *Histoire des grands criminels*.

was particularly well received. In the background behind the figures was a representation of dens of vice, notably the Hôtel d'Angleterre and the Stock Exchange.

By 1840 the Porte-Saint-Martin was in decline, now alternating circuses with junk plays such as *La Duchesse de la Vanbanlière*. The manager, Harel, was in dire straits when Lemaître came up with the suggestion that *Vautrin* should be played. Spurred on by Lemaître it was Balzac who wrote the play based on his character from *Le Père Goriot*, in turn based on Vidocq. It was, it seems, an exhausting process. Balzac complained about the rehearsals and, despite assurances by the actor of immediate fame and fortune, he was thoroughly unhappy with things:

> As for myself, I began to despair ten days ago; I thought the play was stupid and I was right. I have completely re-written it and now I think it might do. But it will always be a poor play. I yielded to the temptation to transfer a character from the novel to the stage, and that was a mistake.

In fact he had delayed writing the piece for so long that, with the opening night approaching, he suggested friends should write an act apiece.

There were also troubles with the censor. *Vautrin* was turned down three times and was finally given a license on the specific understanding that if there were disturbances it would be immediately banned. The dress rehearsal passed off well enough. In the play Lemaître was required to appear in a variety of disguises and, in the fourth of five acts, masqueraded as a Mexican, General Crustamente. He wore a fine uniform and a cone-shaped wig. The censors made no comment but the stage manager, Moëssard, remarked that in the wig Lemaître looked a good deal like Louis-Philippe whose coiffure could be described as pear-shaped. Harel was delighted and instructions were given to play up the resemblance. Unfortunately Vidocq also looked a great deal like Louis-Philippe and in the previous years there had been cartoons of them both.

The first night was talked up as being the greatest theatrical event since Victor Hugo's dramas. It seems the only person not to have heard that it would open at the Porte-Saint-Martin on March 14, 1840, was the politician and poet Lamartine, who would become just about Vidocq's last employer. He invited Balzac to dine at his home on the opening night and was rebuffed with the comment:

Monsieur, the politician in you has absorbed the writer to such an extent that I can well understand your not knowing what is happening in a little Boulevard theatre.

If, as Balzac said he rather hoped it would, the piece failed he would hurry round to Lamartine for supper and consolation.

The first three acts passed quietly but when Lemaître appeared as Crustamente, the theatre erupted in shouts of "The King," catcalling, laughter and abuse. The duc d'Orléans left his box in disgust and, it is said, went back to the Tuileries where he woke his father, telling him what had happened and saying the play should be banned. It was. The next day a notice appeared in the official Government paper that the Minister of the Interior had suspended further performances.[13]

Lemaître sent out a mourning card to his friends:

FREDERICK LEMAITRE

Regrets to inform you of the loss which the most productive of our novelists has just suffered in the person of Monsieur Vautrin, alias Trompe-la-Mort, ex-convict, who has died suddenly at the Théâtre de la Porte-Saint-Martin, where he has been buried in the prompter's box.

Recriminations and blame promptly set in. Balzac laid the blame at Lemaître's door. He believed that it was he who had manufactured the wig in an attempt to bring about the downfall of Harel.[14] He was probably wrong. Lemaître went to the Ministry to try to have the ban lifted. He was greeted with roars of laughter.

It is doubtful if the play would have lasted long in any event. The critics were unanimous in their praise of Lemaître and damning of the piece. Jules Janin described it as "a work of desolation, barbarism and ineptitude, completely lacking in wit, style, urbanity, invention and common sense."

But, once again, Vidocq's name was on the lips of the public. If indeed it had ever left them.

---

[13] *Moniteur universel*, March 15, 1840.
[14] Harel went mad and died in 1846, two months after Deburau. Lemaître, born in Le Havre in 1800 the son of an architect, and who played all the great roles including Hamlet, Falstaff, Ruy Blas and Kean, written for him by Dumas père, died of cancer in 1876.

Chapter 19

VIDOCQ
IN LONDON

*In which our hero opens an exhibition – gets some good and bad
publicity – sells some paintings – travels to and from Brussels – sues
for libel – and thinks about some more publications*

V IDOCQ ARRIVED IN London in 1845 at a time when society
was undergoing one of its periodic bouts of Francophilia. He
had been in England a decade earlier when, in 1835, he had given
evidence to a committee of the House of Lords on prison discipline,
speaking on a topic dear to his heart, the detention of convicts in
prison hulks and the problems they faced on release. In 1841 Lord
Mahon told the House:

> The evidence of M. Vidocq, a thief who afterwards turned thief taker,
> was not very creditable perhaps but it was important . . . He found great
> difficulty in obtaining employment. Whenever he met any of his former
> associates, they insisted on his joining them in their criminal projects.

Mahon had made inquiries in France as to the truth of Vidocq's
evidence and had found "there was not a word of exaggeration."[1]

Now, in 1845, there were a number of reasons for the visit. One was
the remote possibility of opening a branch in London of the now declining detective agency. This ultimately came to nothing but Vidocq
did manage to conduct a little piece of business while in London. Jean
Diemer, a former cashier from Antwerp, had been embezzling money
from his firm and with the proceeds had come to London where
he was working as a laborer, at the same time forging a few more

---

[1] *The Times*, March 24, 1841.

promissory notes. Vidocq tracked him down and Diemer was arrested after a struggle at his home in Ranelagh Street, Pimlico. One
of the partners came over from Antwerp and gave evidence at the
committal proceedings but, after the case went to the Central Criminal Court where Diemer faced twelve charges of forgery, and there
were no more appearances by the victims, the case was dismissed.
Vidocq also gave evidence in a bankruptcy case at Guildhall.[2]

Some writers have also suggested that Vidocq was trying to sell the
patent to his agency notepaper to the paper manufacturers De La
Rue. It may be that he was involved in an approach but in 1834 he had
sold his interest to a M. Mozard who launched a public company two
years later and had so mishandled things that, by 1838, there were suggestions that the company was little more than a sham and should be
wound up.[3]

There was also an exhibition to be staged and at the end of it some
paintings to be sold. Vidocq does not seem to have been all that
lucky with his choice of English representatives, the closest of whom
seems to have been Stephané Etiévant, a man who spent a good deal
of the period in the Queen's Bench debtors' prison. Etiévant had,
however, good advice for Vidocq who was at the same time treating with a man named Dawes over the patent for the notepaper.
Another man, Duval, was also looking to Vidocq as a source of funds
and Etiévant, possibly seeing off competition, wrote that Duval had
appeared "drunk as a Pole" and that Vidocq should, on no account,
give him money. He had owed Etiévant £7, had paid it and then
demanded it back.[4]

The immediate reason for Vidocq's appearance in London was the
exhibition and show that he was arranging. Ten years earlier, after
touring for decades, Madame Tussaud had finally pitched her tent on
Baker Street (the exhibition was not moved to the Marylebone Road
until 1884). Now Etiévant advised Vidocq to rent either the Hanover
Rooms or the Cosmorama in Regent Street and he took the latter,
opening in the first week of June in time for the last performance
of the season at Her Majesty's Theatre of *Un bal sous Louis XIV*, in
which Lucille Gattin danced "The Minuet of the Court" and a ga-
votte with Miss Cerito. M. Philippe, the magician, was giving morning
and evening performances of Matinée Mystèrieuse at the St. James's

---

[2] *The Times*, September 12, 1845; Nat. Arch. Crim. 10 22.

[3] *Gazette des Tribunaux*, December 2, 1838.

[4] BHVP, MS 2928; letter dated April 26, 1845, Dossier 55.

Theatre and French plays included Archard in *Le Petit Homme Gris* and *Bruno le Fileur*.[5]

Vidocq's exhibition was a curious mixture but in terms of quantity customers had value for their money. Over the years Vidocq had acquired a handsome collection of paintings, including military scenes by the watercolorist Dirk Langendyk, and these, along with paintings by artists such as Albert Cuyp, Willem van de Velde and Pierre de Laar, were on view, later to be sold. Vidocq had also acquired a large collection of wax fruit of which four thousand specimens of more than sixty varieties were on display. It had originally been purchased for the palace of Louis-Philippe but Vidocq had bought the entire quantity.

Then came much more interesting exhibits and those most likely to appeal to the public: Vidocq's little Chamber of Horrors included the braces belonging to Joseph Fieschi, who had attempted to assassinate Louis-Philippe, and the pen with which Lacenaire had written his memoirs while awaiting execution. They were joined by a collection of instruments of torture and an example of the manacles and weighted boots which Vidocq had worn in his prison days. There was also an object belonging to Papavoine, the child murderer. The English were undoubtedly interested in such things.

Not very much to see for the five shillings entrance fee but there was the star of the show – Vidocq himself. Not only was he on the premises during opening hours but he also put on a little production in which he appeared in various disguises, to the delight of the audience and, for that matter, most of the press. *The Times* was particularly taken with him, simpering:

The principal curiosity in the collection will be found to be M. Vidocq himself, whose appearance is very much what might be anticipated by those who have read his memoirs or heard of his exploits. He is a remarkably well-built man of extraordinary muscular power, and exceedingly active. He stands, when perfectly erect, 5 feet 10 inches in height, but by some strange process connected with physical formation he has the faculty of contracting his height several inches, and in this diminished state to walk about, jump etc. His countenance exhibits in a way not to be mistaken unflinching determination of character, strong powers of perception and that bluffness which denotes animal courage. He is extremely intelligent, communicative and good humoured. From the flexibility of his features and his powers of varying the expression of them

---

[5] *Weekly Dispatch*, June 8, 1845.

he would make an excellent actor in such representations as require an actor to sustain several parts. He is now seventy-two years of age, but possesses all the strength, vigour and buoyancy of a man 25 years his junior.

Their correspondent also liked the paintings:

> Very clever watercolours and sepia drawings representing many of the great battles in which the French armies have been engaged . . . some of the drawings are of a high character for accuracy of delineation, cornerstones of outline . . . They are very clear and certainly the works of no indifferent artists. Those who admire the marvellous and wish to witness its illustration will be gratified by this exhibition.[6]

The *Morning Post* was also delighted with the exhibition. "Amongst the "delicate monsters" and other curiosities which are now exhibiting in London Vidocq is pre-eminent." The exhibits were admired – their correspondent could not tell the difference between the real and wax fruit in the bowls – and there were comments on Vidocq's "wonderful mobility of features and powers of transmutation. It is thought only a chameleon, Sir Robert Peel or Proteus could surpass him."[7]

For their money visitors to the exhibition also received a small brochure which served as a catalogue modestly entitled "Vidocq, Chef de la Sûreté (Detective Force) de Paris, which was created by him and which he directed for twenty-nine years with extraordinary success." In the front there was the well-known picture of Vidocq by Achille Devéria, which was now signed by him in light blue ink.

There were, however, critics of the exhibition, notably the *Weekly Dispatch*:

> All Frenchmen and a vast number of Englishmen have heard rather too much of M. Vidocq. We have nothing to complain of this police officer's autobiography; he is very candid and impartial and makes himself out the most consummate rogue in Europe. From being an excessive criminal in France where crimes are of a far worse nature than in England or even in Ireland, Mons. Vidocq became an expert police officer and finally suggested, matured and commanded the secret police in Paris or was head of what we, in England, call "the police in plain clothes" a corps

---

[6] *The Times*, June 9, 1845.
[7] *Morning Post*, June 9, 1845.

to belong to which implies talents of a by no means amiable nature. But Mons. Vidocq takes compassion on the dull crazy-skulled English and has opened a most extraordinary exhibition in Regent Street. He has hit our national character accurately and knowing that we are the most dupable and gullible of the human race he equally well knows that we are not a mean, shabby and vulgar people and that the English will not stoop to be cheated at low prices.

Accordingly M. Vidocq charges five shillings as an admission price and those who know the charges for sight seeing in Paris must conclude their 5/- in London is about equal to 35/- in the French Capital.

Unfortunately for this practical French philosopher he has hit upon a wrong period for all our 5/- and 10/- paying classes are now raving after mesmerism and clairvoyance.

But what do our patient and tractable people get for their 5/-? First two good and large rooms one hung with water colours, Indian ink, sepias and bistre; and candour, truth, our inherent love of justice, and of course our love of English generosity compel us to acknowledge that we never saw anything equal to them in England, not even at a country fair or in a cathedral town.

The pictures were, the paper reported, miraculous – modern subjects by long-dead artists. They did not like the fruit much either. Then came the real exhibits:

Spread out on a table with a good light. First there are two knives used by French assassins in murdering children in the woods. Next there is a large clumsy pruning hook used by French murderers in killing gardeners.

The writer was not impressed by the collection of manacles and weighted boots either, concluding:

We wish that Sir James Graham would shut up the show for assuredly the French ambassador will threaten war if our Government suffer such an awful exposure of the torture system of France.[8]

The review was by a journalist called Williams, writing as Publicola, and it was not one Vidocq could possibly accept. The issue of the following week reported that Vidocq had called and threatened a lawsuit over a description of the paintings of "very old works by very young

---

[8] *Weekly Dispatch*, June 8, 1845.

masters." It seems Vidocq had also threatened a whipping to the correspondent:

> He has put us in such a terror that we do not know whether to stand on our head or our heels. He calls us infamous calumniators, odious liars with a base and malevolent spirit. His pictures of the French Revolution are stated to be painted by the great Dutch Masters all of whom were dead 150 years at least before the French Revolution was born or thought of.
>
> He asserts in the newspapers that he is full of the most interesting anecdotes. We must be very stupid for Mons. Vidocq told us nothing superior to what might be found in a page of Joe Miller.[9]

There was support, however, for Vidocq from the *Dispatch*'s rival, *The Era*, which spoke of Williams' despicable conduct. He had, it seems, been given a personal tour, shared a bottle of wine and promised to write a favorable puff. Now to write this was deplorable. As to the exhibition itself *The Era* liked it, thinking it "well worthy of the cognoscenti," and would return to give a full review the next week, but by then, as they say, space did not permit. There the matter seems to have ended. No flogging and no writ.[10]

While in London Vidocq took the opportunity to visit a number of prisons, including Pentonville, Newgate and Millbank, which he was told he could inspect on any day of the week between eleven and noon except Saturday and Sunday. He also paid a call on Professor Robert Longbottom at the Royal Polytechnic who, sadly, was out. A note from the Professor suggested that next time he should make an appointment.[11]

One thing that did annoy him was a poster he saw advertising him as the Master of Ceremonies at a ball in Windmill Street. It called for a visit to Maltby, the Marlborough Street magistrate, to try to lay a charge that the public were being deceived. He might, he said modestly, be a master of disguise but he was never going to descend to disguising himself as a Master of Ceremonies at a shilling a hop. Maltby was reasonably sympathetic but, pointing out that there might even be another Vidocq who had genuinely lent his name, he said he could do nothing. He thought the newspapers reporting the application would

---

[9] Ibid., June 15, 1845.
[10] *The Era*, June 15, 1845.
[11] BHVP, Dossier 50, Authority from Sir John Stevens to Prison Governor.

sufficiently clear Vidocq's name.[12]

Next it was off to Brussels and a continuing correspondence with Etiévant. There were signs that Vidocq was now dyeing his hair for his passport of November 6 gives the color as chestnut. It was Etiévant who advised him on the sale of his pictures, recommending Foster and Christie, both of whom he considered perfectly satisfactory, if anything coming down on the side of Christie. Both wanted to handle the sale. Despite the doubts of the *Weekly Dispatch*, some of the pictures were good in themselves and there was also the added kudos of Vidocq's name. Vidocq went with Foster and three of his pictures, all by Willem van de Velde, sold well. *The Battle of Sale Bay* made £246 15s, *A Small Calm* went for 100 guineas and *A Naval Engagement* made £147, with Lord Northwick, and Messrs Hickman and Lake respectively the new owners.

On February 18, 1846, Vidocq was in Bruges, described by Jean Savant as full of energy and without a gray hair, which is hardly surprising if he was using dye. In May that year, however, Vidocq's death was once again reported, this time by the *Democratie pacifique*. He had apparently died at St-Nicolas, Brussels, in a state of penury following a series of unlucky speculations and the numerous legal actions against him. His death had been caused by his enfeebled state through alcoholism. From Paris Madame Vidocq sent an immediate denial and shortly after, back in London, Vidocq held a dinner for the press to show the reports of his death had again been greatly exaggerated. "There was talk of his flourishing health and that he was sporting two superb diamonds on his shirt front."[13] Vidocq and his wife seized upon one particular paragraph:

> It is affirmed that latterly he sold a Brussels publisher, papers, notes and very curious information about divers French families and personalities on condition that they should not be printed until after his death, for he had been paid to keep their secrets and wanted to keep the bargain and be honest, in his fashion.[14]

The passage was reprinted in other papers including *La Patrie*, to whom Fleuride Vidocq wrote that her husband was in London on important business, that he had never lived in St-Nicolas and that if

---

[12] *The Times*, July 28, 1845.
[13] Jean Savant, *La Vie Aventureuse de Vidocq*, p. 229.
[14] *Democratie pacifique*, May 9, 1846.

they wished to be assured he was still alive they could see a letter she had received that day. She then turned to the meat:

> Finally, those who know him are aware – perhaps no one more so than the author of the libellous article in question – that my husband has preserved the full vigor of his intellect, that he does not indulge in any alcoholic excesses, and that the manner in which he understands honesty will never allow him to authorize the publication, before or after his death, of secrets entrusted to him. The families and individuals whom his discretion concerns need suffer no anxiety on that account.[15]

The London papers picked up the story of his death and Vidocq was quick to write and make a call on the editor of the *Sun* to assure him he was alive and well. In turn the *Sun* was happy to print a retraction. That was sufficient apology for the London papers but Vidocq wanted money from the *Democratie pacifique*. They paid up in court and issued an apology that July. Vidocq was again wearing his diamonds for the occasion.

---

[15] *La Patrie*, May 8, 22, 1846.

Chapter 20

VIDOCQ'S
CRIMINAL FRIENDS

*In which our hero meets a variety of revolutionaries,
assassins, murderers, extraordinary women,
false dauphins and other assorted villains*

H AD IT SUITED HIM Vidocq would doubtless have claimed
the personal friendship of all the crowned heads of Europe.
However, in the preface to his brochure-cum-catalogue to the 1845
London exhibition he more modestly claimed acquaintance with a
number of the lesser, but nevertheless first-class, mortals in their own
field, who decorated the French criminal stage during his career.

First, Vidocq gives the names of two women whom he says he knew.
He is certainly likely to have known, possibly even biblically, Madame
Manson, the so-called heroine of the Joseph-Bernadin Fualdès
murder case, but it is not so likely that he had any close contact with
the equally well-born Madame Marie-Fortunée Lafarge, convicted
of poisoning her thoroughly unattractive husband Charles in 1840.[1]
Her mother was reputed to be the illegitimate daughter of the duc
d'Orléans and she herself was a curious woman. She was something of
a kleptomaniac and had stolen jewelry when staying with the family of
a childhood friend. The evidence in the murder case against her was
strong if not conclusive. Lafarge had met her when he was dowry-
hunting to finance his semi-derelict estate, Le Glandier, in Corrèze,
some 300 miles from Paris. Their wedding night had been a disaster
and she had offered him the dowry to release her from the marriage.

---

[1] The case is extensively covered in the *Gazette des Tribunaux* from February 7, 1840 onwards.
The name is sometimes given as Laffarge.

Now with the marriage a few weeks old, she secretly bought a substantial quantity of arsenic. She certainly had the motive for disposing of her husband, and now the means. Lafarge was taken ill when he was in Paris attempting to obtain an iron-making patent, or, as is more likely, to raise money on false notes, which is how Vidocq may have come into contact with the family. Marie-Fortunée had sent him a cake with instructions that it should be eaten at midnight on December 18, at the same time as she would eat a similar one, minus the arsenic, at her home. After that it was downhill all the way. Lafarge returned to Le Glandier on January 3 and died eleven days later.

Marie-Fortunée was given a suspended sentence for the theft of the jewelry and at her murder trial public opinion, if not the court, was very much in her favor. There was a welter of conflicting scientific evidence, including that of Professor Orfila from the Sorbonne whose evidence had done so much to convict Dr. Edmé-Samuel Castaing years earlier. The question was just how much arsenic was found in the body. The great chemist Raspail declined to come to court on her behalf and, too late, the defense showed that arsenic was present everywhere, even in the chair of the president of the court. There was even an alternative suggestion of another poisoner, a quasi agent-cum-servant Denis Barbier, whose motive was to cover up accounting deficiences. Lafarge's first wife had also died of poisoning, something which could not in any way be attributed to poor Marie-Fortunée. She was sentenced to twelve years with hard labor, the latter part of the sentence being remitted by Louis-Philippe. She wrote several books, including *Heures de prison de Mme Lafarge*, after her release, and, a hysteric, died at the spa town of Ussa on November 5, 1852, probably from tuberculosis following a nervous breakdown.

Much the more interesting of the two women, and certainly one who would have appealed more to Vidocq's tastes, was the very high-spirited and, again, well-connected Marie-France-Clarisse Manson. She also had a short-lived marriage but her real claim to fame is that in 1817 she may have been a witness to the murder of the magistrate Joseph-Bernadin Fualdès, a minor official in Albi. On March 19 his body was found, his throat cut, in the river. It was known that Fualdès had quarrelled with his one-time benefactor Joseph Jausion, telling him that the man's life was in his hands. This was reference to an earlier incident when Fualdès had hushed up a case of infanticide. Blood was found in one of the lowest brothels in town run by a man named Bancal and his wife. Also found in the brothel was someone much more interesting to the general public: Mme Manson. In one version of the story she had apparently witnessed the killing but on her knees had been made to touch the body and swear she would say nothing. And, more or less, she kept her promise. Bancal killed himself in prison but Jausion and Bastide-Gramont, Fualdès, godson, were convicted and sentenced to death. Others also convicted, including Mme Barcal and a laundress who washed the sheets, received life imprisonment. Unfortunately the appeal court quashed the convictions and, in an effort to make her talk and say something approaching the truth, the prosecution now added Mme Manson's name as an accomplice. It was to no avail. She was the only one acquitted and this time Bastide-Gramont and Jausion were executed on June 3, 1818, in Albi.

The case was the talk not only of Albi and the southwest but also of Paris and, says one particular publication grandly, rather forgetting Napoleon was now permanently in exile; of the Empire. Waxworks were made of the principals in a tableau set in the brothel.[2] Apart from publishing her memoirs, Mme Manson received an offer to go to Paris to work behind the bar at the Café de Foy and, when she lost that job, at the café Veron near the Bourse. Later she ran a small bar in the rue Copeau behind the Jardin des Plantes, probably working for Vidocq as an informer since she received a small police pension. She died in obscurity at Versailles in 1847. What she was doing in the brothel was never made clear. She may have been meeting a lover or perhaps she was one of those rare examples of a woman who enjoys sex in such low conditions. She undoubtedly told a number of versions of the story of her involvement and there have been suggestions that she was never in the brothel at all. Other versions of her later life have her dying in 1833 when, on her deathbed, she is said to have confessed to the Abbé de Villiers, in the presence of her son, that she knew nothing whatsoever of the Fualdès murder.[3]

It is very likely that Vidocq knew the assassin Joseph Fieschi, who had, at some time previously, been a *mouchard*. Once the attempted, albeit halfhearted, coup of 1832 had failed, the Republicans took to organizing a series of unsuccessful assassination attempts on Louis-Philippe. Between the autumn of 1834 and the following sum-

---

[2] M. Berthelot, (ed.), *La Grande Encyclopédie*.

[3] *The Times*, January 22, 1818. M-F-C. Manson, *Mon plan de défense dans le procès Fualdès adressé à touts les coeurs sembles*. For a comprehensive account of the case, see Peter Shankland and Lord Havers, *Murder with a Double Tongue*.

mer no fewer than seven plots were uncovered but, despite this, the King refused to cancel the review of the National Guard on July 28.

It was during this procession, which included Maréchal Mortier, duc de Treviso, that Fieschi, who had the arms of Murat, King of Naples, tattooed on his chest, literally concentrated his firepower. There had been strong rumors that the procession was to be the target of another attempt on the King's life and that a bomb had been placed in a house on the boulevard St-Martin near the Ambigu theatre. There was already a warrant out for Fieschi for fraud but Canler's men had been unable to find him. Nor did a house-to-house search to flush out him and his colleagues. In fact, the information was slightly off. Now he and his associates fired a *machine infernale*, a primitive sort of machine gun, at the procession as it passed their house in the boulevard du Temple not far from what is now République. The King and his sons escaped unharmed but eighteen others, including a twelve-year-old girl and the Maréchal, were killed.[4] Much was blamed on the press and Gisquet closed down some thirty Republican magazines and newspapers.

Vidocq does not say how he came to meet Louis Alibaud who, eleven months later, at 6:30 p.m. on June 25, 1836, attempted to assassinate the unfortunate Louis-Philippe. He was taken to the Conciergerie where he was, so the story goes, put in the same cell as that occupied by Fieschi only a few months earlier. He would neither defend himself nor accept the services of a lawyer but, following the efforts of Charles Ledru, he was reprieved. Unfortunately this made Alibaud even more recalcitrant and he explained how regicide was wholly defensible. He was executed on July 11 at 5 a.m. The great-hearted Ledru walked behind his coffin to ensure that Alibaud was buried in consecrated ground.

In London of the 1970s, every summer the Academy, an independent cinema in Oxford Street at the corner of Wardour Street, used to show Marcel Carné's *Les Enfants du Paradis*. One of the central characters was Pierre-François Lacenaire, the great French criminal

---

[4] On the day of the execution of Fieschi and his colleagues, the duc de Brunswick rented space to watch them die, which he did through a lorgnette. He was bitterly criticized. A mock-up of the instrument can be seen in the Museum of the Préfecture of the Police of Paris. A *machine infernale* had earlier featured in the unsuccessful Royalist conspiracy in the attempt on the life of Bonaparte on October 24, 1800, in what was then rue Niçaise between the Tuileries and the Opéra. That explosion was also badly timed and Bonaparte escaped unharmed but a number of people were killed. Felix Orsini also used a so-called *machine infernale* in his unsuccessful attempt on the life on Napoleon III in 1858. He too was guillotined.

of the 1830s, played with some style by Marcel Herraud with kiss curls framing his forehead and a fine mustache. In a way he was the anti-hero of the film, saving Pierre Brasseur, as the actor Frédéric Lemaître, by stabbing the evil count (played by Louis Salou) in a Turkish bath in the boulevard du Temple. In reality there is no record of such an incident but Turkish bath visitor, anti-hero and disciple of Vidocq, Lacenaire certainly was. His criminal career, half of which was spent in prison, spanned only six years but his influence, popularity and fame were enormous.

In December 1834 there were two savage attacks in a Paris now, post-Vidocq, in the grip of a crime wave and with the murder rate running at about two hundred a year. On December 16 the police were called to the very poor 271 rue Saint-Martin, where the widow Chardon and her son were found dead. Chardon fils had given himself the title Brother of Charity and he made his living by writing begging letters. Now came an example of false stereotyping. He was known as "Auntie" and "widely known for his anti-physical tastes so it was on abject creatures known to share these that suspicion first fell."

The second, and attempted murder on New Year's Eve 1834, was that of the clerk Genevau who was attacked at 66 rue Montorgeuil. He had been sent to collect money from a M. Mahossier whose name had been chalked on the door. He fought off his attackers and Pierre Allard was called to investigate.

Louis Canler was by now Allard's Chief Inspector and he commenced the drudgery of making calls on the lodging houses in the district. At 107 rue du faubourg du Temple was an entry for Mahossier and immediately underneath that was the name Fizellier, also known as François, a man described by the lodging housekeeper's wife as tall and with abundant whiskers. The keeper's wife also said that Mahossier had stayed under the name Bâton. She knew Bâton played billiards in a café, the Quatre Billiards, in the rue Bondy and when the man arrived he was arrested by Canler. There was no question of his being Mahossier. Canler found out that he was an associate of a man Gaillard and he obtained a description before releasing him. Gaillard was not an uncommon name and Canler found an entry at a lodging house at 15 rue Marivaux-des-Lombards. He had left behind a package containing Republican songs and a poem which accused Gisquet of being a vicious cur. The handwriting closely resembled that which had chalked the name Mahossier on the door of the house in rue Montorgeuil.

Canler traced Martin François (or sometimes François Martin) to prison and questioned him and out came at least part of the story. François said that he had met a man who had boasted of killing the Chardons, with the lookout being kept by a Victor Avril.

Avril, then in La Force, said that if he was let out he would find Gaillard; no one knew him better. Canler eventually traced Gaillard through a tip by Avril that he had an aunt in rue Bar-du-Bec. The aunt in turn said she was frightened of him and, were he to come to the door, she would not let him in. She knew him as Lacenaire.

A few days later Lacenaire was arrested under the name of Jacob Lévy passing a forged bill of exchange in Beaune. He was brought to Paris where he was questioned by Canler and Allard and made no secret of his involvement in the two sets of attacks. He admitted killing the Chardons and stealing 500 francs and some silver which Avril had sold. Avril had actually finished off Chardon with an axe while Lacenaire had stabbed the widow with a shoemaker's awl. After the double murder they had gone to the Turkish baths in the boulevard du Temple to clean themselves up. Once Lacenaire was told that he had been betrayed by Avril and François Martin he said he would make his own inquiries. For his pains he was beaten up by their friends in La Force.

Lacenaire was born in 1800 at Francheville, near Lyons, the son of a prosperous merchant. He claims to have been neglected as a child in favor of an elder brother and at school he devoted himself to studying Voltaire, something which did not appeal to his teachers. He appears, however, to have been a near model pupil. He got on well with his fellows, created a generally good impression, was never punished and, wrote one master:

> I found him in my class remarkable for his love of work, his gentleness, his success and, above all, for the affection he always showed for me.

Criminologists, eat your hearts out.

He went to Paris to read for the Bar but the family money ran out and in turn he worked as a clerk in an office, as a solicitor's clerk and as a bank clerk before he joined an expedition to the Morea to aid the insurgent Greeks. He returned early in 1829 and deserted from the 16th Infantry of the Line that March. Making his way to Lyons, he found that his father had gone bankrupt and taken the family to Brussels.

Lacenaire was an early example of the angry young man. He had grown up in what he saw as a middle-aged France with a king and administration apathetic to what Stead describes as:

> Those young and generous emotions which had blazed at the Revolution and brightened the legend of the First Empire; and which had burned again on the barricades in those three days in July.[5]

There is no real reason why Vidocq and Lacenaire should have met. Vidocq had completed his short second stint at the Sûreté before Lacenaire really came to notice but in his writings Lacenaire paid substantial tribute to Vidocq's influence on his career.

Finding his parents had left Lyons, Lacenaire continued:

> In fact, within a matter of days, I was reduced to the point at which I almost died of hunger. From that moment I became a thief, and at heart a murderer . . . I resolved to become the scourge of society, but could do nothing alone; I needed associates but where to find them? I had never quite known what it was to be a thief by profession but latterly I had read *Les Mémoires de Vidocq*; this had given me an idea of that class in a constant feud against society . . . It was essential that I should spent some time in the company of those people . . . Thus I crossed my Rubicon. I must next commit some theft which did not bear too heavy a penalty.

This was bad enough but Lacenaire, the professional thief and intellectual, clearly moved in some sort of café society. He then had the misfortune to kill a nephew of the author and politician Benjamin Constant[6] in an unprovoked duel. His misfortunes were, however, further compounded by the view that the equanimity with which he watched the man die showed him to be insensitive to human suffering. This insensitivity would more than suit him in his new profession as a criminal. By August 1829 he was in Sainte-Pélagie serving a sentence for fraud.

The next three years were devoted to his literary career, something which really only blossomed after his death. A literary career is,

---

[5] Philip Stead, *The Memoirs of Lacenaire*, p. 42. It was not only Vidocq who was the inspiration of contemporary authors. Stendhal planned to introduce Valbeyre – who duelled with society and read Molière – based on Lacenaire in his unfinished novel *Lamiel*.

[6] Henri-Benjamin Constant de Rebecque (1767–1830) is best remembered for his short novel *Adolphe* which he wrote in a fortnight in 1807, based on his relationship with Madame de Staël. Politically, he took office under Napoleon during the Hundred Days. After the Restoration he had a brilliant career as a leader of the Liberal opposition.

with very few exceptions, no path to real wealth and since none of his poems and plays was actually published, he was obliged to forage for himself. He had, however, attracted some attention in the form of M. Vigouroux, the editor of the radical publication *Bon Sens*, who was also in prison on political charges. If Lacenaire mended his ways there was a job for him with *Bon Sens*, and indeed on his release he wrote "On the Prisons and Penitentiary System in France."

Lacenaire was released in 1830 and continued his thieving, along with more legitimate work as a legal copyist at the Palais de Justice. Unfortunately his two professions became entwined at the beginning of 1833 when the theft of some stamped paper saw his services dispensed with.

Then it was a version of the old badger game using a boy, and Lacenaire and a colleague appearing at the crucial moment as police officers. He was later caught stealing silver spoons from restaurants and in July 1833 he was back in La Force serving a thirteen-month sentence. It was there that he wrote the best-known of his poems, "Thief's Petition to a King His Neighbor," to amuse some of his fellow convicts who were serving sentences for political offenses. It was in prison that he met his future companion, Victor Avril.

Lacenaire was released in July 1834. Like many another criminal, he had no wish to return to prison, writing that he preferred the prospect of the *bagnes* as at least he would see the sea. He knew, however, that he was not strong enough to endure the *bagnes* and as a result decided that in future he would steal only large sums and take out the insurance of murdering the victim. If he got away with it, well and good. If he did not he accepted he would be executed.[7]

Lacenaire's trial opened on November 12 and shortly before that he gave what amounted to a press conference in which he fielded questions with more dexterity than many politicians:

> Doctor: How is it that your intelligence did not protect you against yourself?
> Lacenaire: There came a day in my life when I had no alternatives than suicide or crime.
> Doctor: Why, then, not choose suicide?
> Lacenaire: I asked myself whether I was my own victim or society's.

---

[7] Of course, not everyone thought the same way about the hulks. On May 22, 1824, Antonio Brochetti, an Italian unwilling to face a life in the hulks, murdered a guard at Bicêtre and was sentenced to death. "I would rather die a thousand times than go to the hulks," he told the executioner Sanson.

From the start he admitted his guilt and took an interest in the proceedings only so far as seeing whether or not Avril and François would be convicted. His hope, so far as Avril was concerned, was realized. François was sentenced to life imprisonment and on July 19, 1838, was a member of the chain that went to Brest.

Lacenaire was kept in the Conciergerie where he wrote his autobiography *Mémoires d'un assassin*. In contrast with Vidocq's there is little doubt that his memoirs were indeed his own. He began them in La Force but this version was destroyed and he wrote his memoirs as they exist in the Conciergerie, finishing on January 8, 1836, and correcting page proofs sent by his publisher.[8] He was under guard day and night to prevent him killing himself but it seems never to have crossed his mind. What he wanted was to complete the memoirs. Canler would visit him regularly. After their convictions, perhaps surprisingly Avril and Lacenaire became firm friends to such an extent that Allard and the Governor of the Conciergerie gave them a dinner at which they joked about the blood of the undercooked meat. On January 9 they were transferred to the Bicêtre for execution the next day.

What the authorities did not want was Lacenaire to be seen as going out in style. He was not to "die game." It was better to present him as a coward at the end.

A crowd of around five hundred watched the executions in the place Saint-Jacques and, according to the *Gazette des Tribuneaux*, while his companion Avril displayed admirable courage, Lacenaire did not:

> At a quarter to nine the mournful procession reached the foot of the scaffold, which had been erected an hour after midnight by torchlight. Lacenaire hurriedly descended from the vehicle, the pallor of his face was frightful, his glance vague and uncertain, he stammered and seemed searching for words, which his tongue refused to articulate. Avril got out after him, with a quick decided step, and took a tranquil glance at the public; perfectly resigned, he walked up to Lacenaire and embraced him.
>
> "Good-bye old fellow," he said; "I am going to open the ball." He firmly ascended the scaffold steps, was fastened to the fatal plank, and then turned round and said, "Come Lacenaire, old fellow, be courageous, and imitate me." It was his last remark, and the knife sent his head rolling on the planks of the scaffold.

---

[8] They were probably finished by Hippolyte Bonnelier who visited him in prison. Bonnelier also wrote for and appeared on the stage of the Odéon under the name Max. He died in 1868 or 1869.

According to the *Gazette*, Lacenaire had to be diverted from the spectacle by the Abbé Montès and although he had announced an intention to address the crowd he had not the strength left:

> . . . his legs gave way; his face was changed; he ascended the steps, supported by the executioner's assistants, and the fatal stroke soon put an end to his anguish and his life.[9]

According to Canler, who was present, Lacenaire behaved far, far better. He had to be turned away from watching the death of Avril and he mounted the steps boldly.[10] The executioner Henri-Clément Sanson confirms that Lacenaire died game and also denies the story that for twenty seconds the guillotine blade stuck, allowing Lacenaire time to twist around to watch it drop.[11] According to Stead, Lacenaire wanted to kiss Canler but the policeman was led away. It was feared the kiss might turn into a bite.[12]

After their deaths the heads of Avril and Lacenaire were examined by phrenologists:

> The face of Avril expresses nothing but a stupid ferocity. The skull presents the following conclusions – The forehead is very low and strongly inclining backwards, being otherwise rather open. A marked projection commences on a level with the external orbitary apuphysics of the crania, extending and enlarging till it reaches the auditory conduit, where it is considerably developed. This in craniology is a decided indication of a thief and murderer. Phrenologists will no doubt avail themselves of this as evidence of the truth of their system.
>
> To this, however, the head of Lacenaire forms a direct contradiction. Lacenaire, whose cold-blooded cruelty and want of feeling under the most frightful circumstances has astonished and disgusted all France was phrenologically endowed with all the qualities of a good, kind, mild, sensible and religious man; holding injustice and robbery in horror, and a hundred thousand leagues from being an assassin. This is what we should be taught by phrenology, if we had not facts to correct the conclusions it would lend us to.[13]

---

9 *Gazette des Tribunaux*, January 10, 1836.
10 C. Moreau-Christophe, *Le Monde des Coquins*, p. 234; *Sunday Times*, December 14, 2003.
11 Louis Canler, *Mémoires de Canler*, Fouquier, *Causes célèbres*, Vol. 1., p. 32; H. Sanson, *Memoirs of the Sansons*.
12 Canler tells the same story but this time with the murderer Jadin asking him to embrace him on the scaffold. "Here?" I said. "What are you thinking of? It is quite out of the question."
13 *The Times*, January 22, 1836.

Phrenology was a fashion of the time but exponents never seemed to learn. When the next year Charles Ledru had the celebrated Fossati examine the cranium of Vidocq, whom he did not know, he described the subject as having the characteristics of a lion, a diplomat and a Sister of Charity. "A monkey, a fox and a tall-story teller," commented Moreau-Christophe.[14]

Lacenaire's hope was that he would ultimately stand side by side with Fieschi in Curtius' Salon.[15] He may never have achieved that distinction but at least some of his effects ended up in Vidocq's little Chamber of Horrors when he visited England. Certainly Vidocq claimed that the pen he exhibited belonged to Lacenaire. Some accounts have him also in possession of Lacenaire's frock coat with its bloodstained collar. If so, he obtained this from Lord Durham. It had passed to His Lordship first through the hands of Sanson and then Benjamin Appert.

It was not only Lacenaire's head which suffered. One of his hands was also cut off and ended up in the study of the journalist Maxime du Camp, where Vidocq's friend, the poet Théophile Gauthier, saw it, yellow and mummified.

As a final footnote to Lacenaire, Sanson took considerable umbrage with the newspapers who had been calling him *le bourreau et ses valets*. He maintained that under a law of January 12, 1787, confirmed by the Convention of 1792 he should be called *l'executeur des arrêts criminals* and that his assistants should be described as aides.[16]

The murderous Edmé-Samuel Castaing, born in Alençon in 1797, a doctor with a well-connected mistress by whom he had two children, is another whom Vidocq almost certainly actually met. In 1823 Castaing had been approached by Auguste Ballet whose elder brother, Hippolyte, was dying and had just cut him out of his will. For a share in the estate Castaing was to gain possession of the will and then kill Hippolyte. Castaing did just this and then insinuated himself into Auguste's trust to such an extent that he had a will made in his own favor. Just how much was genuinely trust and how much was blackmail on his part is perhaps a moot point. Some time later the two men drove to an inn, L'Auberge

---

[14] C. Moreau-Christophe, *Le Monde des Coquins*, p. 230.

[15] Curtius, the "uncle" and instructor of Madame Tussaud, had at least two waxwork museums one of which, appropriately enough, was on the boulevard du Temple, "the Boulevard du Crime." Fieschi remained as a tableau applying a match to his *machine infernale* until at least 1918 in the Tussaud London exhibition.

[16] *The Times*, January 22, 1836.

de la Tête Noire at Saint-Cloud where, in the first recorded instance of the drug being used to kill, the good doctor laced Auguste's wine with morphine. Dying, Auguste asked for another doctor and Pigache, a local man, and Dr. Pellatan of the Paris School of Medicine both recognized the pinpoint condition of the eyes as morphine poisoning. Once the contents of the will were known an autopsy was ordered on both bodies. There were signs, but no more, of morphine in the case of Hippolyte and clear signs in the case of Auguste.

It is amazing how old friends turn up time and again. Taken to Versailles, Castaing looked around for a prisoner who might act as an intermediary between him and witnesses and unfortunately his choice was Vidocq's old master of savate and one-time police agent, Jean-Pierre Goupil, who was back in prison when the doctor arrived there. Castaing suggested that Goupil write to Castaing's mother but, with his eye on more favorable treatment from the authorities, Goupil was acting as a *mouton*. The trial took place on November 10, 1823, and Castaing's defense was that he had bought the poison to kill stray cats and dogs whose noise at night was depriving Auguste of much needed sleep. Castaing created a very favorable impression in court and was acquitted of the murder of Hippolyte and only convicted of the murder of Auguste by a majority verdict. The general opinion was that Castaing was guilty but that Dr. Pellatan had not done a good autopsy. He was particularly criticized for not bringing the intestines to Paris for general examination. Alexandre Dumas père was so disturbed by the verdict that he became an opponent of capital punishment. Castaing was executed by Sanson at 2 p.m. on December 6, 1823. Unsurprisingly his condition was described as "extremely dejected, his mental resolution appeared overpowered, and his bodily strength entirely prostrate, apparently unable to support himself." His conviction broke his family. His father resigned his place in Government and his brother his commission in the Guards.[17]

One of the other well-remembered murders during Vidocq's tenure was the killing by Louis-Auguste Papavoine of two children on a Sunday morning while they were walking with their mother in a wood. Initially his defense, managed by Alphonse-Gabriel-Victor Paillet who had defended Mme Lafarge, was that they were political killings. Papavoine had, he said, been under the illusion that the children were royal heirs

---

[17] *The Times*, December 9, 1823. For an account of the case see Pierre Bouchardon, *L'Auberge de la tête noire*.

but his defense was changed to the more probable one of insanity. He also asked to see the duchesses of Angoulême and de Berri as he had important news for them. Neither his defense nor his request did him any good and he was also executed by Henri-Charles Sanson at 4 p.m. at the place de Grève on March 25, 1825. The execution had been delayed three days and it had been thought that a reprieve was possible. A delighted crowd of 100,000 watched the proceedings. Sanson noted that he would rather be the executioner of Papavoine than the jury that sentenced him.[18]

Vidocq also knew Louis Ulbach, the murderer of his eighteen-year-old mistress, Aimée Millot, the so-called Shepherdess of Ivry. This was a crime of passion committed by a youth who was another with a disturbed upbringing. The papers were sympathetic towards him because, for a murder committed in very similar circumstances, another young man, Sureau, had been sent to the galleys earlier in the year. Now it was reported that Ulbach had received religious consolation for the three weeks he had been in Bicêtre and on the steps of the scaffold, after declining a handkerchief soaked in vinegar, "he recited a prayer and a few seconds later was in eternity."[19]

Then there were the faux dauphins. One of the abiding legends of the Terror was that somehow the Louis-Charles de France who became Dauphin on the death of his brother in 1789, and almost certainly died at the age of ten in 1795 of a scrofulous infection while imprisoned in the Temple, had instead been smuggled out and was alive and well and living under a variety of guises.[20] The basis of the story is that the Revolutionary leader Pierre-Gaspard Chaumette, with the help of Antoine Simon and his wife, smuggled the Dauphin out of the Temple on the night of January 19, 1794. Chaumette's intention was to gain control of the Dauphin and so ensure his own survival when Revolutionary fever had subsided. Instead he was guillotined before the plan could be put into execution.

Many, however, claimed that another child had been substituted and he had been spirited away. The production of lunatic and other unlikely dauphins was really in the King's interest, so discrediting any

---

[18] The Times, February 28, 1825.

[19] *Journal des Débats*, September 10, 1827; *Gazette des Tribunaux*, September 11, 1827.

[20] In April 2000 scientists from the University of Münster announced after taking DNA samples from a lock of Marie-Antoinette's hair that other samples from the boy's dried heart closely matched those of other members of the French Royal Family. *New York Times*, April 20, 2000. See also G. Lenôtre, *Le Roi Louis XVII et l'énigme du Temple*, Philippe Delorme, *Louis XVII la verité: Sa mort au temple confirmée par la science*.

lingering belief that the Dauphin might have survived. The first such Dauphin to surface seems to have been in 1810 when a drummer in the garrison at Tortona in Piedmont was sentenced to run the gauntlet three times for some minor infringement. As he was about to be flogged he said he had something important to communicate to the Commandant and that something was that he was the Dauphin. He had intended to tell no one except his sister but he could not allow the royal body to be subjected to such a punishment. He was sent by the Commandant to Turin where he was apparently recognized by an old Swiss retainer of the Palace of Versailles who fell to his knees. For some time he was held in awe by what passed for a court in Turin but later an inquiry was ordered and he was again sentenced to run the gauntlet three times. The Ladies of the Court interceded, as they had done for Cartouche, and the punishment was reduced to a single run. As he stripped off his shirt he is said to have exclaimed, "What an indignity for a Bourbon!" Following the punishment he disappeared.[21]

After that the false dauphins came, if not thick and fast, at least steadily. There were probably around forty in all, each with a story, some less improbable than others. Among them was Jean-Marie Hervagau, son of a Baisse-Los tailor, born in 1780 who died in Bicêtre where he had been sent by Napoleon in 1812. Then there was Mathurin Bruneau, a Normandy peasant, the so-called singing shoemaker, who was sentenced to five years with an additional two for contumacy as well as being fined 3,000 francs in February 1818. Then came Henri-Louis-Hector Hébert known as the baron de Richemot and duc de Normandie. There was also an English lunatic and Eleazar Williams, a missionary from the United States, but the claimant who had the greatest following was Karl-Wilhelm Naundorff, at one time represented by Vidocq's lawyer Jules Favre, who unsuccessfully took his claim to the French courts.[22]

Last but not least in Vidocq's pantheon was one of the great criminals of the time, Anthelme Collet, described by him as "by turn, a bishop or a general but always a thief." Born at Belley on April 10, 1795, he is regarded as being the equal of Cartouche and Mandrin. His ability to turn himself into a monk or an army inspector must have appealed to Vidocq as much as it did to the general public who saw him as a harmless anti-hero. He was, it is said, "a rogue of enormous skill with

---

[21] "The Pretended Dauphin of France," in *The Times*, January 10, 1816.
[22] *The Times*, February 25, 1818; Jules Favre, *Louis XVII, Plaiderie de Me. Jules Favre*.

unparalleled daring and in addition the art of the actor." He travelled through France for some fourteen years working one swindle after another, very often on municipal officials until retribution followed and he died in the *bagne* at Rochefort on November 24, 1840.[23]

A trio he did not mention – but one of whom mentioned him just before stepping up to the guillotine – was Chaudelet, Bardon and Guérin, convicted in November 1829 and executed on February 2 the next year for the robbery and murder of Chaudelet's uncle at 47 rue Charonne. Even though he was no longer Chef de la Sûreté at the time Vidocq's name was never far from criminals' minds. Trying to dance a *bourée* on the scaffold Chaudelet complained bitterly about police spies and informers, additionally blaming Vidocq for some of his troubles. *The Times* reported, "The notorious Vidocq came in for his share of abuse and the criminal Chaudelet expressed a hope that vengeance would soon be taken in his infamous body."[24] He was probably referring to an earlier five-year sentence he had received with the help of Vidocq.

---

[23] M. Berthelot (ed.), *La Grande Encyclopédie*.

[24] *The Times*, February 3, 1830; *Gazette des Tribunaux*, February 3, 1830, recounts the dance and the general vilification of the police but omits Vidocq's name.

Chapter 21

VIDOCQ'S
LAST MISSIONS

*In which our hero still dreams of future glory – takes up spying
again - is arrested over yet another trick – sets up and then gives
evidence against some conspirators – stands for President – and
for the last time changes his political coat*

N OW IN HIS SEVENTIES, Vidocq was still only too happy to
manipulate and play politics in the hope that he might yet again
become Head of the Sûreté, replacing Allard. His final opportunity came
with the events leading up to the 1848 Revolution when the Orléans
monarchy was overthrown and the Second Republic proclaimed.

Before that, however, Vidocq's wife, Fleuride-Albertine, had died at
their home at Saint-Mandé at 9:30 on the morning of September 22,
1847, after seventeen years of marriage. She was aged fifty-three and
had been suffering from cancer. Some sections of the press reported
that she had committed suicide:

On Thursday being alone with the nurse who attended her she asked for a
glass of *eau sucré*. This being brought she told the woman to bring her from
the cupboard a little phial which she said contained essence of orange flower
but which was in reality laudanum. She poured some of this into the glass
and, in consequence of taking it, expired in an hour afterwards declaring that
she had put an end to her existence in order to escape from the intolerable
sufferings which she endured. The clergy of Saint-Mandé having refused to
receive the body into the church it was carried direct to the cemetery under
the surveillance of the commissary of police. Some workmen and the poor
of the commune, to each of whom Vidocq distributed an 8lb loaf, followed
the corpse.[1]

---

[1] *Gagliani's Messenger*, quoted in *The Times*, October 7, 1847.

The rumor was quickly denied although it is correct she received no church service.

There had been unrest following acute food shortages between 1845 and 1847 and the Government was also unpopular for its intransigent attitude to democratic reform. The Revolution began on February 22, 1848, following the Government's refusal, backed by military force, to allow a so-called patriotic banquet – itself a way round the ban on political meetings. Things turned sour the following day and on February 24 Louis-Philippe abdicated in favor of his ten-year-old grandson, the comte de Paris. This was in no way regarded as sufficient and the Chamber of Deputies was invaded with insurgents demanding a provisional government which, when constituted, had the poet Alphonse Lamartine, François Arago and Alexandre-Auguste Ledru-Rollin at its head. In time they were joined by the Republican socialist Louis Blanc.

Alphonse Prat de Lamartine was born in Mâcon in 1790 and divided his career between politics and literature. In 1816, when he went to Aix-les-Bains for his health, he fell in love with the young wife of a doctor. She travelled with him to Paris, but, too ill to go to the spa the next year, she died in the autumn. His work, *Méditations poétiques*, inspired by her death, was immediately popular. The scientist François Arago was born near Perpignan in 1786 and from 1809 was on the staff of the Observatoire, becoming its director. Involved in politics from 1830 he was, as Minister of Marine, responsible for the abolition of slavery in the French colonies. Louis Blanc, born in 1811, worked initially as a journalist and came to notice with his 1839 pamphlet *L'Organisation du travail*, which advocated a system of state work for the unemployed. His work, *L'Histoire de Dix Ans*, published in 1841, was a highly critical study of the July monarchy and brought him into political prominence. Ledru-Rollin, born in 1807, was an out and out politician.

Lamartine's rise to power came with the publication in 1847 of his *Histoire des Girondins*. Its Revolutionary fervor catapulted him into the first division of politics. As a member of the provisional Government he was, for a few weeks, the true leader of France. This was Vidocq's chance. Lamartine and the others needed men like him to do their spying on the extreme left. The political police were put in the hands of Carlier, a man with an undoubted talent for breaking conspiracies.[2] Well versed in the tricks of the trade he received Vidocq with open arms. They would

---

[2] Pierre Carlier, born in 1799, worked under Gisquet. He dealt strictly with Government employees. In 1849 he was named Préfet. After the return of Napoleon III he faded into obscurity and died in 1858.

work together. Vidocq's particular task was to spy on the activities of the proliferating political societies of the hard-line Republicans.

One particular society, the Société Républicaine Centrale, was regarded as particularly worthy of investigation. It was run by a Revolutionary theorist, Louis-Auguste Blanqui, a man suspected of preparing a strike force and who claimed that it was not possible to change society peacefully.[3] It was this society which Vidocq was set to infiltrate. There was no question of his doing it himself; master of disguise though he may have been in his younger days, he was now far too well known. Instead he selected a young man, Daniel Borme, former chemist, former marine surgeon and wholly unbalanced, saying that the society members wanted a red revolution and he was to see what they were planning. Borme was himself well to the left politically and had no problem in joining the society.[4]

Given that he would attach himself to anyone who appeared to give credit to his rantings he was easy prey for a skilled operator like Vidocq. It was not long before Borme was explaining to his sympathetic employer that he had put together a plot to assassinate Lamartine and other deputies with a *machine infernale* he had made. His weapon was not exactly secret either in France and abroad for *The Times* had printed a report describing it as:

> . . . capable of destroying by an explosion without noise at all, all of the enemy's troops at a distance of 1000 yards from the town to be attacked.[5]

The plot arose out of a demonstration on May 15 when a crowd around 50,000 strong marched on the Chamber on the pretext of garnering support for the Polish oppressed. The march was led by Blanqui, Raspail and Barbes, with Bormes in the wings if things went well for the demonstrators.[6] Overall they did not. At first they created confusion at

---

[3] Blanqui was effectively a professional Revolutionary. Born in 1805 he had a long history of membership of Republican secret societies and was imprisoned following the insurrection of 1839. His elder brother Adolphe (b. 1789), an economist, unlike Louis-Auguste supported the Louis-Philippe Government. In 1840 he carried out an inquiry into the conditions of the working classes later published as *Des classes ouvrières en France.*

[4] Born in 1822 at Roqué-Bru in the Var, in March 1848 Borme tried to set up a group of women, the Vesuviennes, who were to be leaders in the fight for what he saw as freedom.

[5] *The Times*, March 25, 1844.

[6] François-Vincent Raspail was born at Carpentras in 1794. He made his name in the field of organic chemistry and was instrumental in the 1830 and 1848 revolutions. At the beginning of the Second Empire he served a long sentence before going to live in Belgium. He returned to France in 1869 and sat in the Chamber of Deputies, first for Lyons and then Marseilles. He died in 1878.

the Palais Bourbon but when they marched to the Hôtel de Ville they encountered the National Guard in a less than receptive mood. Some of the leaders, including Blanqui and Raspail, were arrested, as was Borme, who was questioned and then released. It was that evening that he explained his plan to Vidocq, something which was music to the old manipulator's ears. Now Borme seemingly was going completely mad. What he envisaged from his machine was to have nothing less than a hell fire in advance of a sort of last judgement. Vidocq encouraged him in the project which Borme planned for May 21, the day of *the fête de la Fraternité ou de la Concorde*. There was even a demonstration at the Château d'Eau. Of course, when it came to it Borme was never going to get near his goal. Vidocq denounced him and it was off to await trial at the court at Bourges to join Blanqui, Raspail and the others.

On May 27, 1848, Vidocq gave a deposition before the *juge d'instruction*, M. Haton. He had known Borme, he said, three or four years before but had lost touch until he met up with him quite by chance in April that year near to the Préfecture. It was then that Borme had told him about his *machine infernale* and his dislike of politicians, particularly Lamartine and Lamartine's wife against whom he held a personal grudge for having been thrown out of an atelier.

After his arrest on May 15 Borme had been released and he had turned up at Vidocq's home, quite unaware that he was in the hands of a master spy, to tell him that he was to be appointed Secretary General of the Provisional Government. And what of Borme's mental stability? "If he's mad he's dangerous. If he's criminal all the more reason to be on one's guard."[7] With this little coup Vidocq was, he thought, up and running once more. The old man was still dreaming of taking over the Sûreté from Pierre Allard.

To a certain extent he was in favor, for, meanwhile, on the other side of the channel, another baby eagle was flexing its talons. There was still another Bonaparte with whom to contend. Charles-Louis-Napoleon was the third son of Louis Bonaparte, King of Holland and a younger brother of the Emperor. This made him Napoleon's nephew but he was also a grandson of the Empress Josephine. After the fall of the First Empire his mother, estranged from Louis, took him to live in the Château d'Arenenberg in Switzerland. After the death of the unfortunate due de Reichstadt he became the Pretender and led two conspiracies to overthrow Louis-Philippe.

---

[7] Arch. Nat W. 569.

The first, on October 30, 1836, led by an artillery officer, Colonel Vaudrey, ended abruptly. After effectively seizing the city Charles-Louis, who apparently spoke with a thick German accent, rode into the military barracks. There he was met with a mixture of hostility, devotion and a good deal of uncertainty. A quick-witted officer, loyal to Louis-Philippe, called out that it was not the Pretender the soldiers were meeting but Vaudrey's nephew. In the confusion the barrack gates were shut; the Prince was separated from his supporters and arrested. A trial was too embarrassing and he was simply deported to America but – and this shows the extent of Bonapartist support – Vaudrey and the others were acquitted of conspiring against the state. Charles-Louis remained in America for little more than a year before coming to London where he wrote *Les idées napoléoniennes*, setting out what he saw as his duty to realize his uncle's social reforms. It was published in 1839 in Paris where, selling for half a franc, it had significant success.

Emboldened, his second attempted coup came the following year when, with the French in political disarray, he decided to attack from Boulogne. Although General Magnan, in command of the region, was initially tempted to support him, it was even less of a success. For a start Boulogne was not a Bonapartist town as was Strasbourg and Charles-Louis Napoleon and his troops were routed. They fled to their boats but were easily captured by the National Guard. This time there could be no avoiding the embarrassment of a trial and as a result the Prince was imprisoned at Ham, near Peronne.

Six years later, in May 1846, disguised as a mason named Badinguet, he escaped and made his way once more to London, arriving on May 27, where for a time he lived at the Brunswick Hotel in Jermyn Street as the count of Arenenberg. Badinguet was afterwards his nickname.

Now Vidocq was contacted by the publisher Pierre-Jules Hetzel, a friend of both Balzac and Lamartine, who worked for Bastide, the new Foreign Minister. Would Vidocq find out what Prince Charles-Louis-Napoleon Bonaparte was up to in London? Of course he would. His first letter to Hetzel is suitably ambiguous but his report from London shows he had lost none of his old bombast:

> There have been difficulties without number but my temerity has been crowned with a fabulous success. I knocked and all doors were opened to me.[8]

---

[8] Bib. Nat (Département des Manuscrits), NAF 17047: Arch. Hetzel, fols. 140–1.

Charles-Louis had been very much playing a waiting game. After the 1848 February troubles the future Emperor had indicated he would return to France but Lamartine informed him that the law sending him into exile had not been abrogated and he should stay away from Paris. Nevertheless he put his toes in the political water. In June his agent Persigny put up his name in four departments in the provisional elections. He was elected without canvassing or even appearing before the electorate. Now he stood down and remained in London where he was living at 3 King Street, St. James's from where he would go to the wine merchants Berry Brothers and Rudd to be weighed on their scales. It was then that Vidocq was sent to London to spy on him. The detective reported back that:

> He sees little of the world and is doing nothing important. He is too well advised to compromise himself. Why should he concern himself when he has such a number of supporters whom he can hardly contain?

Vidocq went on to warn that he was simply biding his time and that this sensible period of calm would end when there was an opportune moment. It was, he thought, absolutely vital to keep him under observation. The best way was to gain not only his confidence but also that of the valet de chambre and Vidocq was well in with him.[9]

Charles-Louis' next step was to win the September election for the Seine. Now he came to take his seat at the Assembly. Things may have quieted down in comparison to the summer but Hetzel was uneasy. Vidocq was to get hold of some compromising documents which would enable them to expel the Pretender. Hetzel was convinced the evidence would be in London.

Vidocq pleaded for time and money. He may have received the latter; indeed it is doubtful if the old rogue would have done anything without it. But was there anything to find? We shall probably never know. What was certainly lacking was time for, at the end of October, Charles-Louis announced that he was standing as presidential candidate, and on December 10 he was elected overwhelmingly. Vidocq himself stood in the election for the 2ème arrondissement, polling just one vote, presumably cast by himself. He was not the only candidate who garnered a single vote. Nor did the Prince de Joinville exactly receive ecstatic support in doubling Vidocq's tally.[10]

---

[9] Ibid. There is no record of Vidocq's entry into England in 1848. Either this is a clerical omission or, more probably, he was travelling on a false passport.

[10] *The Times*, December 14, 1848.

The election marked the end of Lamartine's political career.[11] Hetzel disappeared with him and that meant the recall of Vidocq and with it went any lingering hope of a return to the Sûreté in a dominant role.[12] However, Vidocq now completely changed sides yet again. Defeated in the elections he now became an enthusiastic supporter of Charles-Louis.

The great man had yet one more court appearance to make to give evidence but before that he was arrested again. This time there was another accusation of fraud against him and once more he was deposited in the Conciergerie, on February 9, 1849. It was while he was there that he was taken under police escort to Bourges to give evidence against the unfortunate Borme who was now on trial with Blanqui, Raspail, Barbes and Louis Blanc. Vidocq was quite the dandy in white glacé gloves, diamond studs, gold watch chain and gold earrings. He and Borme blamed each other. Vidocq told of the demonstration. Borme was asked why he should want to blow up nine hundred deputies. It was all part of Vidocq's plan to supplant Allard. Vidocq had sought him out because he knew of the invention which fired three hundred bullets a minute. The idea was to market it in England. Borme had turned him down and so made an enemy of the ex-chief. Wasn't it true that Borme had quite improperly been wearing a ribbon of the Légion d'honneur and received fifteen days imprisonment? Yes, that was Vidocq's fault as well. Borme had the medal pinned on his overcoat in the office in anticipation of being awarded it for his invention and Vidocq had denounced him. Then, on March 30, for Vidocq it was back to the Conciergerie – stopping on the way for a meal at the restaurant in the gare d'Orléans – from where he wrote to Carlier, now Head of the Municipal Police, thanking him for sending an escort and offering to pay the expenses.[13]

---

[11] Ten months was a very long time in French politics of the mid-nineteenth century. The hero of the previous February, Lamartine now received rather fewer than eight thousand votes. He retreated to private life and literature where, to pay his enormous debts, he published a series of historical works, novels and biographies. In 1867 he received a life annuity from the *Corps legislatif* and died in Paris two years later.

[12] Pierre-Jules Hetzel was born at Chartres in 1814. He played an active political part during the Second Republic but was banished in 1851. He was later given an amnesty and died in Monte Carlo in 1886. In addition to the large number of novels he wrote under the pseudonym P-J. Stahl, he founded *Le Magasin d'education et de récréation*. He also "discovered" Jules Verne.

[13] The escort duly reported back that there had been no trouble on the journey. Blanqui, who later founded his own party, the *Blanquistes,* continued his Revolutionary ways and helped to bring down the Second Empire after the fall of Sedan in the Franco-Prussian war. After the defeat of the Commune in May 1871 he was imprisoned for life but was released in 1879.

But what had our hero been doing in the Conciergerie anyway? The answer was that he had been up to his old tricks. He was there for another swindle. And what was this one all about? He was there at the request of the duc de Valençay who was having difficulties with a lady who had some compromising letters from him and as a result he had been having problems with the duchess. The Abbé Grimaud from the parish of Villedieu had called on the lady, a Mme L., explained to her how sorry the duke was for any misunderstandings there might have been and would pay 3,000 francs on His Grace's behalf in return for the letters. Mme L. seems to have known her left hand from her right and to have taken advice, because she met the Abbé that evening for a second time, on this occasion at the house of a business intermediary and was paid – the reports vary – either 1,000 or 3,000 francs. Unfortunately the letters appear to have gone straight to the duchess. The police were called and it was discovered that the priest, although mannered and elderly, had yet to be ordained. In fact he was a M. Bourgeois, a name then once again being used by Vidocq. Arrest at Vidocq's home in the rue Saint-Louis followed.[14]

Philip Stead thinks that the police may also have taken the opportunity in this piece of deception to force Vidocq into the position of police spy yet again. In the Conciergerie at the time several of the leaders of the May riot, including Blanqui, were being kept awaiting trial. No doubt Vidocq was to spy on them. In any event the process was dropped and Vidocq was non-suited. Whether this was because the duke and duchess came to an arrangement or whether he had done his bit for the authorities is not altogether clear. Whatever was behind the arrest Vidocq's evidence did not count. Borme, along with all but the ringleaders, was acquitted.[15] It is possible that Victor Hugo had something to do with Vidocq's release because in *Choses vues* there is mention of Vidocq coming to see him to thank him for his help in the affair.[16]

After his final court case Vidocq, who always could recognize on which side his bread was buttered, executed a last public volte-face. The words uttered back in 1811 that he would act for whoever paid him most, or for whom he thought might profit him most, were

[14] *L'Estafette*, February 8, 1849. In the dossiers relating to his evidence in the Borme case Vidocq, described as aged seventy-five, is referred to as *dit Le Bourgeois*. Arch. Nat. W. 569.
[15] Philip Stead, *Vidocq*, pp. 229–30.
[16] Victor Hugo, *Choses vues*, t. II, pp. 21–2.

yet again proved true. Buried in the past were the days when he had been paid to spy on Charles-Louis-Napoleon. Now, in the windows of his apartment in boulevard Beaumarchais was a splendid banner:

> Louis-Napoleon
> Messiah of 2 December 1851.
> Be blessed.
> You have saved and regenerated France.
> Long live the Empire.

Chapter 22

VIDOCQ
AGAINST DEATH

*In which our hero struggles for a pension – against
cholera – fights off predatory women – and puts
his feet on the soil for one last time*

V IDOCQ ALWAYS BELIEVED he was going to die in Saint-Mandé aged one hundred at midnight on July 22, 1875, but it was not to be. There were, however, still a few years left in him. With the coup d'état of December 2, 1851, which dissolved the Assemblé Nationale *Législative,* Prince Charles-Louis Napoléon repaid his former tormentors. Now he was no longer simply the President of the Republic, he was Napoleon III. In his turn Vidocq, now in his late seventies and a vociferous loyalist, was becoming something of a nuisance. Indeed, no one could be more loyal than he. He began reporting people wearing false decorations and would appear at the Ministry of the Interior clutching seditious pamphlets he had discovered. As a result he was given small assignments including one touring the north of France. His aliases now included Monsieur Jules from the old days but also the far grander baron de Saint-Jules. He took to calling out *"Vive Napoléon"* when he saw the Emperor driving on the boulevards. Now, Saint-Mandé sold, he was living with Anne-Heloïse Lefèvre and her upholsterer husband at 9 boulevard du Temple.

Financially, he was certainly not in good shape. "Abject poverty," says Brayley Hodgetts,[1] but that was far from the case. Reduced circumstances would be more accurate. Nor was he averse to sending out begging letters intended to give the impression of the rats nibbling

---

[1] E. A. Brayley Hodgetts, *Vidocq: A Master of Crime*, p. 319.

his toes as the candle guttered. On February 21, 1853, he wrote from his home with the Lefèvres to the Préfet de la Sûreté:

M le Président

I created the Police de Sûreté which I ran for 20 years. The services which I rendered to Society and notably the Ville de Paris are too well known for me to need to list them.

Fifteen to sixteen thousand criminals of every category went under the hand of justice during my tenure. The most dangerous were arrested by me; referred to tribunals they were condemned to expiate their crimes or to the *bagnes*.

I am more than 80 years old and on the verge of starving in the Paris I have served long and loyally. If I am abandoned in this trying position in which I find myself I have no alternative than begging or suicide. I would have already taken this drastic course if I had not been held back by religious scruples. But, before I take this step I come with trust to demand help to exist in the little time I have left to live. The sacrifice in favor of an octogenarian could not last long. In view of this I hope that my demand will not be rejected.

To this plaint he attached a number of documents underlining the role he had played in the heady days of June 1832. He was never averse to reminding those he thought might be able to assist him. What he really wanted was a life pension but the then Prefect of Police, called on to give an opinion, while accepting the value Vidocq had given was not going to forget "certain tiresome incidents." "Moved to pity," there would nevertheless be financial assistance until his death.[2]

Vidocq cannot have been entirely destitute because on May 13, 1851, he paid 25 million francs to the Companie d'Assurance Générales in return for an annuity of 3,470 francs. However, Bruno Roy-Henri suggests that Valizé, a nephew of his late wife Fleuride-Albertine, persuaded him to sink a substantial amount into a wild scheme to provide the fuel for the heating for all the bakers' ovens in the Paris region and he lost his entire investment. The irony was that, after all his years routing out fraudsters, Vidocq would say that he and Valizé had been swindled. He had also lost money on the Bourse slump at the time of the 1848 Revolution.[3] Vidocq was, however, carrying out a little private detective work and was still acting as an auxiliary for

---

[2] *Des Chercheurs et Curieux*, May 30, 1910.

[3] B. Roy-Henry, *Vidocq du bagne à la préfecture*, p. 306.

the police, something he did up to the last few months of his life. In 1852 he gave some advice to a Mme Deshayes whose daughter had disappeared. The next year he was in Naples to assist the marquis Papin on an unspecified venture. There were also querulous letters to the authorities over the return of books and to a picture restorer about canvasses he had left with the studio, but, not unnaturally, he was slowing down. He was also lonely and Ledru often received notes asking him to call.[4]

For female company, after the death of Fleuride-Albertine Vidocq contented himself with a string of young actresses. Claiming he was very much in reduced circumstances he followed the lines of Volpone: there could be no immediate gift of money or jewelry but there would be a will in the girl's favor – pie in the sky when he died.

On August 6, 1854, now aged seventy-nine, Vidocq was taken ill with suspected cholera and his friend Dr. Dornier, who lived at 57 rue de Rivoli, was sent for. It was not thought that at his age he would survive. After all, the epidemic had in previous outbreaks carried off such apparent indestructibles as Marshal Bugeaud and Mme Recamier.[5] Dornier wrote to the police on August 20 explaining that he would not be able to work for several weeks.[6] But Vidocq must have had the constitution of an ox, as well as a very good doctor, for within a short time he was up and out and about on the Paris streets.[7]

Towards the end of Vidocq's life there seems to have been a surprise visitor. The illegitimate offspring of Marie-Anne-Louise Le Chevalier, Emile-Adolphe Le Chevalier, now Emile-Adolphe Vidocq, reappeared. Thinking that Vidocq was wealthy and that he might inherit he had changed his name. Now, though, he was willing to be bought out and in return would renounce his rights under the estate. The elderly harpy Marie-Anne-Louise was evidently still alive at this stage because Emile-Adolphe indicated that she would be quite prepared to make a statement that her son was a bastard. The putative son was shown the door. His mother died two years before the great man.

---

[4] For documents relating to Vidocq's last years see BHVP, MS. 2928, which contains more than sixty files relating to the years of his agency and after.

[5] Both died in the outbreak of 1849. Thomas Robert Bugeaud de la Piconnerie had commanded a troop which tried, and in 1848 failed, to defend Paris and the Crown. Mme Jeanne-Françoise Bernard (Mme Recamier) was a *saloniste*.

[6] BHVP, MS 2928, Dossier 66.

[7] BHVP, MS 2928, Dossier 41.

Le Figaro reported Vidocq's final collapse in grand style:

> On April 30, 1857, his legs would no longer carry him. He was in a state of extreme feebleness. He developed the idea that he would regain his strength once his feet touched the ground. The good people trying to satisfy the wish of the ill man placed before his bed a bed of earth. Vidocq lifted himself feebly . . . He extended his old Herculean emaciated legs and suddenly, when he felt the ground under his bare feet, a ray of life lit up his face. He demanded they let him alone. He fell inert and cold. He was put back to bed with a deal of difficulty.[8]

From then on it was only a matter of time. Dr. Dornier made out prescriptions including, appropriately enough, one called "four-thieves vinegar," at a cost of two to five francs. Later he wrote that the vinegar played a part in Vidocq's life up to the end.[9] Vidocq died on May 11, 1857, at the age of eighty-two.

Shortly after his death a disparaging piece appeared in *L'Indépendance Belge:*

> A man who was never able to climb from the lower depths of society but acquired universal recognition Vidocq has just died at the age of 78 amidst great sentiments of piety in the arms of an ecclesiastic friend of Father Ventura.
>
> One thought that this man of such strange individuality left some fortune among a variety of people including among others a boulevard actress; they produced wills signed by him but their hopes were not crowned with great success.
>
> Before dying Vidocq wrote the names of three people from whom he would wish sentiments of esteem and recognition. The three people are M. de Lamartine (one recalls that in 1848 Vidocq was obscurely mixed up in some political matters), M. Zangiacomi and M. Pécourt, counsel to the Court of Cassation which acquitted him after his conviction.[10]

And it continued along those lines. In reply the comment drew a long article of special pleading from Charles Ledru addressed to the editor, something with which he was so pleased that he later had it printed.[11] It began:

---

[8] *Le Figaro*, May 21, 1857.

[9] For a list of the expenses at Vidocq's death which included the church ceremony at 290 francs and a donation to the Sisters of Charity of 300 francs, see Dossier 71. Candles cost three francs. BHVP, MS 2928, Dossiers 42 and 71.

[10] *L'Indépendance Belge*, May 11, 1857.

[11] Charles Ledru, *La Vie, la mort et les derniers moments du Vidocq après sa confession à l'heure suprême.*

If justice should be done to the living it is all the more reason to do justice to the dead. So with all the virtue of right and endeavor I have given to defending the accused, I now address you a prayer.

It rehearsed all the old stories of the great man: how he had first unjustly been imprisoned; Vidocq's defense of the Procurator-General in the 1830 Revolution; his examination by the phrenologist Fossati; how he, Ledru, did not wish to appear for Vidocq; Vidocq's gift to the Sisters of Charity which secured Ledru's services; why Vidocq chose Ledru in the first place:

I chose you to defend me because you are one of the lawyers who have attacked my administrative acts with the most severity.

In fact, all the tried and tested defenses the great m*ouchard* had used over the years.

Ledru explained away the arrival of the actress who had come wanting the magistrate to put seals on Vidocq's property, so preserving her legal rights, and how the magistrate had found more recent wills than hers.

He then went on to give a touching account of the death throes of his old friend. He had, apparently, been paralyzed and almost unable to speak for eleven days. Vidocq had confessed and received absolution and afterwards had a letter sent to Ledru saying he wanted to see him on Monday, May 4. Ledru rushed round and immediately called on the priest M. Orssant, the vicar of the Church of Saint-Denys de Saint Sacremont, rue Saint-Louis. Ledru was there when Vidocq had these words to say; that is if Ledru heard him correctly:

I have passed my life in chasing criminals and delivering them to the justice of men. I would be worse than the worst rascal of all if I didn't tell the truth and the whole truth to God's representative in my confession.

It is said that no sensible man can help laughing at the death of Little Dorritt. Anticipating the great novelist, Ledru does what he can to make this scene as mawkish as possible:

The attentive eye of the invalid was fixed upon the priest.
Choking, he said, "was at the bottom of the abyss. I hadn't been to church for 70 years. I had forgotten God himself."

I liked duelling and women too much but I never debauched a single one. Without women and duelling I'd have had the Cross of Honor.

Calling to the priest to come as close as possible Vidocq whispered in his last breath: "You, you . . . my only Doctor."

Which all things considered was a bit hard on Dornier who had kept him alive well beyond any reasonable expectation.

Ledru concluded his open letter with what might unkindly be called a good deal of religious guff about Vidocq being with Christ in Paradise, and signed off:

To the Editor:
Your article inspired me and I have dedicated it to you.

As for M. Orssant, he is reported as having said that Vidocq's death was one of the two best with which he had ever been involved. The other was a General Despeaux, at his death the senior officer in the French army, who had died the previous year.

As far as Lamartine was concerned Vidocq need not have bothered about naming him. The politician and poet had effectively been retired from public life and he met Ledru on the way to see the dying Vidocq. Lamartine expressed the wish to see him saying that, as far as he was concerned, he was a faithful and honest servant and an honest man. He is also quoted as saying of the events of 1848 that had he been given a clear field and had only Vidocq been with him he would have controlled the situation. It was right that he should pay his last respects to his old friend.

He made it as far as the front door where he encountered Louis Ulbach of the *Revue de Paris*. Afraid that there would be other members of the press outside the house who might make unflattering comments, Lamartine went into a swift retreat. "My dear fellow, you'll never guess where I'm off to. I'm going to see Vidocq. He is dying." A moment later he continued:

All things considered I won't go. I've only to meet some mischievous journalist there and there'll be some fine gossip. Vidocq and Lamartine. Can't you see what they'd make of it? He's not expecting or asking for me, poor Vidocq! He will die well enough without me. It's a pity. I liked him very much.[12]

---

[12] Bartélemy Maurice, *Vidocq, vie et aventures*.

Vidocq's body was taken to the church of Saint-Denys.[13] The funeral service was not well attended. The nuns marshalled some one hundred of the poor of the neighborhood to attend the service to supplement Dornier, Ledru, the Lefèvres and, among the few other non-conscripts, a young woman who cried throughout the service. *Le Figaro* reported that Vidocq, who wanted a good send-off, had set aside a sum of money to give everyone who attended three francs for so doing.[14]

After Vidocq's death, Emile-Adolphe Vidocq made a further claim on the estate but Vidocq had left sufficient proof to thwart it and it was withdrawn on August 25, 1856. Others claimed small amounts of money owed and yet others wanted papers returned to them.[15]

Surprisingly, as far as is known, Vidocq had no children, at least whom he acknowledged. Such money as he had was left to Anne-Héloïse Lefèvre (whom it has been suggested was his last mistress) in a will of January 1, 1857, which was sufficient to defeat the claims of some eleven women who were apparently in possession of earlier wills. His fortune consisted of 2,907.50 francs from the sale of his goods at Drouot's, the Paris auction house, and 867.50 francs, the arrears of his annuity. The sale took place in the summer of 1857 and there was no formal catalogue.

---

[13] Curiously in the register his age is given as "*85 (ou 89) ans.*"
[14] *Le Figaro*, May 21, 1857.
[15] BHVP, MS 2928, Dossier 44.

Chapter 23

"A LA RECHERCHE
DU TEMPS VIDOCQ"

In which our hero meets Honoré de Balzac, Alexandre Dumas
père, and many others – is metamorphosed into Vautrin,
Jean Valjean, Inspector Javert, Monsieur Lecoq and many,
many more – and influences a host of other writers

V IDOCQ HAS NEVER CEASED to fascinate the French public even if the Paris police have sometimes regarded his place
in their Valhalla as suspect. In September 1905 the police put on
an exhibition of portraits of the former chiefs of the Sûreté, beginning with Vidocq's successor Allard. When this omission was queried
by the press it was said, quite wrongly, he had never been Head.[1]
It was some time before he was credited with his due. His name was,
however, used as a stick to beat the police over the years. So when,
a century after Vidocq, some members of the terrorist Bonnot Gang
were killed in a shoot-out with the police, Vidocq and his methods
were held up as a shining example of how they should have been
caught.[2]

What legacy did Vidocq leave? His most notable impact was on
the police, British and American, as well as the French. For all but a
few months of Vidocq's time with the Sûreté there was no equivalent
police force in either country. London had the Bow Street Runners
and New York a system of watchmen. One of the problems which
Sir Robert Peel had when trying to establish a Metropolitan Police
Force in 1829 was the opposition to a Fouché-Vidocq style secret

---

police.[3] In 1818 members of a Select Committee, set up three years earlier to consider the "state of mendacity in the Metropolis," reported that they would "deprecate a severe system of policing as inconsistent with the liberties of the people."

As a result, when the first London's finest paraded in Old Palace Yard on September 29, 1829, they were kitted out in blue swallowtail coats, broad leather belts fastened with brass buckles, half-wellington boots and specially strengthened top hats, on which the officers could stand, the better to view the surrounding countryside. Each man had his divisional number and letter sewn to the collar of his coat to make him readily identifiable to the public.

It did not, however, take the officers long to understand Vidocq's theory of the necessity of proactive policing. Undercover officers were soon in operation. The first of these, a William Steward Paul Popay, a sergeant sent in 1831 to infiltrate a trade union, came only two years after the establishment of the force. Passing himself off as an out-of-work coalman he was a typical police spy. His speeches were the loudest; he damned the ministers for villains; he wanted to establish a shooting gallery and gave lessons in the use of the broadsword. He marched arm in arm with trade unionists to a meeting to celebrate the French Revolution. All in all, he behaved exactly as the police of the estaminets of 1816 had done. Unfortunately he was recognized by a union member when Popay was working at the police desk at Park House and all hell broke loose.

His conduct described as "highly reprehensible," poor Popay was dismissed from the force "with ignominy." It did not help him to argue that the plain clothes were for his own protection. His superiors, who argued that Popay had been working at the request of the Home Office but only to watch meetings, were criticized for not keeping him under closer control. The Select Committee, while recognizing the need for a plainclothes force, deprecated:

> any approach to the Employment of Spies, in the ordinary acceptance of the term, as a practice most abhorrent to the feelings of the People and most alien to the spirit of the Constitution.

But there had been other Popays, disguised:

---

[3] Fouché and Vidocq became almost synonymous in English eyes. Writing of the American Civil War, one reporter commented on the "unscrupulousness of a Fouché or a Vidocq," *The Times*, June 14, 1865.

. . . in clothing of various descriptions, sometimes in the garb of gentlemen, sometimes in that of tradesmen or artisans, sometimes in sailors' jackets.[4]

Vidocq would have been proud of Popay and the others.

The difficulty was, so far as English detectives were concerned, in the attitude of Commissioners such as Sir Charles Warren who thought, as the historian Bernard Porter writes:

. . . policing should be open, visible and by the book, rather like cricket, where everything was governed by the rules of fair play. Plain-clothes policing was like taking off the bails at the bowler's end without a warning whilst the batsman was backing up. It was also a temptation to corruption as history showed very well.[5]

But, there again, the French never did understand the summer game.

What is more amazing is how long it took for the Metropolitan Police to introduce women officers. The French police had used them as spies long before Vidocq put a series of women on a more or less formal footing. There is little doubt that his auxiliaries were carrying on the same profession they had under the Restoration and before.

Society women, more or less ruined, were in great demand:

The Minister of Police had ready and waiting to act young baronesses and old vicomtesses who, launched into the world of fashion, and possessing no other income but their monthly payments from the secret funds, were delighted to prove their devotion to the Minister, by informing him of the way of living and the opinions of the majority of Government officials.[6]

In England there were isolated incidents of their use such as the 1880 arrest of Thomas Titley in which a policeman's wife was employed in an effort to flush out an abortionist pharmacist;[7] but the first official

---

[4] Report from Select Committee on Metropolitan Police (675), Parliamentary Papers (1833), Vol. 13, pp. 401, 409–11; James Morton, *Bent Coppers*, pp. 28–30. For other early examples of the police spy in England and Wales see Bernard Porter, *Plots and Paranoia*, p. 74 and *The Refugee Question in Mid-Victorian Politics*, pp. 114–15. One of the first long-term undercover police officers was a Superintendent English who was used against rural incendiarists in East Anglia in 1844. John Archer, *By a Flash and a Scare*.
[5] Bernard Porter, *Origins of the Vigilant State*, p. 84.
[6] N-T. Desessart, *Dictionnaire universel de police*, quoted by Jean Galtier-Boissonière in *Mysteries of the French Secret Police*, p. 166.
[7] This brought charges against the police which were dismissed at the Old Bailey. James Morton, *Supergrasses and Informers*, pp. 201–4.

policewoman was an Edith Grant from Grantham who was used to keep London's Hyde Park free of sexual misbehavior so that the wildlife was not frightened. It was not until the end of the First World War that a force of women was created, subject to the same discipline as the men. Again, initially, it was used for cleaning up streets and parks.[8]

During the First World War an undercover worker, employed on a more or less casual basis, was used to infiltrate the increasing drug traffic. A Mrs. Garner or Gardiner:

> disguised herself as a prostitute, got to know her supposed colleagues, moved in circles where she was in constant danger from the drug-runner, and obtained information of a most important kind, both in connection with drug-running and spying.[9]

So far as the Sûreté is concerned Vidocq's influence was immense. He ensured that his detectives went to the prisons, as he had done, to see the new intake of convicts so they could recognize them in the future. It was a practice later adopted and still maintained in England until the late 1980s when detectives would go to court in particular cases to see who was in the public gallery and could therefore be linked as an associate of the suspect.

Samuel Edwards tells the story of Vidocq's understanding of ballistics.[10] In 1822 the tall, red-headed comtesse Isabelle d'Arcy was found dead in her bed. The comte, twenty-five years older than his wife, was arrested but despite the fact she had almost certainly been killed with one of d'Arcy's duelling pistols, which had since been cleaned, Vidocq accepted his story that he had not murdered her and soon discovered she had an Italian lover, one Deloro. Vidocq persuaded a doctor to remove the bullet from the comtesse's skull and was satisfied that it was too large to have been fired by a duelling pistol.

The story has all the hallmarks of a Vidocq production. Next he hired a red-haired actress to insinuate herself with Deloro and when the Italian was out, she let him into their apartment where he discovered a larger pistol and jewelry which d'Arcy identified as having been given to his wife by him. Vidocq, now in disguise, found the fence who had purchased a diamond ring from Deloro a short while before. As for the

[8] See Joan Lock, The British Police Woman, p. 47; Daily Mail, October 3, 1918.
[9] Mary Allen, Lady in Blue, p. 38.
[10] Samuel Edwards, The Vidocq Dossier, pp. 66–9.

bullet, although flattened, Vidocq believed it fitted the pistol. Deloro was arrested and, no doubt with a little help, confessed.

Edwards quotes Alexandre Dumas père as the source – it does not appear in other versions of Vidocq's life and Sanson does not name Deloro as one of his clients for the guillotine that year. If the story is correct, Vidocq was a decade and a half early for the development of ballistics. Not until 1835 did Henry Goddard, one of the Bow Street Runners, take a bullet with a curious ridge from the body of a householder. In those days bullets were often homemade and at the home of the suspect Goddard found a bullet mold with a slight gouge and a ridge on the bullet which matched the mold.[11]

Vidocq also began a card system for recording the physical characteristics of criminals and suspects; as well as that he had at least a rudimentary understanding of fingerprinting, something which did not become accepted in France until 1914 after the death of Alphonse Bertillon, whose rival system of classification of criminals had gradually replaced Vidocq's cards. In fact, fingerprinting as a means of identification was nothing new. It had been used for centuries in India, Japan and China as a prevention against fraud in claiming pay twice over. Chinese orphanages took the fingerprints of abandoned babies and a handprint was common on a Chinese divorce contract. The problem was really categorizing fingerprints and introducing a system so that the data could be easily searched.

In Europe two early observations on fingerprints had come to nothing. The first was in 1686 when Marcello Malpighi, Professor of Anatomy at the University of Bologna, put down his thoughts which were promptly ignored, as were those of John Purkinje at the

---

[11] Probably the first fully recorded case of an identification through ballistics came when on December 9, 1860, a laborer, Thomas Richardson, stood trial at Lincoln charged with the murder of Constable Alexander McBrian on October 25 that year. At about 4 a.m. McBrian had been on duty patrolling near the churchyard at Wyberton when he saw Richardson wearing a billycock hat pulled over his eyes and with something in his pocket. When McBrian went to question Richardson he shot the officer and fled. Badly wounded, McBrian managed to arouse the vicar but he died later that morning after given a description of his attacker.

This time the murder was solved not by matching the bullet but with the paper plugs used to stuff powder and bullets into the barrels of muzzle-loaders. Superintendent Manton found the singed remains of a tampion made from a page of *The Times*. The home of Richardson was searched and he was found to have a double-barrelled pistol, one barrel of which had been fired and the second contained a matching piece of *The Times* of March 27, 1854. At his trial the jury was invited to return accident, manslaughter or wilful murder with the judge seeming to favor a manslaughter verdict. They returned a verdict of wilful murder and Richardson was sentenced to death. The sentence was respited on December 20. *The Times*, December 10, 21, 1860.

University of Breslau, who did the same in 1823.[12] So far as Vidocq was concerned he had difficulty in finding a suitable ink. His own indelible ink took too long to wear off the fingers and it also dried too quickly to take a proper impression. Again, as with footprints he understood that impressions could be made in clay but it was impossible to store, let alone index, clay impressions.

There was, of course, no system of classifying fingerprinting in existence and Vidocq's original card index expanded over the decades until it was completely unwieldly. Nevertheless when the young Alphonse Bertillon endeavored to establish his own system which involved the measuring and recording of a criminal's features – the nose, eyes, length of ears, etc. – so that he could establish the percentage chance of a suspect having all the same measurements, he met with very considerable resistance from his superiors. What had been good enough for Vidocq in the 1820s was still good enough for his successors such as Goron in the 1890s. Edwards believed that Vidocq also understood the possibilities of blood-typing.

Certainly Vidocq's method of interviewing suspects survived him. In the years when the New York police were giving beatings, using sweat boxes and locking suspects up with the bodies of their alleged victims, and the German police were putting rats in the cells of female suspects, Vidocq's successors continued to obtain confessions with rather more grace. Not that the occasional slap could be ruled out. Eugène Roch describes Vidocq's treatment of the convict Fossard's brother, when he was investigating the Cabinet de Médailles, as *"quelques caresses."*[13] Overall, however, he seems to have subscribed to the view of some police that if the criminal will not confess after the shock of the first blow and the resulting feeling of helplessness, then he will not confess at all in the face of further brutality. It was easier to feed them and ply them with drink to obtain a confession, which could itself be rewarded by a visit from a prostitute.

In the case of Rata and Malaguti, Vidocq recognized the need for a parade instead of mere confrontation as a more reliable way of making an identification of suspects. The police of Paris under Vidocq may

---

[12] For a highly readable account of the early development of fingerprints and the science of ballistics, see Jürgen Thorwald, *The Marks of Cain*. See also James Morton, *Manhunt!*

[13] Eugène Roch, *L'Observateur des tribunaux*, t. I, p. 86. Culled from the pages of the *Gazette Roch*, this provides a thoroughly entertaining commentary on politicians, crimes and manners, from the secret marriage and arrest of the duchesse de Berri and false dauphins to a civil claim between a pharmacist who claimed to have a delipatory soap for women's mustaches, and his clients.

have been as corrupt as any other force in any major city but in terms of dealing with criminals they were light years ahead of London and New York.

One thing of which there can be no doubt is Vidocq's influence on literature. "The massive silhouette, now reassuring, now terrifying, not only loomed in the background of the major contemporary works, but also dominated the people's fears and beliefs."[14] Ten years after the success of *Les Voleurs* he again turned his hand to fiction. In 1843 Eugène Sue had written *Les Mystères de Paris* – some suggested that Vidocq provided the first chapter. It had not been wholly well received. The reviewer for *L'Univers* thought, "You must have forgotten that we read the Memoirs of Vidocq at high school." The next year Vidocq went one better writing *Les Vrais Mystères de Paris*, or at least providing the framework and detail for some of the stories. Some real characters, such as the police agent Ronquetti, appear under their own names and Appert wrote that he had met the hero, Salvador, on one of his visits to the galleys. *Les Vrais Mystères* caused Vidocq a few more visits to the courts. First, inconveniently, the rather mediocre writer Horace-Napoleon Raisson decided that he was the real author. He claimed he had provided the synopsis and had put the suggestion to Vidocq that he might like to lend his name to it. He had written the first part and when he had shown it to the detective, Vidocq had confiscated it and taken it to another publisher, Cadot. A court case naturally followed with Raisson suing Cadot rather than Vidocq. Without any considerations as to the merits he lost on this technical ground and was obliged to pay the costs. After that Raisson reproduced the first volume as his own novel, *Une Sombre Histoire*. There was more trouble for Raisson because he changed his name to Mortonval so annoying another man of the same name.[15]

The problems caused by *Les Vrais Mystères* did not end there. M. Caron, manager of the Café Divan in the passage de l'Opéra, now decided he had been libelled by being named as a receiver and the associate of fraudsters and asked for the book to be suppressed. In the

---

[14] The book was to be entitled *The Revelations and Recollections of Vidocq*, containing "every unpublished fact connected with his remarkable career and which were suppressed in Paris – the whole embracing a period of fifty-seven years from 1788 to 1845 and written since his arrest in this country."

[15] *Gazette des Tribunaux*, April 24, June 6, 1844; Philip Stead, *Vidocq*, pp. 202–3. Horace-Napoleon Raisson (1798–1854) was first employed at the Ministry of Finance and from 1822 devoted himself to literature. He wrote *L'Histoire impartiale des Jésuites* in association with Balzac and *Code des gens honêtes*, sometimes attributed to that writer. In his *Histoire de la police de Paris de 1697 à 1844* he defends Gisquet.

end Vidocq was fined 100 francs, and 500 francs damages were awarded to Caron. There was also an order for the offending passages to be deleted.[16] Another action was settled for a more modest 25 francs. But, just as Vidocq cheated or at least imposed on his borrowers over the publication of *Les Voleurs*, so did Cadot over *Les Vrais Mystères*. The arrangement had been for an edition of twelve hundred copies but Cadot printed more and had them sold in Germany.

After *Les Vrais Mystères* came the last of Vidocq's novels and memoirs, *Les Chauffeurs du Nord*, written probably with the considerable help of Auguste Vitu who was said to have later collaborated with Baudelaire. The first two volumes appeared in 1845 and the remaining three in 1846. In it Vidocq returns to the tales of his early days in and around Lille and with it come the old stories of Salembier, Albert Labbe and Calendrin with whom Vidocq had shared a cell. The stories are those of Vidocq; the trials and tribulations of the heroine are undoubtedly Vitu's.

However, at his London exhibition in 1845 Vidocq announced the proposed publication of his *Revelations*:

> Besides establishing for some time my residence in England, the classic land of freedom and the press, my chief motive was to be able to write that work with all liberty, and tell all I know of many high placed persons; to reveal a multitude of abuses, and indicate the remedies to evils, that men, guided by motives that I shall tell, do all in their power to maintain.
>
> That work, which will form at least six volumes in 8vo., will, at first, be published in English, for which purpose I have engaged one of the most distinguished translators of Great Britain.[17]

It never appeared. The project foundered over the question of money. It worked out that Vidocq would receive £40 and he thought he should have £70. There was also the curious item of the expense of £40 worth of wine.[18] Frederick Tolfrey might have thought he was to be the distinguished translator. Vidocq had been negotiating with him and he hoped to translate the exhibition catalogue. Vidocq had also been dickering with the publisher Newby of 72 Mortimer Street about the six-volume venture and Tolfrey, who had a number of books to

---

[16] *Gazette des Tribunaux*, August 10, 1844; *Le Moniteur*, August 11, 1844.
[17] E-F. Vidocq, *Vidocq*.
[18] BHVP MS 2928, Dossier 48.

his name, was anxious to have the work.[19] He was already acting as negotiator and general translator for Vidocq. Newby made an offer of £70 per volume for a limited edition with £117 per volume for a second edition. Vidocq wanted a serialization first and ultimately nothing came of the project. In the meantime he was obliged to fund Tolfrey who was desperate first for £5 and then for £3 to pay the week's rent. When it came to it Tolfrey did not even get the job of translating the catalogue.[20]

In fact it was not until the middle of the twentieth century that Vidocq's contribution to literature in general and detective fiction in particular was accepted. For example, the early Penguin edition of *Old Goriot* makes no mention of the Vautrin–Vidocq axis. In Victor Hugo's *Les Misérables* he forms the basis of both the heroic convict Jean Valjean and his nemesis the detective Javert. Modesty was never his long suit and, according to the critic Charles-Augustin Sainte-Beuve, Vidocq believed that he should have been credited as co-author of Hugo's *Notre-Dame de Paris*. He had, he said, provided the details for the *Cour des Miracles* and it was acknowledged that this was the best part of the book.[21]

Balzac's master criminal Vautrin owes a great deal to Vidocq. It is not surprising that Balzac took to the detective. Graham Robb describes the author as:

A social observer who turned characters into real people and the real people he loved, seduced or exploited into characters; a brilliant business-man who was always on the edge of bankruptcy; an expert fantasizer who believed that the vital fluid known as will power diminishes with every desire; a defender of the Family with at least one illegitimate child and a wide repertoire of sexual appetites, a man with a phenomenal capacity for self-deception who can be treated (according to Henry James) as a "final authority on human nature."[22]

He sounds really rather like the great man himself.

It is difficult to know exactly how Vidocq came to meet Balzac but it is likely that they had met at the house of Gabriel de Berny and

---

[19] His work includes such classics as *The Sportsman in France* (1841), *The Sportsman in Canada* (1845) and *Jones's Guide to Norway* and *Salmon Fisher's Pocket Companion* (1848).

[20] See BHVP, MS 2928.

[21] *The Times*, August 13, 1883.

[22] Graham Robb, *Balzac*, p. xi. The quotation is from Henry James, *French Poets and Novelists*, p. 117.

his wife Laure, the goddaughter of Marie-Antoinette, who was more than twenty years older than Balzac. Apparently Balzac, on all fours, "playing both the huntsman and the hound," used to enjoy chasing her naked through the rooms of her apartment.[23]

Given that Balzac had a character, Annette, who provides a good influence for the hero in his 1822 novel *Annette et le pirate*, it is likely they met in the days when Vidocq's mysterious mistress was at least being mentioned.

Balzac was accused of having dreamed up Vautrin from his diseased imagination. He pointed out that he had been inspired by a meeting with Vidocq. Graham Robb comments that this might not have pleased the detective but this self-aggrandizing publicity seeker would surely have welcomed any literary acknowledgement.[24]

Vidocq had told Balzac that "all the criminals he had arrested went from one to five weeks before recovering the ability to salivate" and the comment appears in *Traite des Excitants Modernes*.[25] Sanson confirmed that this was true. He had never, he said, seen a man spit on the way to the guillotine. Balzac turned this somewhat on its head, writing of Vautrin in *Le Père Goriot:*

> The very way in which he spat out a stream of saliva revealed an imperturbable *sang-froid*. Suggestive of someone who might commit a crime in order to wriggle out of a tight spot.[26]

Given Vidocq's antipathy to homosexuals it is ironic that in *Splendeurs*, Vautrin, who has reappeared as the Abbé Herrera, has obviously homosexual feelings towards Rastignac. Nor does it stop Balzac taking a sideswipe with his remark that a private police force was "morally and institutionally unacceptable" given that those who were the targets were from the same milieu as the hunters. In *La Cousine Bette* Vidocq appears as M. de Saint-Estève.

Nor is it clear how Vidocq came to meet Victor Hugo. He must have known him in the 1820s because *Notre-Dame de Paris* was published in 1831. He was by no means as close to Hugo as he was to Balzac and there was certainly a gap in their relationship. Shortly after his release

---

[23] Balzac apparently met her in 1822 when he was twenty-three. She died in 1836. Robert Baldick (ed.), *Pages from the Goncourt Journal*, p. 216.
[24] G. Robb, *Balzac*, p. 256.
[25] Chapter XIII, p. 323–4.
[26] Chapter III, p. 61.

from the Conciergerie in 1849 Vidocq wrote to Hugo, by now a *pair de France*, reminding him of how, the previous year, he had saved him by calling out "Long live M. Hugo" when he was being harassed by a crowd throwing stones at his windows. There was no mention in the letter of any part that Hugo had played in Vidocq's release.[27]

Hugo, however, made good use of the stories Vidocq told him and wrote down. Indeed, incident after incident in the early parts of *Les Misérables* has a parallel in Vidocq's life. Jean Valjean is condemned – as was Boitel – for stealing bread for a starving nephew. He escapes, as Vidocq did, from the *bagne*. When, now living as the kindly and respectable M. Madeleine, Valjean gives himself up after hearing of a man being tried under his name, it is a reconstruction of the incident in which Vidocq went to save the gatekeeper at St-Omer prison. The scene of lifting the cart comes from an incident in January 1828 when Vidocq lifted a cart at Saint-Mandé to release one of his employees who had become trapped. The commitment of the detective Javert in chasing down Valjean is an echo of Vidocq's tenacity in tracking down criminals.

Vidocq was source material for a host of other writers. The basis of the short story by Wilkie Collins, *A Terribly Strange Bed*, is probably from Vidocq's account of a case in Nanterre while whole passages are lifted from *Les Vrais Mystères*. He was also used by Melville in *Moby Dick*. Balzac's *Une fille d'Eve* came from an idea suggested by Vidocq, as did Alexandre Dumas père's *Gabriel Lambert*.

As for the detective novel, it is impossible to overstate his influence on the genre. Edgar Allan Poe's detective Dupin is based on Vidocq. Gérard Dôle wrote a number of Dupin stories in which Vidocq also features, rather mischievously giving Vidocq's tormentor, the journalist Saint-Hilaire, a part as well. He is the basis of Monsieur LeCoq, the investigating detective in the novels of Emil Gaboriou. There is more than a hint of him in Magwitch in Dickens' *Great Expectations*, as there is in Sherlock Holmes and his French rival, Arsène Lupin, in the immensely popular novels and short stories by Maurice Leblanc. Lupin, a master criminal and tormentor of the police – particularly the detective, Ganimard, assigned to capture him to whom he constantly refers as Light of my Heart – is another who finally becomes Head of the Sûreté.

---

[27] BHVP, MS 1055, fol. 133. In his biography of Hugo, Graham Robb makes no reference to Vidocq.

From the moment a translation of his memoirs appeared in English, London was fascinated by Vidocq and on July 6, 1829, Robert William Elliston, the manager of the Coburg Theatre, put on *VIDOCQ! The French Police Spy*. It was a splendid melodrama culled from the memoirs and with great staging. T. P. Cooke was Vidocq and he was given a foil, Fanfan, an escaped baker's apprentice, as the action moved from the port of Brest to the Pont Neuf, the baroness's mansion and finally to the farmhouse which was the thieves' den. His clothing and persona changed with each scene: a smock; frock-dress of galley slave; French sergeant; modern plain suit; brown wide dress and jackboots; a dress of tatters; a monk; a gendarme. The dialogue was suitably hammy. He is unmasked in Act 1, Scene V, in the baroness's apartment.

> Coitel: Ha! That mark! You are a galley-slave! You are –
> Thierry: Vidocq?
> All: Vidocq!

All good stuff, particularly the raid on the farmhouse in the last act. *The Times*, for one, although sorry there was not the usual spectacle associated with melodramas, thought:

> The whole gave great satisfaction to a crowded audience attracted by the announcement of the novelty and the curtain fell amidst loud applause from all parts of the house.[28]

The play was performed nine times that month but then faded from the repertoire. It was possibly played elsewhere because the volume of collected plays in which it appears says "at London Theatres."

It was not until after Vidocq's death that another piece based on his memoirs played in 1860 at the Britannia in Hoxton. This was an enormous theatre which, at its peak, housed 3,921 spectators and which opened on Easter Monday 1841 featuring strong drama with special effects.[29] In December 1860 *VIDOCQ or THE FRENCH JONATHAN WILD* by Mr. F. Marchant opened in a package which included the Wonderful Bedouin Arabs, Ritter and Crocker's Nigger Entertainment and Mrs. W. Cranford as *Eily O'Connor, The Bride of Killarney*.

---

[28] *The Times*, July 6, 1829.
[29] It was run first by the impressario Sam Lane and on his death by his wife. In 1912 it became a cinema and was destroyed in the 1940 bombing.

Vidocq seems to have lasted only a week – unlike *Eily O'Connor*, who was a staple production at the theatre – before giving way to the Christmas spectacular, *The Prince and the Ogre*.

In 1909 Emile Bergerat's play, *Vidocq, Emperor des Policiers*, in five acts and seven scenes, was rejected by the French producers Hertz and Cocquelin on the grounds that it had been set in the Napoleonic era. He successfully sued for 8,000 francs damages and it was performed the next year at the Théâtre Sarah Bernhardt. Diamonds have always been a useful device in melodramas and the plot centred around the loss of a collar loaned by the duchesse de Berri to her friend, the marquise de Madiran. Naturally it offered Jean Kemm as Vidocq the opportunity for numerous changes of appearance.[30] In the 1920s it was thought that the celebrated and, if the truth be told, hammy actor, Bransby Williams would play Vidocq on the English stage. He did not.

By the time of Vidocq's death he may largely have passed from public consciousness but there was still interest in him. In the summer of 1857 it was announced that a series of articles was imminent, beginning on August 1 that year. These would be written by B. Maurice and would be based "on the most carefully authenticated documents and for the most part issued by him."[31] Since then there has been a string of reissues of his memoirs along with strip cartoons, films and television series with him as the hero. In 1967 a long-running television series began with Bernard Noël as the detective. On his death the role was taken by Claude Brasseur. Novels such as Pierre Castex and Georges Neveux's 1967 *Vidocq – d'après le scénario du feuilleton* were published to complement the series. Just as with Sherlock Holmes, new adventures including Neveux's *Les Nouvelles Aventures de Vidocq*, written in 1970, have been invented for him. Jean Kemm, who appeared on the stage as Vidocq, first played him on the screen and over the century there were regular new films made of his life. Then in 2000 Gérard Depardieu appeared in a sci-fi film version with Vidocq, already dead in 1830, challenging a criminal mastermind, known as the Alchemist, from beyond the grave.

Nor has Vidocq's fame been confined to France. In Philadelphia the Vidocq Society, whose members include forensic professionals, meets on the top floor of the Public Ledger Building at Vidocq luncheons.

---

[30] *Le Matin*, July 31, 1909; *Le Théâtre*, June 1910.

[31] B. Maurice was Barthélemy Maurice.

These meetings aim, often successfully, to apply the collective minds of the members to cold cases with a view to providing a new focus for a stale investigation. Vidocq would have been proud of them.

At the far end of the small *cimetière nord* at 26 avenue Joffre, Saint-Mandé Nord, is a grave, near that of the actress Juliette Drouet, the mistress of Vidocq's friend, Victor Hugo. It is marked with a headstone, Vidocq 18. There is no other inscription and no indication that his last wife, Fleuride-Albertine, is buried there, although at the entrance to the cemetery on the small map indicating the graves of famous people it is her name rather than that of Vidocq which is recorded. As for the headstone itself, a visit in the spring of 2003 showed that someone had recently picked out the detective's name and a partial date in gold.

Bibliography

Abbott, G., *Sanson, Family of Death* (1995) London, Hale.

Allen, M., *Pioneer Policewoman* (1925) London, Chatto & Windus.

— *Lady in Blue* (1936) London, Stanley Paul.

Année, A., *Le Livre noir de Delavau et Franchet* (1829) Paris, Moutardier.

Anon, *Histoire authentique du célèbre Brigand Cartouche et de ces confrères* (n.d.) Paris, Ancienne Maison Gautrun.

— *Histoire des grands criminels* (n.d.) Paris, Le Bailly.

— *Relation fidèle et détailée de l'arrestation de S.A.R. Madame, Duchesse de Berry* (1852) Nantes, n.p.

Appert, B.N.M., *Bagnes, prisons et criminels* (1836) Paris, Guilbert.

— *Dix Ans à la cour de roi Louis-Philippe* (1846) Paris, J. Renouard.

Arasse, D. (trans. Christopher Miller), *The Guillotine and the Terror* (1989) London, Allen Lane.

Archer, J., *By a Flash and a Scare: Incendiarism, Animal Maiming and Poaching in East Anglia 1815–1870* (1990) Oxford, Clarendon Press.

Baldick, R., *The Life of Frederick Lemaître, Lion of the Boulevard* (1961) London, Hamish Hamilton.

— *Pages from the Goncourt Journal* (1962) London, Oxford University Press.

Ballantine, W., *Some Experiences of a Barrister's Life* (1881) London, R. Bentley & Son.

Berry, M., *A Comparative View of the Social Life of England and France* (1828) London, Longman, Rees, Orne, Barry and Green.

Berthelot, M. (ed.), *La Grande Encyclopédie* (n.d.) Paris, H. Lamirault et cie.

Bertil, G., *La Louve de Rainecourt,* Montdidier, Ed. Collection Santerre.

Bland, J., *Crime Strange But True* (1991) London, Futura.

Bleakley, H., *Hangmen of England* (1929) London, Chapman and Hall.

Borowitz, A., *Which the Justice, Which the Thief* (1997) Kent, Ohio, Kent State University Press.

— *Blood and Ink* (2002) Kent, Ohio., Kent State University Press.

Bourchardon, P., *L'Affaire Lafarge* (1924) Paris, Albin Michel.

— *L'Auberge de la tête noire* (1926) Paris, Perrin.

Bowring, Sir J., *Autobiographical Recollections* (1877) London, Henry King.

Bru, P., *Histoire de Bicêtre* (1890) Paris, Lecrosnier et Babé.

Burton, R. D., *The Flaneur and His City: Patterns of Daily Life in Paris, 1815–1851* (1995) Durham, University of Durham.

Cadbury, D., *The Lost King of France, Revenge and the Search for Louis XVII* (2002) London, Fourth Estate.

Canler, L., *Autobiography of a French Detective* (1862) London, Ward & Lock.

— (ed. Jacques Brenner), *Mémoires de Canler* (1968) Paris, Mercure de France.

Carlyle, T., *The Diamond Necklace* (1913) Boston, Houghton Mifflin.

Carné, M. (trans. D. Brooke), *Les Enfants du Paradis* (1968) London, Lorrimer.

Castanié, F., *L'Histoire vue par la police. Les indiscretions d'un préfet police de Napoléon* (1912) Paris, Tallandier.

Castelot, A. (pseud. A. Storms), *Le Duc de Berri et son double mariage* (1951) Paris, Presence de l'histoire.

— *L'Aiglon : Napoléon Deux* (1959) Paris, Le Livre Contemporain.

— (trans. R. Baldick), *Napoleon's Son* (1960) London, Hamish Hamilton.

Caussidière, M., *Mémoires* (1849) Paris, Michel Lévy.

Chateaubriand, F-R., Vicomte de, *Mémoires … sur le duc de Berri* (1820) Paris.

Chenu, A., *Les Conspirateurs* (1850) Paris, Garnier Frères.

Chevalier, L., *Le Choléra* (1958) La Roche-sur-Yon, Société d'Histoire de la Révolution de 1848.

Childs, J. R., *Casanova* (1961) London, George Allen & Unwin.

Claveau, A-G., *De la police de Paris et ses abuses et des reformes dont elle est susceptibles* (1831) Paris, Chez A. Pilot.

Cobb, R., *The Police and the People: French Popular Protest 1789–1820* (1970) Oxford, Oxford University Press.

— *The French and Their Revolution* (1998) London, John Murray.

Cobban, A., *A History of Modern France* (1961) Harmondsworth, Penguin.

Collingham, H. A. C., *The July Monarchy* (1988) London, Longman.

Crawley, C. W., (ed.), *The New Cambridge Modern History* (1965) Cambridge, Cambridge University Press.

—*La Justice enchainée* (1934) Paris, Albin Michel.

Creissels L., *XVII et les faux dauphins* (1936) Paris, Albin Michel.

Crook, M., *Revolution France* (2002) Oxford, Oxford University Press.

Davies, C., *Recollections of Society in France and England* (1872) London, n.p.

De Cleron, T., *Abrège de la vie de Louis Mandrin, chef des contrabandiers de France* (1755) Paris, n.p.

Delarue, J., *Le Métier de bourreau* (1979) Paris, Fayard.

Delayen, G., *L'Affaire du Courrier de Lyon* (1905) Paris, Librarie d'éducation nationale.

Delorme, P., *Louis XVII la verité: Sa mort au temple confirmée par la science* (2000) Paris, Pygmalion/Gérard Watelet.

Demartini, A-E., *L'Affaire Lacenaire* (2001) Paris, Aubier.

Dermancourt, General, *The Duchesse de Berri in La Vendée* (1833) London, Bull & Churton.

Desessart, N-T., *Dictionnaire universel de police* (1786–90) Paris, Montard.

Doyle, W., *The Oxford History of the French Revolution* (1989) Oxford, Clarendon Press.

Edwards, S., *The Vidocq Dossier* (1977) Boston, Houghton Mifflin.

Ensley, C., *Crime and Society in England 1750–1900* (1987) London, Loughman.

Excoffon, A. (trans. R. H. Sherard), *Le Courrier de Lyon* (1903) London, Greening & Co.

Favre, J., *Louis XVII, Plaiderie de Me. Jules Favre* (1884) Paris, Librairie nationale.

Forbes, E., *Mario and Grisi* (1985) London, Victor Gollancz.

Fortassier, R. (ed.), *Peines de cœur d'une chatte anglaise* (1985) Paris, Flammarion GF.

Foucault, M., *Surveiller et Punir: Naissance de la Prison* (1975) Paris, Gaillimard; (trans A.Sheridan), *Discipline and Punish* (1979) London, Penguin Books.

Fouquier, A. *Causes célèbres* (1858–74) Paris, Les Procès du Jour.

Fréigier, H., *Des classes dangereuses de la population dans les grandes villes* (1840) Paris, Chez J. B. Baillière (II).

Froment, M., *La Police dévoilée depuis la Restauration et notamment sous MM. Franchet et Delaveau* (1829) Paris, Levasseur.

— *Vidocq* (1830) Paris, Lerosey.

Gaboriau, E., *L'Ancien Figaro* (1861) Paris, E. Dentu.

Galtier-Boissière, J. (trans. R. Leslie-Melville), *Mysteries of the French Secret Police* (1938) London, Stanley Paul.

Gisquet, H-J., *Procès de M. Gisquet contre Le Messager* (1839) Paris, Pagnèrre.

— *Mémoires de M. Gisquet* (1840) Paris, Marchant, Editeur du Magasin Théâtral.

Greenwood, J., *The Wilds of London* (1874) London, Chatto & Windus.

Gronow, R. H., *The Reminiscences and Recollections of Captain Gronow* (1964) London, The Bodley Head.

Gury, C., *L'Honneur professionel d'un bourreau homosexuel en 1847* (1999) Paris, Editions Kime.

Guyon, L., *Biographie des commissaires de police et des officiers de la paix de la ville de Paris* (1826) Paris, Groullet.

Harvey, P. and Heseltine, J. E., *The Oxford Companion to French Literature* (1959) Oxford, Oxford University Press.

Hay, D. et al., *Albion's Fatal Tree* (1977) London, Peregrine Books.

Henry, G., *Cartouche, le bandit de la Régence* (2001) Paris, Tallendier.

Heppenstall, R., *French Crime in the Romantic Age* (1970) London, Hamish Hamilton.

Hibbert, C., *The French Revolution* (1982) London, Penguin Books.

Hilliaret, J., *Gibets, pilories et cachots du vieux Paris* (1956) Paris, Les Editións de Minuit.

Hobson, H., *French Theatre Since 1830* (1978) London, Calder.

Hodgetts, E. A. B., *Vidocq, A Master of Crime* (1928) London, Selwyn & Blount.

Hugo, V., *Things seen* (1887) London, G. Routledge & Sons.

Hutton, O., *The Poor of Eighteenth-Century France 1750–1789.*

Irving, H. B., *Studies of French Criminals* (1901) London, William Heinemann.

Jacob, Y., *Mandrin, le voleur d'impôts* (1983) Paris, Eds Tallendier.

Jagot, H., *Vidocq* (1928) Paris, Eds Berger-Levrault.

James, H., *French Poets and Novelists* (1878) London, Macmillan.

Janin, J. G., *Deburau: histoire du théâtre à quatre sous* (1881) Paris, n.p.

Jephson, H., *The Real French Revolution* (1899) London, Macmillan and Co.

Jones, C., *The Longman Companion to the French Revolution* (1998) London, Longman.

Kalifa, D., *Naissance de la police privée* (2000) Paris, Plon.

Kershaw, A., *A History of the Guillotine* (1958) London, John Calder.

Lacour, M-B., *Trente-six espèces de vols en 1838* (1838) Paris, Chez les Marchands de Nouveautés.

Lafarge, M-F., *Lafarge ses mémoires* (1841) Paris, Levy Frères.

— *Heures de prison de Mme Lafarge* (1855) Paris, Librairie Nouvelle.

Lamartine, A-M-L., *Histoire des Girondins* (1847) Paris, Fourneerae.

— *Balzac et ses oeuvres* (1866) Paris, Levy, Librairie Nouvelle.

Langeron, R., *Decazes, ministre du roi.* (1960) Paris, Hachette.

Larousse, P., *Grand dictionnaire du XIXe siècle* (1990) Nimes, Collection Rediviva.

LeClère, M., *Histoire de la police* (1947) Paris, Presses universitaires de France.

— *La Vie dans les bagnes* (1974) Paris, La Cercle Histoire.

— *La Vie quotidienne dans les bagnes* (1979) Paris, Hachette.

Lecomte, L-H., *Un comédien au XIX siècle, Frédérick Lemaître; étude biographique et critique d'après des documents inedits* (1888) Paris, Chez l'auteur.

Ledru, C., *Mystères du procès de l'Abbé Contrafatto* (1846) Paris, Edmond Albert.

— *La Vie, la mort et les derniers moments du Vidocq après sa confession à l'heure suprême* (1857) Paris, Dentu.

Lefebvre-Filleau, J-P., *Vidocq contre "les chauffeurs" de la Somme* (1999) Luneray, Bertout.

Lemaître, F., *Souvenirs* (1880) Paris, Paul Ollendorff.

Lenôtre, G., *La Guillotine et les executeurs des arrêts criminels pendant la révolution* (1893) Paris, Perrin et cie.

— *Le Roi Louis XVII et l'énigme du Temple* (1921) Paris, Perrin.

Levy, B., *Legacy of Death* (1973) Farnborough, Saxon House.

Lock, J., *The British Police Woman* (1979) London, Robert Hale.

Lucas-Dubreton, J., *Louis-Philippe et la machine infernale* (1951) Paris, Presence de l'histoire.

Lurine, L., *Histoire secrète et publique de la police ancienne et moderne* (1847) Paris (n.p.).

Maurice, B., *Vidocq, vie et aventures* (1858) Paris, Jules Laisne.

Mansel, R., *Paris Between the Empires, 1814–1852* (2003) London, Phoenix.

Manson, M-F-C., *Mon plan de défense dans le procès Fualdès adressé à touts les cœurs sembles* (1818) Albi, Baurens et Radière.

McPhee, P., *The French Revolution 1789–1799* (2002) Oxford, Oxford University Press.

M. G., *Histoire complète du Procès de Louis-Pierre Louvel* (1820) Paris, P. Plancher.

Milligan, J. C., *The History of Duelling* (1841) London, Richard Bentley.

Morain, Alfred, *The Underword of Paris* (1930) London, Jarrolds.

Moreau-Christophe, L.M., *Le Monde des Coquins* (1864) Paris, E. Dentu.

Morris N. and Rothman D.J. (eds.), *The Oxford History of the Prison* (1995) Oxford, Oxford University Press.

Morton, J., *Bent Coppers* (1994) London, Warner Books.

— *Supergrasses and Informers* (1996) London, Warner Books.

— *Manhunt!* (2002) London, Ebury Press.

Munthe, A., *The Story of San Michele* (1929) London, John Murray.

Nauroy, C., *Le Premier Mariage du duc de Berry* (1880) Paris, Charavay Frères.

O'Brien, D. H., *My Adventures During the Late War, A Narrative of Shipwreck, Captivity, Escapes from French Prisons, and Sea Service in 1804–14* (1902) London, Edward Arnold.

Oman, C., *The Lyons Mail* (1945) London, Methuen & Co.

Opie, R. F., *Guillotine: The Timbers of Justice* (2003) Stroud, Sutton.

Orczy, Baroness, *The Turbulent Duchess* (1935) London, Hodder & Stoughton.

Palmer, R. R., *Twelve Who Ruled: The Year of Terror in the French Revolution* (1941) Princeton, Princeton University Press.

Panola, E., *Petition à MM. les députés sur l'excès du journalisme* (1839), Paris, G. Pissin.

Parinaud, M-H., *Vidocq, le Napoléon du police* (2001) Paris, Ed. Taillandier.

Pasquier, E-D., Duc de, *Memoirs of Chancellor Pasquier* (1892) London, T. Fisher Unwin.

Perrin, E., *Vidocq* (1995) Paris, Pocket.

Petit, J-G. et al., *Histoires des galères, bagnes et prisons* (1991) Toulouse, Biblio Historique Privat.

Peuchet, J., *Mémoires tiré des Archives de la Police* (1838) Paris, A. Levasseur.

Philip, A. M., *The Prison Breakers* (1927) London, Philip Alan and Co.

Phillips, R., *Family Breakdown in Late Eighteenth-Century France 1792–1803* (1980), Oxford, Clarendon Press.

Pierre, M., *Le Dernier Exil, histoire des bagnes et des forçats* (1989) Paris, Gallimard.

Porter, B., *The Origins of the Vigilant State* (1977) London, Weidenfeld & Nicolson.

— *The Refugee Question in Mid-Victorian Politics* (1979) Cambridge, Cambridge University Press.

— *Plots and Paranoia* (1989) London, Unwin Hyman.

Pringle, P., *The Thief Takers* (1956) London, Museum Press.

Quérard, J. M., *Les Supercheries littéraires dévoilées* (1847–53) Paris.

Raban, L. F. and Saint-Hilaire, M., *Mémoires d'un forçat ou Vidocq dévoilé* (1829) Paris.

Raisson, H-N., *Histoire de la police de Paris de 1697 à 1844* (1844) Paris, B. Dusillion.

Réal, P-F., *Indiscretions* (1935) Paris.

Rémy, T., *Jean-Gaspard Deburau* (1954) Paris, L'Arche Editeur.

Rheinstein, M., *Marriage, Statutory Divorce and the Law* (1970) Chicago, University of Chicago Press.

Rives-Child, J., *Casanova* (1961) London, George Allen & Unwin.

Robb, G., *Victor Hugo* (1997) London, Picador.

— *Balzac* (2000) London, Picador.

Robiquet, J., *Daily Life in the French Revolution* (1964) London, Weidenfeld & Nicolson.

Roch, E. (ed.), *Procès complet de Lacenaire et de ses complies* (1836) Paris, Bureau de l'Observateur.

— *L'Observateur des tribunaux* (1840) Paris, Bureau de l'Observateur.

Roy-Henry, B., *Vidocq du bagne à la préfecture* (2001) Paris, L'Archipel.

Rudé, G., *The French Revolution* (1988) London, Weidenfeld & Nicolson.

Saint-Edmé, M. B., *Biographie des Lieutenants Généreaux* (1829).

Sanson, H., (ed.), *Memoirs of the Sansons* (1881) London, Chatto & Windus.

Saunders, E., *The Mystery of Marie Lafarge* (1952) New York, Morrow.

Sauval, H., *La Chronique scandaleuse de Paris; ou histoire des mauvais lieux* (1883) Brussels J. J. Gay.

Savant J., (ed.), *Les Vrai Mémoires de Vidocq* (1950) Paris, Editions Correa.

— *La Vie fabuleuse et authentique de Vidocq* (1950) Paris, Hachette.

— *Tel fut Ouvrard, le financier de Napoléon* (1954) Paris, Fasquelle Editeurs.

— *Le Procès de Vidocq* (1956) Paris, Club de Meilleur Livre.

— *La Vie aventureuse de Vidocq* (1972) Paris, Hachette.

Shankland, P. and Havers, M., *Murder with a Double Tongue: The Enigma of Clarissa Manson* (1978) London, William Kimber.

Slipper, J., *Slipper of the Yard* (1981) London, Sidgwick & Jackson.

Sophianopoulo, Dr. *Relative des épidémies du choléra en Hongroie* (1832) Paris, Delaunay.

Spearman, N., *Executioners All* (1962) London, Neville Spearman.

Stead, P. J. (trans.,ed.), *The Memoirs of Lacenaire* (1952) London, Staples Press.

— *Vidocq: Picaroon of Crime* (1953) London, Staples Press.

— *The Police of Paris* (1957) London, Staples Press.

Sue, E., *Mystères de Paris* (1992) Edinburgh, Thomas Nelson.

Symonds, J., *Bloody Murder* (1972) London, Faber & Faber.

Thorwald, J., *The Marks of Cain* (1965) London, Thames & Hudson.

Vermorel, A. J. M., *Les Mystères de la police* (1864) Paris Librarie Centrale.

Vidalence, J., *La Societé francaise de 1815 à 1848* (1973) Paris, Eds Marcel Rivière.

Vidocq, E-F., *Memoirs of Vidocq* (1828) London, Hunt & Clarke.

— *Le Paravoleur où l'art de se conduire prudement* (1830) Paris, Roy-Terry.

— *Les Voleurs* (1836) Paris, Author.

— *Quelques mots sur une question a l'ordre* (1844) Paris, Author.

— *Les Vrais Mystères de Paris* (1844) Paris.

— *Les Chauffeurs du Nord* (1845) Paris, Comon cie (comoar).

— *Vidocq* (1845) London, Printed Alfred Dod.

— *Vidocq: The French Police Spy* (1848) London, G. Routledge.

Watelet, J., *L'Histoire des bagnes* (1978) Geneva, Eds Famot.

Wensley, F., *Detective Days* (1931) London, Cassell & Company.

Wild, N., *Dictionnaire des théâtres Parisiens aux XIXe siècle* (1989) Paris, Aux Amateurs des Livres.

Wills, A., *Crime and Punishment in Revolutionary Paris* (1981) London, Greenwood Press.

Wright, G., *Insiders and Outsiders* (1981) San Francisco, W.H. Freeman & Co.

Zweig, S., (trans. Eden and Cedar Paul) *Joseph Fouché* (1930) London, Cassell & Co.

Selected Articles etc.

"Cartouche — Histoire de sa vie et de son procès" in *Le Figaro*, May 21, 1857, et seq.

Robert Darnton, "High Enlightenment and the Low- Life of Literature in Pre-Revolution France," in *Past and Present*, 1971.

Catherine Decouan, "Vidocq un peu affabulateur" in *Historia mensuel*, September 1, 2001.

Jean Galtier-Boissière, "Mystères du police secret" in *Crapouillot*, May 1936.

Gazette des Tribunaux, 1825–57.

Hubert d'Havrincourt, "Le Bagnard Incorruptible" in *L'Evénement*, March 1967.

Marcel Herrand, "Lacenaire parle" in *Conferencia*, June and July 1946.

Eric Pincas, "La Brigade de sûreté était payée sur des fonds secrets!" in *Historia mensuel*, September 1, 2001.

Tristan Rémy, "Sur Jean-Gaspard Deburau et son fils Jean-Charles" in *Revue d'histoire du théâtre*, Paris, Année 3, no. 2.

C-H. Sanson, "Rapport de Charles-Henri Sanson au ministre de la Justice sur le mode de décapitation" quoted in *Revue retrospective*, Paris, 1835.

Jean Savant, "Vidocq et Alexandre Dumas père" in *La Tribune Littéraire*, March 1951.

— "Le Cabinet de Médailles" in *Les Oeuvres Libres*, Vol. 81, Librairie Arthème Fayard, Paris, February 1953.

— "Le Créateur de la Police de Sûreté" in *La Tribune Littéraire*, October 1955.

Jaroslav Svehla, "Jean Gaspard Deburau: the immortal Pierrot" in *Mime Journal*, 5, 1977.

Annabel Thomas, "To what extent, if at all, did women gain a voice in the era of the French Revolution?" Unpublished MS.

Sources

Archives de la Préfecture de Police de Paris (APP)

Archives de la Somme (Amiens)

Archives de Lyons

Archives de Paris

Archives du Nord (Lille)

Archives Nationale

Bibilothèque Historique de la Ville de Paris (BHVP)

Bibliothèque Nationale

Lilly Library, University of Indiana at Bloomington

Index

JAMES MORTON practiced law for twenty-
five years before becoming editor of *New Law Journal*
and *Criminal Lawyer*. He is the author of many books,
including the bestselling Gangland series and a biography of actress and courtesan Lola Montez.

OF SIMILAR INTEREST
AVAILABLE FROM THE OVERLOOK PRESS

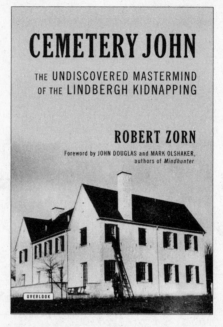

CEMETERY JOHN The Undiscovered Mastermind of the Lindbergh Kidnapping
by Robert Zorn • 978-1-59020-856-4 • $26.95 • HARDCOVER

"Prompted by his father's belief in a boyhood brush with history, Robert Zorn is now offering a fresh take on the cold case, plausibly arguing in Cemetery John that, despite the execution of the odious Bruno Richard Hauptmann, the real mastermind of the crime escaped unpunished. . . . Mr. Zorn offers much more detail, and he consults FBI profilers, psychologists, high-tech handwriting experts and others to establish that Knoll almost certainly wrote the ransom letters and had the borderline psychopathic personality to hatch the scheme." —*Wall Street Journal*

"Through some incredibly persistent sleuthing, consultation with specialists in modern criminal investigative analysis, and a good dose of luck, author Robert Zorn has solved what has been correctly called 'the crime of the century.'"
—*The Daily Caller*

"*Cemetery John* by Robert Zorn isn't only a book I strongly recommend, especially for history buffs such as myself, but one that earns a permanent place on my bookshelf—which regular readers know this means I didn't just like it, I loved it." —*True Crime Zine*

THE OVERLOOK PRESS
NEW YORK, NY
WWW.OVERLOOKPRESS.COM

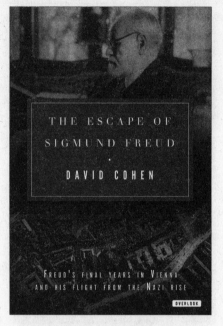

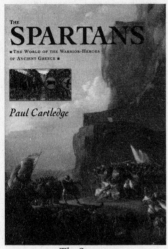
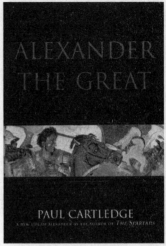

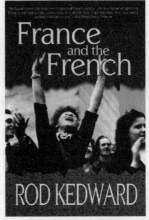

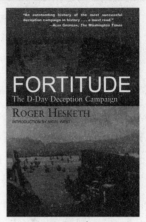
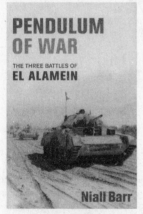
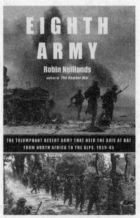

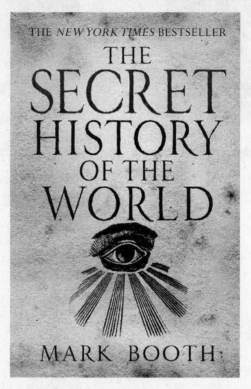

THE *NEW YORK TIMES* BESTSELLER

THE SECRET HISTORY OF THE WORLD

MARK BOOTH·

The Secret History of the World
MARK BOOTH
978-1-59020-162-6

OVER 100,000 COPIES IN PRINT

An enthralling and mind-opening journey through our world's secret histories. Starting from a dangerous premise—that everything we've been taught about our world's past is corrupted and that the stories put forth by the various cults and mystery schools are true—Booth produces nothing short of an alternate account of the past three thousand years.

"This is the most controversial book I have ever read . . .
This important new book is a masterpiece and quite clearly inspired."
—COLIN WILSON, author of *The Outsider* and *From Atlantis to the Sphinx*

THE OVERLOOK PRESS · NEW YORK · WWW.OVERLOOKPRESS.COM